Canadian Indian Cowboys in Australia

Canadian Indian Cowboys in Australia

Representation, Rodeo, and the RCMP
at the Royal Easter Show, 1939

LYNDA MANNIK

UNIVERSITY OF
CALGARY
PRESS

© 2006 Lynda Mannik.

University of Calgary Press
2500 University Drive NW
Calgary, Alberta
Canada T2N 1N4
www.uofcpress.corn

No part of this publication may be reproduced, stored in a retrieval system or transmitted, in any form or by any means, without the prior written consent of the publisher or a licence from The Canadian Copyright Licensing Agency (Access Copyright). For an Access Copyright licence, visit www. access copyright. ca or call toll free to 1 (800) 893 • 5777.

Library and Archives Canada Cataloguing in Publication

Mannik, Lynda, 1957–
Canadian Indian Cowboys in Australia: representation, rodeo, and the RCMP at the Royal Easter Show, 1939 / Lynda Mannik.

Includes bibliographical references and index.
ISBN 10: 1-55238-200-1
ISBN 13: 1-978-55238-200-4

1. Indian cowboys — Canada. 2. Indian cowboys — Australia. 3. Race discrimination — Canada. 4. Race discrimination — Australia. 5. Indians of North America — Canada — Government relations — 1860–1951. 6. Royal Easter Show.   I. Title.

E78.C2M336 2006   305.89707109'043   C2006-901626-7

The University of Calgary Press acknowledges the the support of the Alberta Foundation for the Arts for this published work.

We acknowledge the financial support of the Government of Canada through the Book Publishing Industry Development Program (BPIDIP) for our publishing activities.

Canada Council for the Arts / Conseil des Arts du Canada

Printed and bound in Canada by AGMV Marquis

∞ This book is printed on acid-free paper.

Front cover photo courtesy Glenbow Archives, NA-481-10.
Back cover photo courtesy Glenbow Archives, NA-1241-69.
Cover design by Mieka West
Interior layout by Jeremy Drought, *Last Impression Publishing Service*, Calgary, Alberta

*To my daughter, Dylan Mannik-Zulinski,
my father, Meinhard Mannik,
and my mother, Rosemary May Mannik (d. 1997)*

Table of Contents

- **LIST OF ILLUSTRATIONS** ix
- **ACKNOWLEDGMENTS** xi
- **INTRODUCTION** 1

1
THE AUSTRALIAN REQUEST
11

- The R.A.S. and its Ambassadors 12
- Modernity at the Royal Easter Show and the Accompanying Brochures 17
- Economic Depression, WW II and the Unspoken Political Motivations of the R.A.S. 30
- Conclusions 31

2
THE CANADIAN RESPONSE
35

- The Beginning of the Negotiations 36
- The Preferred Performance 37
- The Second Canadian Preference 38
- Schmidt's Bottom Line 44
- Handicraft Sales as Government Income at the Royal Easter Show 46
- Conclusions 49

3
CANADIAN INDIAN COWBOYS AT THE ROYAL EASTER SHOW IN SYDNEY: CELEBRITIES, CITIZENS, AND WARDS
53

- Life on the Reserves in Alberta, 1930s 60
- Life as an Indian Cowboy 63
- The Trip to Australia in 1939 67
- Indian Cowboys as Celebrities 70
- Indian Cowboys as Wards of the State 76
- Indian Cowboys as Equals 79
- Conclusions 83

4
CONSTABLE LEACH AT THE ROYAL EASTER SHOW IN SYDNEY: TOURIST, AMATEUR ANTHROPOLOGIST, AND CHAPERONE
87

- The Unique Relationship between First Nations and the RCMP 91
- Constable Leach and a Touristic View 93
- Primitivism Discourse within Constable Leach's Commentary 98
- Constable Leach as Chaperone and Representative of Canada 102
- Conclusions 110

5
THE AUSTRALIAN AUDIENCE
115

- "Noble Savage" and Savage Ideology in North America and Australia 117
- Press Reports from Australia 121
- Conclusions 131

- **CONCLUSION** 135
- **ENDNOTES** 141
- **BIBLIOGRAPHY** 171
- **INDEX** 187

List of Illustrations

1 • "Two of the First Nations Cowboys Relaxing at the Easter Show."
2 • "Two Australians Visit City in Quest for Cowboy Riders."
3 • "Two Australians Visit City in Quest for Cowboy Riders."
4 • "Front Cover of *Souvenir Ring Programme*."
5 • "Page One of *Souvenir Ring Programme*."
6 • "In the Ring."
7 • "Collage of First Nations Cowboys."
8 • "Cover Page of *Rodeo Brochure*."
9 • "Collage of First Nations Cowboys" (*Rodeo Brochure*).
10 • "Clements Tonic Advertisment."
11 • "Picture of Red Indian Chiefs sent from Canada."
12 • "A New Thrill: Chuckwagon Races at the Royal Show."
13 • "Indian Village at Royal Easter Show."
14 • "Straight From the Canadian Indians."
15 • "Canadian Pavilion at the Empire Exhibit in Glasgow, Scotland."
16 • "Water Power Statue, Canadian Pavilion, New York World's Fair."
17 • "Two Totem Poles designed by Mungo Martin, outside the Canadian Pavilion atthe New York World's Fair."
18 • "Joe Crowfoot at the Calgary Stampede, 1939."
19 • "Joe Bear Robe at the Calgary Stampede, 1940."
20 • "Left, Ted Brave Rock; right, Joe Young Pine; woman and child unidentified, 1920."
21 • "Chief Jim Starlight, 1965, *Calgary Herald*."
22 • "Eddie One Spot at the Calgary Stampede, 1941."
23 • "Frank Many Fingers at the Calgary Stampede."
24 • "Left, Joe Crowfoot; right Duck Chief, prior to leaving for Australia, February 1939, Calgary."
25 • "Troupe Leaving for Australia."
26 • "Troupe's arrival in Open Cars with Flags Titled, 'Pontiac Welcomes the Red Indians'."

27 • "Canadian Troupe Walking up Stairs at City Hall upon Arrival."
28 • "Posing at Moore Park for the Press."
29 • "Eddie One Spot, Sarcee, Tsuu T'ina, in Australia."
30 • "Cowboys in Grand Parade at the Royal Easter Show."
31 • "Constable Leach Leading Grand Parade."
32 • "Constable Leach Prior to Leaving."
33 • "Lance Corporal Leach with his charges at Sydney, NSW."
34 • "Lord Gowrie with 'Mountie'."
35 • "Crowfoot and Leach in Sydney."
36 • "Constable Leach, Col. Somerville and A.W. Skidmore on the deck of the SS *Niagara*."
37 • "Alberta Indians and Cowboys Return from Australia."
38 • "Making Real 'Whoopee'."
39 • "Show Window of the State: Always Something New at the Royal Show."
40 • *Daily Telegraph* Staff Reporter; "Meaty Man are these Braves of the Prairie....'Whoo'!"
41 • "Wild West at Woolloomooloo: Eddie One Spot Visits Day Nursery."
42 • "Constable Samuel Leach Raising Horse in Salute at the Royal Easter Show, Sydney Australia."
43 • "A Paleface Listens."

Acknowledgments

I HAVE ACCUMULATED MANY DEBTS in the course of researching and writing this book. I am grateful to everyone who has helped me in this regard. Particularly, I would like to thank Peggy Maxwell for allowing me access to her father's private papers and for graciously inviting me to her home to talk about this event. Chapter Three would not have been possible without the help of Cecil Crowfoot and Floyd Many Fingers, who agreed to share their memories of this trip. I would also like to thank Deanna Crowfoot and Amelia Crowfoot-Clark for spending time with me while I was in Alberta and, as well, Geraldine Many Fingers for graciously allowing me to spend time with her and her family in Cardston. Many thanks to Sandra and Colin Campbell for their offer of time while on vacation in Australia and to Elizabeth Nannelli, archivist for the Royal Agricultural Society of New South Wales Heritage Centre, for her conscientious help.

My perspective on national identity, colonialism, Canadian culture, and ideology was developed through many conversations and exchanges with the faculty associated with the Frost Centre at Trent University. I especially want to thank Keith Walden, Julia Harrison, and Jim Struthers for their patience, intellectual stimulation, and moral support throughout this project.

The staff at the University of Calgary Press deserves a special thank you for their time and support. They not only made the process of publishing very enjoyable, but also quite painless.

I also want to thank my family for their support, Steve, Sil, Andrew, Lisa, and Jennifer, and all of my wonderful friends. The writing of this book would not have been as successful or as enjoyable without the companionship and encouragement of my daughter, Dylan, and the support of my father, Meinhard Mannik. Thank you both for remaining tolerant and thoughtful throughout.

Introduction

> The theatricality of history making will always demand that the many voices of every cultural moment be heard. It will discover that the interpretative genius of the audience can cope with these paradoxes and multivalences.[1]

IN JULY OF 1938, the Royal Agricultural Society (RAS) of New South Wales (NSW) approached the Canadian government with a request for a "small group of Indians as a rodeo attraction"[2] for their annual Easter Show in Sydney, Australia. The Indian Affairs Branch, under the direction of C. Pant Schmidt, inspector of Indian Affairs in Alberta, conditionally accepted, but stipulated that First Nations representatives must be supervised by a Royal Canadian Mounted Police (RCMP) officer at all times, and also be seen in a traditional tipi-village, selling handicrafts. Joe Crowfoot and Joe Bear Robe from the Blackfoot Reserve, Frank Many Fingers and Joe Young Pine from the Blood Reserve, Edward One Spot and Jim Starlight from the Sarcee Reserve, and Johnny Left Hand and Douglas Kootenay from the Stoney Reserve, all decided to accept this offer with the understanding that they would be representing Canada in international competition against other Canadian, American and Australian cowboys.[3] All were accomplished and professional athletes; some were also businessmen, politicians and well-known entertainers. Constable Samuel Leach and his wife, Dorothy Leach, were hired to escort these men. Mrs. Leach was trained as a nurse and was also responsible for all bookkeeping and money distributions pertaining to the First Nations men's wages, expenses and handicraft sales.

On 14 February 1939 all eight First Nations cowboys and the Leaches boarded a train in Calgary. They arrived in Vancouver on the morning of the following day and at noon set sail on the SS *Niagara* for Australia. Canadian newspapers in Vancouver and Calgary published small articles about this adventure, which appropriately described the First Nations men as accomplished rodeo performers and inappropriately described them as "ambassadors of commerce,"[4] who were opening up new export markets for Canada. Ironically, the relatively small shipment of 525 items they were referring to, consisting of hand-beaded clothing and various other articles worth approximately one thousand dollars, had been solely instigated and arranged by the Indian Affairs Branch for sale in Sydney.

The voyage took three-and-a-half weeks. The SS *Niagara* was a well-known luxury liner and it provided very comfortable facilities. Other than seasickness and the fact that Johnny Left Hand required an operation for an ear infection, the trip seemed to be enjoyable for all. There were three brief stops: Honolulu, Hawaii; Suva, Fiji; Auckland, New Zealand. At each port this Canadian group was greeted by the press and local officials, and then treated to sightseeing tours, lunches and evening entertainment.

On 11 March 1939 they landed in Sydney, were welcomed by RAS representatives and given a civic reception on the steps of City Hall. Members of the party were interviewed by the press and posed for publicity photos for two days. Afterwards, they travelled 245 miles by train to T. B. MacFarlane's ranch in Merriwa. There they joined up with the other cowboys and cowgirls from Canada and the United States to train horses and prepare for the Easter Show. Most of their thirteen-day stay was spent brushing up on their rodeo skills. On two occasions all of the North American athletes were invited to lavish banquet dinners, one at MacFarlane's ranch, and the other at the home of Frederick McMaster, a wealthy station owner.

This Canadian troupe returned to Sydney on 26 March 1939 and immediately went to the show grounds at Moore Park, to look over the area where the "Indian Village" would be built. A bell-tent and a makeshift Sun Dance Lodge were erected on this site alongside eight tipis brought from Alberta. This Indian Village became the troupe's residence for the duration of the show, as well as the place where beaded handicrafts were sold. During this preparatory period the First Nations cowboys were informed that they would not be allowed to compete in two main rodeo events, the bulldogging and buckjumping contests. They were very disappointed. Leach spent a great deal of time negotiating with RAS officials, yet they would not alter their decision on this matter.

The Royal Easter Show took place between 1 and 12 April. This annual event was the largest in Australia. It was organized by the RAS in order to promote excellence and innovation in all aspects of agriculture. Throughout, the First Nations cowboys spent most of their time in the Indian Village, except on Sundays when they went sightseeing. Twelve different rodeo events took place each afternoon and evening. The well-advertised "big new thrill" at this 1939 show was the "Clements Tonic International Chuck Wagon Race," which pitted "Red Indians" against white Australian, Canadian and American riders.[5] Canada's team of First Nations men suffered more accidents than usual throughout, chiefly because some of the horses that they had trained in Merriwa were taken from them and given to Australian cowboys by RAS officials. The Australian crowds loved the "Red Indian" cowboys and swarmed the Indian Village constantly in attempts to get autographs and talk to the men. Another popular daily event was the "Grand Parade" in which Constable Leach led all of the North American cowboys and cowgirls on horseback around the show-ring. The handicraft endeavor was less successful; only small, inexpensive items were sold, partially due to high prices created by a 70 per cent Australian tariff.

The First Nations cowboys were able to win quite a few of the events despite multiple hindrances to their success. On the last day of the show, five of them were publicly awarded silver trophy cups for their achievements. The RAS announced that they made a record 850,000 Australian pounds in paid admissions to the show. All of the cowboys and cowgirls were invited to a farewell party at the Hotel Grand Central; however, Constable Leach did not allow the First Nations cowboys to go because liquor was being served.

The SS *Aorangi* sailed for Vancouver on 13 April at 4:30 p.m. The trip home was particularly turbulent because the ship was travelling at full throttle due to the threat of impending war. The trip home, though shorter, did not seem as jovial as the earlier journey. There were altercations on board, and at all three stopovers, as the First Nations men attempted to resist restrictions on their activities. Constable Leach asserted his authority by further isolating the men to curtail any freedom they tried to attain. His actions created a great deal of tension within the troupe.

The SS *Aorangi* docked in Vancouver on 5 May at 9:45 p.m. All of the passengers immediately departed except Joe Crowfoot, Joe Bear Robe, Frank Many Fingers, Joe Young Pine, Edward One Spot, Jim Starlight, Johnny Left Hand and Douglas Kootenay, who were forced to spend the night on board. On Leach's recommendation, Corporal Floyd of the RCMP, immigration authorities and the ship's purser detained them because a few of the men had boasted that they were going to go out drinking as soon as they landed. They passed through customs the next morning, collected their baggage and their wages from Leach, and boarded a train to Calgary. Honor dances and other public celebrations greeted them upon their return to their individual communities. The legacy of this adventure has remained very important to all of the families of this group. Leach, exhausted and relieved, returned to normal duty. The story of the trip remained memorable for his family as well.[6]

This story constitutes an important moment in Canadian history for a variety of reasons. First, it is a unique occasion when a First Nations team of athletes represented Canada in international sport; therefore it sheds light on the construction of national identity. Although there has been a wealth of scholarly work linking international competition with national identity, little has focused on Canada specifically. Recently scholars have also recognized the ways that athletes belonging to marginalized groups have challenged mainstream ideologies supported by the state. This Canadian example provides substantial material for analyzing cultural interactions of a colonial nature, which affected notions of national pride for First Nations. It also demonstrates how mainstream notions of national pride were promoted in 1939.

Secondly, First Nations people in Canada were legally wards of the state at this time; therefore this instance of international competition provided a way for these "Indian cowboys" to gain cultural recognition as citizens. Athletic competition differs dramatically from other forms of public performance such as ethnographic displays and/or "Indian Villages," because aspects of human action, skill and determination supersede mere symbolic representation. As well, my research with the family members of two of the men, Joe Crowfoot and Frank Many Fingers, revealed specific efforts to publicly declare themselves as Canadian citizens to a foreign audience. This was only one of the ways they purposefully disrupted both legal and symbolic categories of state-induced subordination.

Generally, there have only been a handful of authors who have written about the role rodeo has played in First Nations communities.[7] This story adds to a discussion concerning rodeos as places where resistance to, and recovery from, colonial imposition can and does occur. It was also a unique historic moment for this sport due to the fact that four distinct cultural groups, Australians, Americans, white Canadians and First Nations Canadians, competed against each other. Professional international rodeo was limited at this time; consequently the events of 1939 can be considered glamorous and unusual.

However, this story is not just about rodeo. It is a complex tale of real and imaginary relationships, both on a national and an individualized scale. The ultimate purpose of this book will be to elaborate on the events of this story in order to bring out the multiple and often contradictory meanings concerning human bodies, identities and space that shift through the acts of travelling and performance. It will attempt to delineate shifts in identity, both individual and national, which were restricted by colonialism, but nevertheless altered through international public performance and international travel. The inclusion of both views, colonizing and colonized, will emphasize that visual representation is, in varying degrees, intercultural, social in nature and based on relationships of power.

Raymond Williams' explanation of "lived hegemony" will underlie the ambivalent nature of colonial relationships that is central to this story. Williams states, "lived hegemony is always a process" and also a "complex of experiences, relationships and activities" that are continually "renewed, recreated, defended and modified."[8] Here, acts of resistance that impinged on dominant colonial hegemony in Canada, Australia and the rest of the Western world, which allotted the "North American Indian" a certain racial, legal and economic status, will be recognized as equally dynamic. Through their participation in rodeo, eight First Nations cowboys from Alberta employed forms of counterhegemony to present themselves as individuals and as competitive participants in a popular sport. Constable Leach also negotiated an alternative hegemony in his insistence that RAS officials treat these men fairly as equal competitors. I will argue that these acts of resistance to hegemony allowed not only for the exploration of its limits, but also for subtle, yet noticeable, shifts in dominant ideology. In particular, shifts were made within the Australian public's view of "Red Indians," suggesting that colonial, stereotypical beliefs are more easily challenged when compared cross-culturally.

Theatre production will be used as a metaphor to establish the perspectives of all parties involved. When applied to historic analysis, the dialectic nature of the interaction that occurs between producers, actors and audience members draws out the wider meanings of single events. As stated by Dening, the writing of history should demand that every voice involved in a cultural moment be heard.[9] Multiple truths shift the balance of power by the very nature of their multiplicity. The final outcome, or the final view, is reflected in the audience's reaction, often the most objective interpretation of a cultural production.[10]

Chapters One and Two will present the viewpoint of the producers of this story, the RAS of NSW in Australia, and the Indian Affairs Branch in Canada. As prominent organizations within colonial nations, they were motivated by imperial doctrine, which focused on the establishment of profitable commercial relations as the best means for the promotion of modernity and progress. For both, the power of popular culture was used in their decision to attract an audience and to verify the legitimacy of their messages.

From the RAS's point of view, the First Nations men's bodies, their traditional costumes, and rodeo skills became popular vehicles for the production of positive nationalist ideals and imperialist principles. The early twentieth-century proliferation of American popular culture, and in particular images from the many Wild West shows that ran in tandem with the development of cattle ranching and rodeo, guaranteed them audience interest. The combined spectacle of "Red Indians" driving a chuckwagon was the "unforgettable turn of events"[11] that promised to thrill the Australian public due to its ironic nature. "Indians" skillfully driving stagecoaches was something truly unexpected in their eyes.[12] Their request to hire a "small group of Indians as a rodeo attraction"[13] followed a two-month tour of North America taken by A.W. Skidmore and T.B. MacFarlane, two RAS officials. This tour was also intended to aid in solidifying political ties with Canada during an economic depression and amidst serious threats of impending world war.

The Canadian government's quick acceptance of the RAS offer followed approximately forty years of disallowing First Nations performers work overseas. Although rodeo competitors were athletes and not simply performers, according to the Canadian government's agenda they represented the same cultural commodity. C. Pant Schmidt, the inspector of Indian Agencies for Alberta and spokesperson for the Indian Affairs Branch, continually attempted to erase rodeo performance from the RAS agenda. The final decision to allow these men to go was based on the short-term economic needs of Alberta's Indian agents, and also on long-range goals of establishing a national/colonial identity. Making money and gaining political recognition through racial ordering and subjugation was a well-known reality in larger imperial projects. The Royal Easter Show in 1939 was simply one more instance when the Canadian government attempted to promote this ideal. Constable Leach's presence guaranteed official representation that symbolically suggested successful colonial authority.

Chapters Three and Four will assume the perspective of the main participants in this story: Joe Crowfoot, Joe Bear Robe, Frank Many Fingers, Joe Young Pine, Edward One Spot, Jim Starlight, Johnny Left Hand, Douglas Kootenay, Constable Samuel J. Leach and Dorothy Leach. Their individual motivations varied greatly, yet they shared the same desire to represent Canada as proud, competent and productive citizens. These First Nations men wanted to go to Australia to compete internationally as Canadian athletes and to demonstrate the distinct qualities of their traditions. A desire for adventure, money and prestige were secondary factors. Interviews with the family members of Joe Crowfoot and Frank Many Fingers demonstrate how cultural identity, duty and the determination to overcome colonial oppression were reinforced through involvement in professional rodeo. The participation of these eight First Nations cowboys in Sydney reveals an early twentieth-century model of colonial resistance when counterhegemonic declarations of cultural value were authenticated through international presentation.

Constable Leach played the complex role of officially representing the Indian Affairs Branch and the RCMP, while symbolically representing the Canadian state. He became the mediator, who was supposed to make sure everyone's needs, preferences and concerns were met. His correspondence and reports regarding the trip reveal many tensions, yet also stress the fluidity of identity recreated through notions of "others" and "self," which can occur through the experience of travel and performance. Mrs. Leach played the supporting role of wife, nurse and bookkeeper.

The power of individual agency can be clearly seen through the complex perspectives of these actors. While their differences accentuate incompatibilities between colonizers and the colonized, the intimacy encouraged through travel accentuated both playful and antagonistic interactions. The sense of relationship that developed within this Canadian troupe facilitated resistance to nationalist ideals by all its members. It was at such moments that these opposing representatives of a colonial state came closer together. The journey to a foreign land, combined with the performance of national identity for a foreign audience, allowed for altered representations of citizenship.

Chapter Five will assume the perspective of the audience, the Australian public. Their generalized view of this Canadian troupe began with a distinct domestic comprehension of internationally popular cultural stereotypes. Constable Leach was supposed to be a noble officer, courteous and brave in every thought and action. The "Red Indians" were supposed to be savages. Although their perceptions of Leach were not altered, their perceptions of the First Nations cowboys were. In the end, they viewed them as individuals and not mythological Wild West villains. This revised Australian perspective represents the final effect of the RAS's publicity scheme and, I would argue, an affirmation of reality that altered colonial ideology by favoring equality over subjection.

Fig. 1: "Two of the First Nations Cowboys Relaxing at the Easter Show." April 1939. Courtesy National Library of Australia.

A detailed analysis of each perspective will demonstrate the complex processes inherent to the production of national, cultural and individual identity. Although identities are generally classified according to a "them" versus "us" dichotomy, they also shift, meld and mimic each other, and are constructed through a dialectic process.[14] I argue that this process is made meaningful due to a variety of influences including political, cultural and economic need, individual agency and the approval of others. These interrelational aspects of identity are again complicated through transcultural experience. In this case, the intended political aim of colonial nations was altered by the input of individuals hired to represent them, and then further altered by the audience's response.

Popular culture is a powerful venue for the production of stereotypes that benefit colonial nations. However, the reciprocal nature of their production, which requires an audience and actors to complete the cycle, also allows for alterations to political intent and ideological agendas. While the producers of this story, the RAS and the Indian Affairs Branch, tried to use race to establish political alliances, national recognition and economic security, in the end, the actors, eight First Nations cowboys and one RCMP officer, effected ideological challenges through personal interactions on their travels. Their individuated ideas about what constituted national identity shifted once they left their homes. A new sense of self was reflected in the presentations made available in press reports and at the Royal Easter Show. Consequently, their Australian audience was able to see a new view of "Red Indians," a view where "Red Indians" became average people, "just like them." Ultimately, this story demonstrates how the intercultural transactions of a small group of people destabilized stereotypical beliefs created through larger popular cultural venues and colonial projects.

1

The Australian Request

> The big new thrill at this year's Royal Show will be the Chuck Wagon Races, with Red Indians in full war-paint going helter-skelter around the arena, chuck wagons swaying and jostling perilously, horse teams urged with wild whooping into a frenzy of speed.[1]

Two members of the Royal Agricultural Society (RAS) of New South Wales, A.W. Skidmore, the assistant secretary, and T.B. MacFarlane, a member of the council, arrived in Vancouver on 25 August 1938. This marked the beginning of a 28,000-mile tour across North America, where they intended to investigate and compare exhibitions and rodeos with "a view to improving ring attractions at future Royal Easter Shows."[2] They attended all of the famous shows en route including rodeos in Calgary, Detroit, Chicago and New York, as well as the Canadian National Exhibition, the Pacific National Exhibition and the New York World's Fair. Skidmore and MacFarlane claimed to be searching for "something new in Show entertainment,"[3] something sensational to attract record crowds to the upcoming 1939 show. Every detail of these North American events, from types of promotional materials to display techniques, was recorded for future reference. According to their reports, they finally decided that a troupe of "Red Indian" cowboys from Alberta would be the "most distinctive and thrilling attraction" ever staged in Australia.[4]

Earlier in August, in conjunction with the Toronto Board of Trade, the Canadian Manufacturers' Association, and the Rotary and Kiwanis clubs, a special meeting had been held at the Empire Club of Canada in Toronto. At this meeting the Honorable Sir Earle Page, minister of trade and commerce for Australia, emphasized the desirability of expanding Australia's trade with Canada, Britain and the United States. He also alluded to the desire to cement imperial ties in the face of impending war. An analysis of this speech accompanied with Skidmore and MacFarlane's final report to the RAS demonstrates the intensity of the isolation and fear Australian authorities were feeling at this time. On one level, the request by the RAS to hire "Red Indians" from Canada was considered a promotional tool to entice record crowds to the 1939 show. However, on another level it served the more important purpose of reinforcing political alliances between these two countries.

The RAS and its Ambassadors

The evolution of the RAS fits neatly into the wider Western trend of promoting nationalism, progress and technology through exhibitory venues, which first became popular in the 1850s. Various types of fairs, from local agricultural shows to World's Fairs, were used as instruments of hegemony to support imperialism, to promote burgeoning capitalist endeavors, and to shape "class identities, social spaces and public spaces."[5] Visual culture and the art of display became essential in defining aspects of national distinction. Colonial nations in particular, such as Canada and Australia, were attempting to develop distinct national identities to differentiate themselves from British imperial power.[6] Agricultural fairs in North America originated at the beginning of the nineteenth century and were devoted to educating practicing framers in ways of improving their cultivation of livestock and crops through the use of various technologies.[7] Symbolically, this cultivation was linked to the colonial project of civilizing wilderness frontiers.[8] By the mid-twentieth century, advertisement in various forms was common and included programs or brochures, which were handed out to fair-goers as they entered.[9] These were seen as opportunities for educating the public. Often comments promoting the importance of the fair were based on ideas about patriotism and nationalism. The Royal Easter Show is a good example of an exhibitionary context which grew from a small fair, based on local agricultural competition, to a larger venue that incorporated the mandates of national development and the cultivation of colonial character.[10]

In 1822 the RAS was created on the premise that there was a dire need in Australia for the development of improved farming skills to better support growing urban populations and export markets. Organizations based on agricultural improvement, which were popular in Britain, provided camaraderie as well as political and financial support for their members. Once transferred to the colonies, in this case Australia, they played an integral part in converting and organizing land for colonial purposes. The RAS began as a private club, holding its first public show in 1823. This show lasted only one day, had no entertainment and was designed strictly to educate the public and to create competition among its members.[11] By 1918, the once day-long agricultural exhibitions had grown into ten- to twelve-day shows with multiple pavilions and elaborate display areas. Increasing interest from exhibitors and visitors attracted prestige, substantial awards and prize money. Entertainment features and sideshows enhanced attendance. By the late 1920s, "Ring Events" at what was now called the Royal Easter Show included a "Grand Parade," equestrian contests, sideshows and wood-chopping competitions. Attendance almost doubled in one decade, reaching 642,290 by 1930.[12]

In 1929 the collapse of the US stock market led to bankruptcy and unemployment in Australia. The Royal Easter Show was hit hard. By 1935 revenues had dropped approximately 30 per cent across the board. In order to compensate for this loss and attract more visitors, the "Ring Programme" was improved with acts such as Russian Cossacks, North American cowboys and "Red Indians." These improvements were accompanied by forward-looking policies of expansion and enhancement intended to offset the effects of economic depression and newly felt uncertainties of impending war. In 1938 the largest and most successful Easter show to date included celebratory events to commemorate the 150th anniversary of the founding of Australia. A cavalcade of floats and a massive parade focused on themes of industrialization and commerce opened the show, which was attended by over one million people.[13] The success of the 1938 Royal Easter Show bolstered the royal society's confidence. Plans were made to expand and improve all aspects in the upcoming year with the expectation that the 1939 show would become even more spectacular.

On 8 July, Col. Cosgrave, Canada's trade commissioner in Australia, sent a request to Dr. H.W. McGill, director of the Indian Affairs Branch in Ottawa. It stated, "Royal Show Sydney anxious secure small group Indians as rodeo attraction 1939 Exhibition. Secretary arriving Vancouver August 26. Strongly recommend permission by Indian department. Is demonstration possible Banff or Calgary August 27. Brodie C.P.R. informed willing cooperate. Cable reply. Consider excellent publicity Canada."[14] McGill's response was immediate. He indicated that this would not be a problem as long as all performers' expenses and return fares were paid. His quick acceptance contradicted forty years of government restrictions on travelling First Nations performers, particularly those leaving the country. Consequently, the reciprocal desire of the Canadian government and the RAS to enhance the 1939 show with the presence of Canadian First Nations cowboys was made evident prior to the arrival of Skidmore and MacFarlane.

At the end of July, Skidmore and MacFarlane departed on their two-month excursion to North America. An analysis of their personal backgrounds explains why they were chosen by the RAS. However, the actual purpose of their trip remains a mystery, considering the fact that the decision to hire a "small group of Indians as a rodeo attraction"[15] had already been made. It would seem as though their elaborate and expensive adventure was intended to be a diplomatic tour and research project, with the secondary purpose of finalizing decisions as to what type of "Indians" would be hired.

Born in Scotland and educated in New Zealand, Thomas Brydone MacFarlane was a Corriedale sheep breeder from Merriwa, NSW (see Fig. 2). He was a member of the Australasian Corriedale Society, the NSW Sheepbreeder's Association and the RAS council for many years.[16] MacFarlane was heavily involved in the professionalization of rodeo in Australia and was in fact the person who organized the first "campdrafting"[17] event at the Royal Easter Show in 1935. His efforts are recognized in a trophy for the highest score in this event, which has been presented at the show since 1969. MacFarlane's influence extended to all of the equestrian activities at the 1939 show.

When compared to cattle ranching in North America, cattle ranching in Australia seems more strenuous, dangerous and intriguing. Cattle drives are measured in months as opposed to weeks, and ranches encompass vast areas of rough, desert-like terrain.[18] Competitions involving horses became a part of this lifestyle between 1880 and 1890. They were called "Bushmen's Carnivals" and were primarily predicated on skills inherent to campdrafting. In this event the rider moved into a yard filled with cattle, which was called a "camp." He chose one animal and then proceeded to maneuver this animal through a figure-eight-styled obstacle course. The rider's score was based on his time and skill managing his/her horse.[19] Currently campdrafting remains the only event indigenous to Australia in a sport based on American-styled contests based in turn on far older Spanish and Spanish-American traditions. The inclusion of "buckjumping" and "bullock-riding" to campdrafting competitions in 1929 is remembered in Australia as "the first modern rodeo."[20]

T.B. MacFarlane was the organizer of this original event. He also persuaded a few RAS councilors to attend with the intention of plugging competitive rodeo as

Fig. 2 (left): T.B. McFarlane, and Fig. 3 (right): A.W. Skidmore, "Two Australians Visit City in Quest for Cowboy Riders." *Detroit Free Press*, 3 October 1938.

a spectacle for the Royal Easter Show. The impetus for MacFarlane's persistence in promoting American-styled rodeo was centred on his desire to see Australia become internationally competitive in sporting events related to horsemanship. In 1939 MacFarlane noted that while Australia's "Spirit of Rodeo" had links to American traditions, it had actually originated on cattle stations where "there are no finer horsemen in the world."[21] In an article written about the 1939 Easter show, MacFarlane described in detail his desire to promote international competition: "In setting to make a feature of Rodeo, the Council of the Royal Agricultural Society went in for it thoroughly, to insure it being of a standard well in keeping with other sections of what is now regarded as one of the world's greatest annual exhibitions. With that end in view, the Rodeo was developed into a kind of international tournament, picked teams of cowboys and cowgirls from Canada and America being regularly brought over to pit their skill against leading Australian riders."[22] McFarlane's sincere interest explains why he wanted to introduce chuckwagon races to the Royal Easter Show. These races, which were recognized as distinctly Canadian,[23] had never been seen in Australia before. Besides offering a unique form of entertainment, they also offered a way for MacFarlane to prove the superiority of Australian riders by challenging Canadian and American teams in an event indigenous to their western cultures.

An analysis of Anthony William Skidmore's background suggests a complementary influence. Skidmore had been the secretary and accountant for the RAS since 1934. He was born and educated in England and spent seven years working for the British government (see Fig. 3). He was also a member of the "Citizens of Sydney Organizing Committee," which was responsible for the 150th anniversary celebrations in 1938.[24] During his stint as secretary, Skidmore took on all of the responsibility for the organization and promotion of commercial displays having to do with the Royal Easter Show, particularly the "Ring Programme."[25] His promotional emphasis was based on stereotypical images common to American-styled Wild West shows, very popular in Australia at this time.

Between the late nineteenth century and the early twentieth century, a complex collage of Plains Indian imagery was mass-produced in multiple venues and readily consumed in most European countries. Native "savages" wearing feathered war bonnets and white cowboys driving stagecoaches were commonly recognized symbols of American frontier success.[26] The glorification of this mythology in Wild West shows, dime novels, western music and motion pictures had a profound effect on the Australian public between 1920 and 1930.[27] At this time a complex social fascination was inextricably tied to the development of cattle ranching, agriculture and Australian fantasies about the colonization of empty frontiers. Through the use of stock imagery and sensational commentary, which was applied to all promotional material related to the show, Skidmore was simply following this national and international trend.

On 28 August, MacFarlane and Skidmore attended a demonstration on the Stoney Reserve in Morley, Alberta in order to "choose types of Indians" and to "make selection[s] of teepees, costumes, regalia etc. from the band's full supply"[28] to take to Sydney. They had originally wanted to attend the famous Indian Days at Banff or the Calgary Stampede, but these fairs had already taken place earlier in the summer. This demonstration, which consisted of a handful of First Nations men wearing casual apparel while practicing archery, did not impress them. They claimed that this spectacle lacked "life and dash."[29] Even though a mini-demonstration of rodeo skills was quickly organized, this real "Indian Village" still did not resemble the Wild West shows they were used to and wanted to see.

Following this encounter and several meetings with Schmidt their request was modified to include an "Indian Village" and handicraft sales in order to satisfy the Indian Affairs Branch's preferences. Final decisions followed these criteria:

1) All the Indians should be good horsemen and have full costumes of feathers, buckskin coats and trousers, beads etc.
2) The Indians bring their own saddles and bridles.
3) To add to the interest of these Indians whilst in Sydney we suggest they bring with them as comprehensive a stock of beadwork as is possible. In this regard we would suggest bangles, gloves, belts, handbags, jewelry, headdresses and, if possible, Indian outfits for children. We have no hesitation in saying there will be considerable demand for all articles within the Indian village to be created on the show grounds during the currency of our Easter Show.
4) Three of the Indians should be capable of driving a chuckwagon which events it was agreed upon at our previous conference could be staged.[30]

For publicity purposes they also requested stories and legends of the bands represented, as well as pictures of the men in their costumes.[31]

Throughout four months of negotiations Skidmore and MacFarlane repeatedly made their priorities clear by stressing that "these Indians" must "wear their own costumes of feathers, buckskin, beads, etc."[32] at all times when in public and particularly upon landing in Sydney. The combined emphasis on rodeo and Wild West shows was evident in their insistence that "three of the Indians should be capable of driving a chuckwagon."[33] What they described as an "unforgettable turn of events"[34] would become the highlight of the show (see Fig. 12 on page 28). In their imagination, First Nations men wearing traditional beaded costumes and driving chuckwagons was strangely ironic considering they were "Indians" acting like stagecoach drivers. In reality, First Nations men in Alberta were highly competitive in chuckwagon racing at this time.

Modernity at the Royal Easter Show and the Accompanying Brochures

Skidmore and MacFarlane were also responsible for three brochures created in conjunction with the 1939 Easter Show. The first two, the *Souvenir Ring Programme* and the *Rodeo Programme*, were designed for public consumption. The third, published for the benefit of the RAS council, was a lengthy report of their North

Fig. 4. The Front Cover of the *Souvenir Ring Programme*, Royal Easter Show, Sydney, 1939. Courtesy Peggy Maxwell, private collection.

American tour. In all three, stereotypical images of North American Plains Indians, both textual and visual, were used.

The *Souvenir Ring Programme* was handed out to showgoers as they passed through the gates of the exhibition grounds, Moore Park. The cover highlighted a commercial image of a grimacing Plains Indian in full regalia charging at the audience with spear held high. Below this central figure were very small photographs of equestrian riders, wood-chopping events and free-hand drawings of various agricultural products (see Fig. 4). This elaborate illustration was followed by page one, which was in effect a second cover. It featured an aerial view of Moore Park documenting its large configuration of modern-looking concrete buildings. This secondary cover page was titled, *Ring Programme and Souvenir Book with E.R.D.A.: Electrical and Radio Exhibition, 1939* (see Fig. 5). It provided a startling contrast to the front cover page and suggested a dual purpose for the brochure. The Australian audience was promised both the excitement of primitiveness and the enticement of modernity.

The brochure itself contained maps, ads, short articles and daily timetables of the events at the show. In the schedule of events "Red Indians" were listed as celebrities and their participation in rodeo competitions was made obvious, yet was not exaggerated (see Fig. 6). There were also three separate pages depicting collages of pictures advertising all of the ring events. One was made up solely of images of the First Nations cowboys in action (see Fig. 7).

Themes emphasizing electrical products and radios were predominant. There were multiple ads and a directory outlining in detail thirty-five exhibits of merchandise. The *Souvenir Ring Programme* also contained a lengthy article on the necessary components of "An All Electrical Home." This inclusion seemed particularly unusual considering the fact that none of these exhibits took place in the show ring, but were housed in modern exhibition venues such as the "Commemorative Pavilion," the "Electrical and Radio Exhibit Building," the "Royal Hall of Industries," and the "Manufacturers Hall." The weighty promotion of new electrical advances confirms the observation that savage "Red Indians" were only a minor attraction, used to visually enhance through opposition the main reasons for attending the show. Modernity and progress were the important themes, which would hopefully encourage economic growth and positive nationalist ideals.

The second brochure designed for public consumption was titled, *Rodeo Programme*. On the cover was a standard rodeo image of a cowboy on a bucking bronco (see Fig. 8). This brochure focused on rodeo events; however, it also included advertisements for businesses such as the "Atlantic Union Oil Co."[35] The introduction contained a two-page article written by MacFarlane, which briefly described the development of rodeo in North America and Australia. In

Fig. 5: Page one of the *Souvenir Ring Programme*, Royal Easter Show, Sydney, 1939. Courtesy Peggy Maxwell, private collection.

it he emphasized the high standards of competition that would be seen at the Royal Easter Show, and the fact that rodeo provided both entertainment and a demonstration of the "onerous work being carried out in the cattle lands."[36] His focus was on the heroic riding skills of a legendary Australian outlaw named Alan

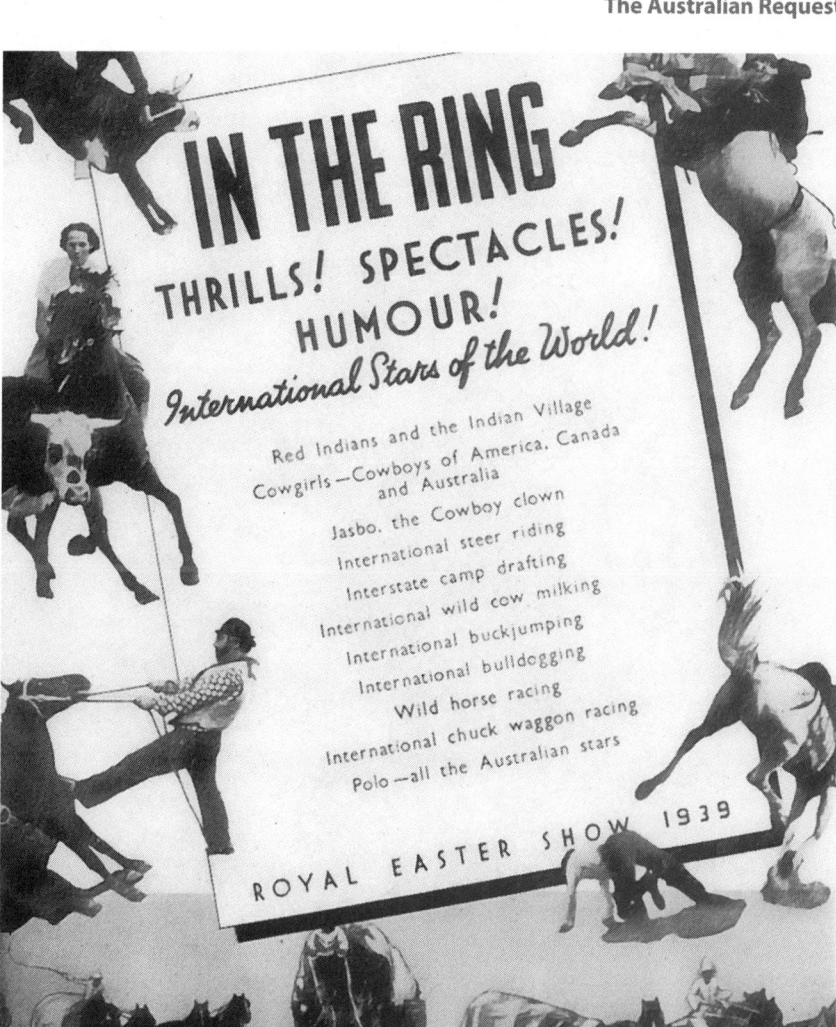

Fig. 6: "In the Ring." Advertisement in the of the *Souvenir Ring Programme*, Royal Easter Show, Sydney, 1939. Courtesy Peggy Maxwell, private collection.

Lindsey Gordon and the innate Australian love of animals. He did not mention any "Red Indians."

The primary indication of the First Nations cowboys' presence was a one-page collage featuring photographs of the men performing in traditional attire (Fig. 9). There was also a scorecard with a description of the "Taronga Zoological Park Red Indian Bareback Race,"[37] and an advertisement accompanied by another scorecard,

Fig. 7: Collage of First Nations Cowboys in the of the *Souvenir Ring Programme*, Royal Easter Show, Sydney, 1939. Courtesy Peggy Maxwell, private collection.

this one for the "Clements Tonic International Chuck Wagon Race" (see Fig. 10). While the Clements ad epitomized stereotypical representations and described the men as "American Red Indians" who would provide "hair-raising stunts,"[38] the accompanying scorecard positioned them as legitimate competitors. Such contradictory emphasis followed in all other references to this Canadian team.

The third brochure was made available only to the RAS council and its political affiliates. It was intended to demonstrate the vital part that the RAS was playing in "the many phases of Australian national and educational development."[39] This thirty-six-page brochure presented information Skidmore and MacFarlane had obtained on their tour and primarily resembled a travelogue of landscapes

Fig. 8: Cover Page of the *Rodeo Brochure*, Royal Easter Show, Sydney, 1939. Courtesy Peggy Maxwell, private collection.

and exhibitions. It also devoted several pages to the inspiring new "show entertainment" they found in Alberta. Curiously, on page two, sandwiched between the table of contents, a list of RAS officers, and a foreword written by

Fig. 9: Collage of First Nations Cowboys in the *Rodeo Brochure*, Royal Easter Show, Sydney, 1939. Courtesy Peggy Maxwell, private collection.

Sir Samuel Hordern (the president of the RAS), was a full-page photograph of the "Red Indians Chiefs on the Morley Reserve, Alberta, Canada"[40] (see Fig. 11). This photograph was strikingly out of place and raised the question: What role did four Canadian First Nations men have in furthering Australian nationalism and educational development?

These men have "NERVES of STEEL"!

Hair-raising stunts—by these daring American Red Indians—will thrill spectators at the R.A.S. Rodeo. If you've never seen a "Chuck Wagon Race," come to the Rodeo and learn what it means to have "Nerves of Steel"! . . . . .

CLEMENTS TONIC *gives you "Nerves of Steel"!*

Fig. 10: "Clements Tonic Ad." *Rodeo Brochure*, Royal Easter Show, Sydney, 1939. Courtesy Peggy Maxwell, private collection.

Detailed commentary about "Red Indians" does not occur until page thirteen. Here substantial descriptions provide insight into transnational racist attitudes of the 1930s. The comments in this section of the brochure seem to have been influenced by imagined Australian stereotypes combined with specific details supplied by the Canadian government.[41] Three subsections exaggerated the primitiveness, savageness and exoticism of First Nations in Canada, while one visually described the "colourful Indian Village"[42] that would be at the show. It also attempted to provide an educated view on tipi construction and decoration.

The first subsection of this brochure was titled, "Red Indians for Easter Show." It began by explaining "warriors [had been] specially selected so that ring-siders [would] be entertained by dashing performances [that were] truly rare North American spectacles reserved for occasions of national festivity."[43] This section went on to state that these Canadian "Red Indians" would "recall fast-moving stories" similar to those involving "Buffalo Bill, Daniel Boone and the beloved Deerfoot."[44] Their presence was described as offering the Australian public "[an] opportunity of seeing for the first time" typical representatives of the vanishing race of "Red Men."[45] In actual fact, a number of North American Aboriginal performers had participated in either Wild West shows or rodeo venues

Fig. 11: Picture of "Red Indian Chiefs" sent from Canada, published in the *Royal Agricultural Society of New South Wales Brochure*, Sydney, Australia, April 1939, p. 2.

in Australia on multiple occasions prior to 1939.[46] Most specifically, a troupe of First Nations performers from Lytton, British Columbia had travelled to Australia in 1911. It performed during the RAS's Grand Easter Show at the same Moore Park showgrounds in Sydney. Interestingly, although the 1911 show was billed as "The Wild West in Australia" and described as the "Real Thing,"[47] there was no mention of this performance in the RAS council brochure of the 1930s. Perhaps this acknowledgment may have diluted the "new thrill" that was promised.

The second subsection was titled, "Famous Blackfeet Tribe." It seems to have been heavily influenced by literature brought over from Canada. In it the Blackfoot were specifically hailed as the most famous and dangerous of all

Canada's first peoples. They were described as being taller and more intelligent than other Aboriginal people.[48] A brief history falsely highlighted their fall from a once noble state, which was precipitated by the decimation of buffalo, elk and antelope herds. Ironically, this description continued by refuting any previous suggestion of intelligence through its explanation of the Blackfoot's reaction to this dilemma. "Dazed and unable to comprehend the terrible calamity which had overtaken them, clinging doggedly to their belief that the buffalo had hidden and would soon return to their loved grass lands, the Red Men were slow to rally."[49] This subsection concluded by stating that the Canadian government had rectified this problem by transforming these "once wild hunters into gentle farmers"[50] within a single generation.[51] In reality, during this time period, many First Nations in Alberta were self-sufficient due to their innate entrepreneurial skills and not the endeavours of the Canadian government.[52] Again, a heavy reliance on false sensationalism was used to impress RAS council members.

Another subsection titled "Fast-Moving Scenes" glorified the thrill of seeing "Red Indians" driving chuckwagons by emphasizing the picturesque traditional attire that the men would be wearing. It promised brilliant "Indians [in] war-paint, flowing feathers headdresses, buckskins, exquisitely hand-made buck skin moccasins and ornamental bead-work trappings." Although they were "well versed in traditional deeds of daring," the real thrill at this show would be watching them drive chuckwagons. Chuckwagons were described as "light four-wheeled conveyors of food supplies and other gear used by North American cowboys on their cattle round-ups."[53] The thrill and spectacle promised by Skidmore and MacFarlane reversed Wild West/rodeo fantasies by placing savage "Indians" in the driver's seat, where they imagined only white cowboys were supposed to sit (see Fig. 12).[54] Although they explained that this event was popular at "Cowboy and Indian stampedes and exhibitions in Canada and America," the excitement of seeing "Australian rough-riders, spurring on their charge and hurling defiance at rivals" would provide an "unforgettable turn of events," which would titillate the patriotic instincts of Australian fair-goers on a twice daily basis.[55]

The final subsection was titled, "Indian Village." It used a great deal of visual description to explain the addition of "a picturesque and colourful Indian village,"[56] which would inevitably add "a touch of Canadian atmosphere"[57] to this splendid attraction. Skidmore and MacFarlane's report stated that eight tipis provided by the Canadian government would form a semi-circle.[58] A Sun Dance Lodge, constructed by the Indians themselves out of "traditional saplings and

Fig. 12: "A New Thrill: Chuck Wagon Races at the Royal Show." Advertisement in *The Sun* (Sydney) 29 March 1939. (This ad was published in a variety of Australian newspapers between March and April of 1939).

green bushes," would be in the centre, and immediately in front there would be a "Canadian Mountie bell tent" with a "Union Jack flag unfurled"[59] on top. The rest of this section described the specifics of tipi construction, and the traditional meanings associated with this construction.

Such details about First Nations culture were not readily available to the Canadian public. In fact, a survey of Canadian textbooks of the late 1930s reveals that comments in the RAS brochure were much more sympathetic. In Alberta high schools, where W. L. Grant's *History of Canada* was used as a standard text between 1924 and 1938, descriptions were minimal and often derogatory.[60] First Nations women were characterized as "drudges" and "mules," and First Nations men were described as "lazy," "ignorant" and "superstitious." In Ontario, descriptions were even more negative. Out of 583 references only 49 were positive. "Friendliness" and "ally" were the only positive terms used, whereas negative terms such as "savage," "warlike," "torturer" and "half-breed" abounded.[61] There was no attempt made to actually explain cultural activities, their purpose or meanings. It must then be assumed that the information used in this section of the RAS brochure was provided by the Indian Affairs Branch and privileged the viewpoint of Albertan Indian agents only. Their paternalistic attitude, which will be discussed in the next chapter, defined their role as government officials and formed a view of First Nations people that was simultaneously sympathetic and protective, yet belittling.

The detailed descriptions in this RAS brochure, which were intended to impress and educate members of the council about First Nations culture, were in actual fact a compilation of popular stereotypes. Some were obviously gleaned from personal and distinctly Australian beliefs. Others were gleaned from reports allocated by Canadian Indian agents and other government sources. None of them came directly from the cultural groups involved, who obviously were not consulted. At the same time, none of the descriptions reflected the generalized negative beliefs of Canada's non-Aboriginal population. Still, all of the comments were obtuse exaggerations, particularly those suggesting that the Canadian government had saved First Nations people from near extinction.

Essentially, all three brochures emphasize the promotion of modernity, technology and industry as key factors in the future economic success of Australia. Images of First Nations from Canada appear as a counterpoint to visually accentuate this goal. Stereotypical portraits replaced commentary about these men's personal identities or career histories. The simple fact that they were not primitive and war-like, but established ranch owners and well-known rodeo competitors, was never considered. Their entrepreneurial accomplishments were ancillary to generalized racist clichés.

Economic Depression, World War II and the Unspoken Political Motivations of the RAS

The goal of Skidmore and MacFarlane's trip to North America, as it was publicly stated, was to investigate and compare exhibitions and rodeos with "a view to improving ring attractions at future Royal Easter Shows."[62] The emphasis in their final report was, however, quite different. During their travels throughout North America it became clear to them that North Americans knew very little about Australia. Skidmore and MacFarlane found it deplorable that there were no comments about Australian affairs in the leading newspapers or any mention of current events or market reports.[63] Their solution was to disseminate as much propaganda to the "right sources" as possible. While touring they distributed nearly a hundred copies of the 1938 Royal Easter Show brochure, and presented an album of photographs from this show at every available opportunity. They attempted to forge as many alliances as possible with North American officials associated with either rodeo or exhibition venues. Promises were made for the future promotion of Australian talent in both Canada and the United States.[64]

Skidmore and MacFarlane were not alone in feeling distressed about Australia's isolation from North America. The economic pressures of the 1930s hit Australia hard. Its reliance on trade and monetary loans from countries other than Britain was essential after 1920.[65] A determined push for increased import trade with Canada began in 1935 when Prime Minister J.A. Lyons of Australia visited Toronto. His speech to the Empire Club was focused on the fact that Australian and Canadian trade alliances had been strong for many years. Nevertheless, Canada consistently exported three times more than they imported.[66] Later, in 1937, Percy Pease, a representative from Queensland, spoke to the Empire Club and blatantly commented on the size of Australia's national debt and the need, which this time sounded more desperate, for increased trade with Canada. He emphasized that considerable amounts of American capital had been invested in Australia and suggested that Canada should follow their example.[67] In 1938, in a public radio broadcast, Sir Earle Page, another Australian politician, lightheartedly focused on trade and borrowing money as the primary ways that Australia made itself known to the rest of the world. On a more serious note he stated that increased international trade and mutual interdependence were the keys to world peace. He proposed that the joined economic forces of the British Empire, Canada, the United States, and Australia would be able to rescue the world from "this welter of chaos,"[68] by which he meant impending world war.

Broken trade alliances with Japan had placed Australia in a particularly vulnerable position. In 1936 the Australian government created a "Trade Diversion Policy" in an attempt to control the balance of imports and exports between its two major trading partners, Japan and the US. This policy resulted in a major trade war with Japan and a minor trade war with the Americans.[69] Broken alliances, accompanied by Japan's imposing presence in the Pacific, created deep-seated fears of an invasion.[70] Between 1935 and 1941, "consecutive Australian governments were aware of their nation's vulnerability and worked anxiously for a commitment of military support from the US, as well as Great Britain."[71] Australia's only hope of security, both economically and politically, was to procure solid alliances within the military web developed between Great Britain, Canada and the US.

Australia's vulnerability in the late 1930s intensified a resurgence of nationalism aimed at eliminating public fears. There was a determined push to create a progressive and competitive nation. Manufacturers advocated for a new economic base focused heavily on industry.[72] As White explains, "The image of Australia as an industrial nation was part of an ideological offensive."[73] It is conceivable that most, if not all, Australian diplomatic visits made during the immediate pre-war period were aimed at solidifying alliances and repairing the damage caused by convoluted trading tactics. Cultural alliances enhanced political alliances. Skidmore and MacFarlane's extended tour of rodeos and exhibitions in North America, which consequently created "amicable relationships,"[74] was also an important diplomatic venture. Their appreciation of western cowboy and rodeo culture contributed to Australia's quest for partnerships within an essential web of military and economic co-operation.

Conclusions

Skidmore and MacFarlane's final speech to the president and councilors of the RAS concluded with the insistent recommendation that a World's Fair should be organized in conjunction with the Royal Easter Show within the next two years. They viewed this recommendation as a brilliant solution to the problem of Australia's global isolation. Skidmore and MacFarlane were greatly impressed by the grandeur of the New York World's Fair,[75] and wanted to "wrap a World's Fair around [their] Royal Show."[76] They saw this American promotion of technology and consumerism as a "stepping stone in the progress and advancement of civilization and the education of the masses."[77] Although they realized that it would be a gargantuan undertaking, they also imagined that a World's Fair would be a "golden opportunity to place before the whole world that possibility of Australia becoming one of the most important continents of the world of the future."[78]

Skidmore and MacFarlane's proposal never materialized and the impact of this suggestion on the RAS council remains unknown. The onset of World War II disrupted any further plans. By the fall of 1939, military authorities had commandeered most of the buildings in Moore Park. By June 1940, six thousand troops were billeted there.[79] In 1941 the RAS produced a much-diminished Royal Empire Show, the last such public extravaganza until 1947.[80]

Throughout the 1939 Royal Easter Show's promotional material there were themes associated with rodeo, modern industry and "Red Indians." What at first glance seemed like a convoluted effort to promote nationalism actually became logical following an analysis of Skidmore and MacFarlane's recommendations and the political/economic context of the time. The romance of rodeo predicated on images Buffalo Bill and the Wild West represented a romantic "narrative of human ingenuity over the non-human world."[81] Rodeo not only glorified the cattle-ranching industry, but also supported this narrative. "Red Indians" provided the perfect visual signifier to support modernity as it opposed primitiveness. The international prevalence of themes related to Plains Indian stereotypes were promoted globally, and therefore easily recognized by Australian audiences.

Throughout their adventure Skidmore and MacFarlane seemed oblivious to the fact that they were responsible for hiring real people to participate in an international rodeo competition. In their requests to the Canadian government they focused on racialized comments that fed into century-old myths. The "Red Indians" they were familiar with from Wild West shows and American films did not translate into real life. Skidmore and MacFarlane's request was based on acquiring popular symbols, not hiring real people. Their request and subsequent promotion of this "small group of Indians"[82] speaks volumes about the power of racial stereotyping during this time period.

Although the importance of the link between popular culture and politics was evident, the question of actual power concerning the production of stereotypes remains complex. Skidmore and MacFarlane's fascination with the idea of "Red Indians" driving a chuckwagon was cultivated by decades of popular imagery that negated such a concept. Rodeo's public appeal as a fun and exciting sporting event made it a viable theme for the promotion of an agricultural show. In the end, although it was the innate reciprocal nature of stereotypes that actually motivated their reproduction, it was the RAS's authority that made this production possible.

They paid the wages and travel expenses of the First Nations men involved and instigated this event through joint political ties. From the Australian show promoters' point of view, the First Nations men's bodies, their traditional attire and rodeo skills were simply popular culture vehicles for the production of positive nationalist ideals and imperialist principles.

2

The Canadian Response

> I am anxious to know what is meant by demonstration. I presume it is an Indian Camp. Teepees, Indians in full Regalia etc. etc. NOT Rodeo Stampede Cowboy stuff![1]

COL. COSGRAVE'S REQUEST FROM SYDNEY, in July of 1938, was first sent to the Canadian Government Exhibition Commission in Ottawa. A.T. Seaman, the assistant commissioner, then forwarded it to H.W. McGill, the director of the Indian Affairs Branch.[2] Within ten days, T.H.L. MacInnes, the secretary of the Indian Affairs Branch, was sending letters out to all of the Indian agents in British Columbia, Saskatchewan and Alberta. At this point the department was claiming to have no objection to the undertaking, provided "the Indians [were] returned home and their expenses [were] paid."[3] MacInnes was also asking for reports "with regard to the advisability of sending a group of Indians to Sydney."[4] Agents from British Columbia and Saskatchewan claimed that they could not find "any Indian riders in their provinces."[5] Agents from Alberta sent lengthy responses indicating multiple reasons why their men should go and explicitly outlined the types of food, equipment and numbers of people they thought should be sent. By 27 July, it had been decided that only First Nations men from Alberta would be chosen and that C.P. Schmidt, the inspector of Indian Agencies in Alberta, would become the coordinator of the expedition.

Schmidt was born in Grandin, Saskatchewan, in 1881; he began work at Duck Lake for the Department of Indian Affairs in 1911. In 1936 he transferred to Calgary to become the inspector of Indian Agencies. Schmidt became the middleman in all negotiations between the RAS and Indian Affairs officials.[6] The telegram outlining his initial response to their request stated, "SEE NO REASON FOR REFUSING REQUEST PROVIDED GENUINE TYPE OF INDIAN ONLY IS SENT NOT MODERN RODEO COMPETITORS."[7] Throughout he repeatedly stressed the Indian Affairs Branch's desire to erase rodeo performances from the agenda. His response must be viewed as representative of the Indian agents under his charge and the officials above him, for it was never challenged. In the end, Schmidt gave permission for a troupe of rodeo competitors to travel to Australia with the provision that an "Indian Village," designed as a primitive/ethnographic display, would also be incorporated into the show. In this way, both the short-term economic needs of Alberta's Indian agents and the long-range goals of the Canadian colonial project were met.[8] Again, the nature of these negotiations demonstrated the influence popular culture had on political decisions. In this case, Wild West shows and the glamour of Buffalo Bill held little appeal. It was the influence of historical pageantry and the patterns of display common to World's Fairs that affected the Canadian response.

The Beginning of the Negotiations

Although MacFarlane and Skidmore had requested an enactment of either the famous Indian Days at Banff or the Calgary Stampede, Schmidt decided that it would be too costly to restage these events, which had already taken place earlier in the summer. The Indian agents involved claimed it was critical for all First Nations men to remain at home and attend to their farming responsibilities.[9] Therefore, it was decided that a quick trip to the Morley Reserve would be a viable alternative that would provide an opportunity for the Australian delegation "to see the Indians at home on their own lands."[10] This, according to Schmidt, would also be a more satisfying cultural experience than rodeo.

At Morley, arrangements were made to have a "half a dozen or more Indians" dressed in full regalia practicing archery skills in front of "3 teepees, with full interior decorating and equipment." It became immediately obvious that MacFarlane and Skidmore were disappointed with this performance and were looking for "rodeo stuff to go along with it." A few horses and steers were quickly rounded up and a mini-demonstration of rodeo skills took place. According to Schmidt, this impromptu display satisfied their curiosity.[11]

From the beginning of his correspondence with the Australian show promoters, Schmidt tried to shift their focus away from rodeo acts towards "real Indian pageantry."[12] He explained to them at a meeting in late August that "we," referring to the Indian Affairs Branch of the Department of Mines and Resources, "favor[ed] the colourful pageantry idea."[13] By this he meant staged historical re-enactments including elaborate traditional costuming and props. In a letter to MacInnes he listed his preferences in the order he imagined others in his department also perceived them.

> My first consideration would be a Group of Canadian Law-Abiding Indians, representing their forefathers who signed the Articles of Treaty No. 7 in 1876 with the representatives of the Great White Mother, the Beloved, Her Majesty, the late Queen Victoria.
>
> Secondly, the Colourful Indian Camp with Indians in full regalia. Primitive mode of transportation. Dog Travois. Horse Travois. Old Cart later known as (Red River Cart). Indians on horse back with Indian Saddles. Cloths, Blankets. Indian Campfires and Tripod. Meat Drying Racks. Willow Frame Sweat Baths, etc. etc. One or more women to display babies or (large dolls) in Moss Bags and Portable Cradles, etc. etc.,
>
> Thirdly, rough rider cowboy stuff, if approved. If 8 Indians only are sent they will be chosen from the Stonys, Bloods, and Blackfoot Bands.[14]

Schmidt also emphasized that there must be an RCMP officer in control of these "Indians" at all times.

The Preferred Performance

Schmidt's first preference can be clearly aligned with the format typical of historical pageantry. In the early twentieth century, such pageantry was a form of public ritual in which citizens acted out understandings of civic or national history. Relative to American examples, similar performances in Canada generally were smaller in scale; however, they remained important local events. Most pageants took place outdoors and were considered representative of real historical occurances. Their plot structures were based on a chronological model, which in North America often began with demonstrations of First Nations culture and ended with an idealized version of modern civil society. Throughout there were only minor conflicts, order and progress were well defined, and the ending was usually happy. Original historic research was combined with dramatic theatrical conventions, as well as amusing comic interludes. In general, these pageants were viewed publicly as artistic renditions of history; however, in actuality they were heavily laden with creative and subtle political meanings.[15]

Schmidt's preferred display clearly resembled historical pageantry. A re-enactment of the signing of Treaty 7, which covered the territories of all the groups involved in the Australian show, positioned First Nations as law-abiding, compliant and respectful of British and, therefore, Canadian rule. It claimed success in solidifying colonial control over western lands. It also glorified this success by suggesting that it had been achieved in a peaceful manner. Such a demonstration would visually assert that all problems associated with First Nations reform were under control.

In reality, political conflicts between First Nations and the Canadian government tell a very different story. Lands were not surrendered with a smile and a handshake. In fact, in 2003, the territories associated with Treaty 7 were still under review. Currently, First Nations elders continue to claim that Treaty 7 was a peace treaty only and not a surrender of land at all. The communities involved maintain that they only agreed to "share" this land with the white newcomers in exchange for education, medical assistance, and annuity payments.[16] Therefore, Schmidt's desired performance would have completely misrepresented the interests of First Nations in Canada.

The Second Canadian Preference

In the early twentieth century, "Indian Villages" were popular attractions in southern Alberta at Banff's Indian Days and the Calgary Stampede. For First Nations they provided an entrance into the tourist economy and a way to promote traditional culture to white audiences.[17] Long rows of painted tipis were adorned with traditional equipment and somewhat resembled Schmidt's lengthy description outlined in his second preference (see Fig. 13). Although Schmidt would have been very familiar with these displays, his second preference would have been based on the desire to mimic ethnographic/primitive village scenes, which were common to World's Fairs.

Between 1878 and 1937, "people shows"[18] served the dual purpose of promoting specific aspects of traditional indigenous cultures, while also promoting colonialism, even though most scholars refer to them as stylized representations only. This is due to the fact that the people involved were rarely consulted, and therefore, stereotypical representations developed through theatrical formats.[19] The first display of this type was constructed in Paris, in 1889, and called a "native village."[20] Four hundred people from various French colonies were situated in a row of constructed pavilions. Each cultural group's position in the row indicated their assumed position within an imagined racial hierarchy.[21] At subsequent fairs, organizers and/or ethnographers recreated similar village scenes, under

Fig. 13: A photograph of the Indian Village at Royal Easter Show. Sydney, Australia, 1939. Courtesy of the Royal Agricultural Society of New South Wales, private collection.

the conviction that they were creating authentic environments. Aboriginal people lived in these mock habitats for weeks, sometimes months, practicing their daily subsistence tasks and recreating ceremonial dances for a constant stream of local citizens and international tourists. "People shows" not only promoted the taxonomy of Darwinism and the rightness of colonialism, but also the anthropological positioning of Aboriginal peoples as traditional, static and vanishing.[22] The implied intentions, outlined by Schmidt in the second preference, can be aligned to this type of display.

Canada has a long tradition of using First Nations cultural symbols to represent itself as a unique nation. Elsbeth Heaman analyzed Canadian participation in international exhibitions prior to the World's Fairs and found that "the primitive" was assumed to be more visually spectacular and exotic than modern civilization.[23] Although the merits of using First Nations cultural materials to promote nationalism was consistently debated by government officials throughout the latter part of the nineteenth century, they proved to be an unfailing way to gain audience attention. Schmidt's image of the

"Indian Village" to be built in Sydney would have been inspired by the ones he saw in Calgary, but his complex negotiations with the Indian agents involved demonstrated the obsessive manner in which this display was to be ordered and arranged for an international audience. J.E. Pugh was the most explicit in describing his preferred presentation. He expounded on Schmidt's description with two full pages of details and calculations concerning the "Indian Village" set-up: "I believe that three teepees holding all 21 Indians would be preferable. I however suggested in my wire, 7–14–21, in one, two or three teepees, selected in sequence, Bloods, Blackfeet at Gleichen, and Morley, if only 7 selected, Bloods, if 14, Bloods and Blackfeet, if 21, take in Morley."[24] He went on to describe a gender and age breakdown that in his eyes would be appropriate: "The personnel, might be, One Head Chief to each Teepee, and 5 other Indians, 2 of these with their wives, and 1 single young Indian....The single Indian might be an older pupil at school."[25] Pugh even outlined the exact amounts of food required on a daily basis:

> Tea, half a pound for three days per person.
> Bread, 1½ lbs. per person per day.
> Fresh Meat 1½ lbs. per person per day.
> Syrup and Jams, 5 lbs. per teepee per 3 days, for seven persons....[26]

His incessant focus on elaborate arrangements was indicative of the lengths that Indian agents went to in controlling First Nations people's lives.[27]

The underlying motive for J.E. Pugh, W.B. Murray, G.H. Gooderham and T.F. Murray, the four agents involved, was the desire for financial gain. Throughout their correspondence the desperate need for financial returns was balanced against moralistic concerns. W.B. Murray expanded on this idea by claiming that "such an event [meaning rodeo competition] would glorify a part of Indian life which is a natural hindrance to their progress." He worried that any people he might send "would come back feeling too important to work," which he claimed was the case after every Stampede show in Banff or Calgary. His central concern was money. Murray was willing to give up moral concerns "if the financial return was considerable."[28] At this time First Nations people in the prairie provinces were legally not allowed to conduct any type of sale, barter or exchange without the written consent of an Indian agent.[29] Therefore, an Indian agent's personal investment in the type of performance seen in Australia would have also been critical to their sense of duty (both to the Canadian government and the First Nations people they were responsible for), and to their sense of pride. Throughout their correspondence it is unclear whether they would have allowed rodeo performers to travel overseas if financial straits had not been so severe.

Ironically, in the early twentieth century, legislation was introduced in an attempt to curtail all public displays of First Nations ceremonial or secular public performance.[30] Canadian government officials believed that these practices hindered the assimilation of First Nations people into mainstream Canadian society. In 1914, Section 149, an amendment to the Indian Act, was introduced to prohibit off-reserve dancing. It stated that any Indian dancer who performed in "any show, exhibition, stampede or pageant in an Aboriginal costume, outside of their own reserve, would be fined twenty-five dollars and/or be imprisoned for one month."[31] This new policy proved ineffective for multiple reasons. Indian agents were reluctant to implement it fully because First Nations performances were so popular, and because they provided much needed income to the participants.[32] In 1933, the words "in aboriginal costume" were deleted from Section 149 in an attempt to acquire greater control. The updated ruling stipulated that any participation, not only that involving traditional clothing, was punishable by the same fine and jail sentence.[33]

Overseas performances were a separate and more serious problem for the department because they influenced Canada's international reputation. In 1893, at the Chicago World's Fair, three groups of Canadian Aboriginal peoples participated in what was described as a "great Aboriginal encampment."[34] An Inuit display and a Kwakwaka'wakw (a First Nation culture from the Alert Bay region of northwestern Vancouver Island) display had been brought to the fair by private promoters. The Canadian government provided its own exhibit consisting of a mock residential school. It contradicted the other exhibits because it mimicked American models of schoolhouse settings where First Nations children demonstrated the industrious tasks of printing, sewing, knitting and spinning. The emphasis on industrial education was another attempt at illustrating how Canada's "savage people" had been brought into a civilized present without any bloodshed.[35]

George Hunt brought the Kwakwaka'wakw group to the fair.[36] He helped organize a dramatic act of resistance, as part of a traditional *hamatsa* dance, where he slashed the backs of two dancers, tied ropes through their wounds, and then ripped the flesh from their backs as they continued to move around the stage. This performance took place on the eve of "Great British Day," when they were assured that an exceptionally large audience would attend. This transgressive act was designed to protest the severe and unfair treatment that the Kwakwaka'wakw had received at the hands of missionaries and government officials in British Columbia. Fear and panic, in an audience of ten thousand fair-goers, was the immediate outcome of this production. The abolition of government-sanctioned out-of-country exhibits was the long-term accomplishment of this group.[37]

Between 1900 and 1931, multiple requests for a Canadian First Nations presence at American and European exhibitions were denied. In 1904, L.O. Armstrong, an agent for the Canadian Pacific Railway (CPR) asked if he could take a few "Indians" down to the New York Sportsman Show to perform as backwoods guides.[38] In 1905 George A. Dodge, from the Eastern Park Construction Company of Boston, requested twelve to fifteen "Canadian Indians" as an amusement for a miniature World's Fair on Nantucket. The Indian Affairs Branch responded by stating that it was "the rule of the Department not to encourage the Indians to leave their reserves for exhibitions."[39] In 1909, Adolf Klinko asked if he could take two First Nations men with him to Germany, Austria and perhaps Russia. He was willing to pay them one thousand dollars per year plus room and board, but his request was also denied.[40] Ironically, there were two very similar requests in 1911, one from the Great Empire Show held in London, England[41] and the other from Col. Stacey, a retired British officer living in Australia. Unlike the London request, Stacey's appeal was accepted and "seventeen red men" performed at the RAS Royal Easter Show.[42] It is difficult to ascertain from these files why one situation was favoured over the other. Perhaps, First Nations performances in Australia posed less of a threat to Canada's national reputation than performances in London might have. Approximately ten other requests were denied during this period.

In 1933, forty years after the Kwakwaka'wakw incident, attitudes in Ottawa began to change. In February, Sergeant Benjamin F. Sced of Clayoquot, BC[43] rekindled the notion that local Indian dancing would make a great attraction at larger international venues. In his letter to a local member of the House of Commons, he referred to the Glasgow Exhibition in 1901 as an example of a "great attraction" depicting "varied native attractions."[44] Deputy Superintendent General H.W. McGill of the Department of Indian Affairs was contacted, and he agreed that "there [was] merit" in the idea to allow "performance[s] of our Indian native dances"⁴⁵ for profit. This renewed enthusiasm was based on the fact that all First Nations had been hit hard during the depression. The idea was described as "timely and good" in terms of money-making, but caution was to be taken in terms of "Indian behaviors" while travelling.⁴⁶

In May, Kalvero Oberg, an organizer for the Century of Progress Exhibition in Chicago, asked for permission to hire eight First Nations people from Clayoquot, B.C. to perform for a period of five months. His idea was to feature "several of the most sharply contrasting of Indian cultures" in "high-class Indian exhibit[s]" within an extensive "Indian village" made up of approximately 150 to 200 people.⁴⁷ Fay-Cooper Cole, an anthropologist at the University of Chicago, backed his request. Cole explained their plans in length, which included reproducing Mayan buildings and a large natural setting which would house "a group of Winnebago," "a group of Sioux" and "the Southwest Navaho and Pueblo."⁴⁸ Private citizens from Chicago were apparently funding this endeavor and the Social Science Division guaranteed their safe return. Although Oberg and Cole's proposal was almost identical to the production that took place at the Chicago World's Fair in 1893, permission was granted immediately.⁴⁹ This "change of heart" reinstated "people shows" at international venues. In the logic of the Indian Affairs Branch, it was a way for Canadian First Nations to make money and become financially independent. At this time the promotion of nationalism was not mentioned.

"Indian Villages" as tourist attractions have always been highly controversial venues, in both First Nations communities and Canadian government circles, because of the identity issues associated with them, and not because of potential monetary gains. On the one hand, these types of performances degrade First Nations identity by perpetuating stereotypes, thus limiting individuality and the realities of cultural diversity.⁵⁰ On the other, they have also historically proven to be excellent venues for the widespread promotion of cultural identity, as well as places where white stereotypes can be challenged and regional land rights and citizenship can be declared.⁵¹ The perceived political impact of the 1939 performances was magnified due to its transnational nature. From Schmidt's and the Indian Affairs Branch's point of view, Joe Crowfoot, Joe Bear Robe, Frank Many Fingers, Joe Young, Edward One Spot, Jim Starlight, Johnny Left Hand and Douglas Kootenay should pose as actors in a visual performance that "complete[d] the script of colonial history"⁵² and colonial success.

Schmidt's Bottom Line

Schmidt's third consideration clearly expressed a limited, if not negligible, desire for "modern cowboy rough and risky stuff."[53] In North America, by the early 1930s, Wild West shows had vanished, to be replaced by an abundance of local and national rodeos.[54] Large, urban venues such as the Calgary Stampede provided the excitement of sporting competitions and the cultural reinforcement of local heritage festivals. They were also immersed in events, clothing and other paraphernalia representative of cowboy culture. From its inception in 1912, the Calgary Stampede promoted a romanticized public discourse about cowboys and ranching that ignored the reality of western Canada's multi-racial past.[55] The cowboy symbolized human triumph over "nature" and, subsequently, colonial mastery over the west. In the popular discourse of this mythology, First Nations represented a prehistoric past, one altered and renewed by Europeans. Cowboy culture, as it was enacted at rodeos, symbolically "re-enacted the 'taming' process whereby the wild was brought under control."[56] Indian agents felt that they were responsible for keeping the west "tame." Allowing "their Indians"[57] to perform as cowboys would defeat this purpose.[58]

Schmidt supported this perspective by describing rodeo in terms of its contradiction to the missionary work that was being done on the reserves. He adamantly claimed that missionaries did not want to see "their pupils being used as showmen in rough rodeo stuff at Stampedes or other places."[59] Missionaries favored the "colourful Historical Indian Pageantry," which went back to the days of treaty signing, "where the glad hand and the smiling lips prevailed."[60] An overview of the history of exhibitions and agricultural fairs demonstrates that the Indian Affairs Branch, as well as the Canadian government, preferred to see First Nations performers either displayed like museum pieces or as controlled, compliant pupils.[61] Static and traditional exhibits suggested a nostalgic view of a tamed frontier. Mock residential schoolrooms suggested that "progress" in transforming First Nations into productive citizens was successful.[62] Rodeo activities, it seemed, had no place in the creation of either scenario.

Rodeo culture was also noted for its connection with alcoholic and rowdy behavior.[63] Indian agents were on constant watch for abuses of alcohol because in Canadian law it was a "serious offence to supply any Indian"[64] with alcohol. There was also a serious concern and scientific belief at the time that alcohol had a biological effect on First Nations people that made them lose all control.[65] Schmidt clearly acknowledged the fear of this happening in his comments concerning the trip to Sydney. In a letter to Skidmore he stated that liquor of any sort was the "one thing that Indians cannot handle"; even one drink would render them unable to perform and quite possibly make them "go wild."[66]

In reality, for First Nations, rodeos began as part of Treaty Days and Indian Days celebrations. Horse races and betting were combined with storytelling, dancing and singing as activities that celebrated tradition and culture.[67] By the mid-1930s, for professional competitors in Alberta, it became a way to transcend the restrictions of reserve life. Practically, it offered opportunities for the acquisition of unmonitored income. Theoretically, it offered a space where First Nations people could transcend stereotypes through individual competition.[68] The blending of Indian identity with cowboy identity in professional rodeo venues reminded the Canadian public that First Nations people could compete on an equal basis.

For Indian agents rodeos were problematic because they inspired independence. Competitors travelled constantly, mingled with all sorts of people, and were less easy to monitor. Although it was difficult to gain complete financial independence, undetected monies were spent without the permission of the government agents involved. During the 1930s, when large amounts of government funding were required to support on-reserve living, Indian agents did not want to see any potential profits passing by them unnoticed.

Even though "Indian rough riders" were the least appealing performance option, in the end Schmidt acquiesced. However, Skidmore and MacFarlane made many concessions to their original request as well. In order to appease Schmidt they included "vaudeville stuff [and] Indian dancing."[69] The final contract allotted a wage of fifteen dollars a week for each First Nations performer.[70] This was considered a decent wage in 1938 and provided further incentive. It also stated that "the party w[ould] bring approximately one thousand (1000) pounds weight of bead-work."[71] By the end of the decade a national project to make all First Nations self-sufficient through handicrafts sales was well under way. This was believed to be a civilized industry that could be easily monitored, was safe, and would not encourage wild behavior. The appeal of handicraft sales justified Schmidt's compromise. Although he would have to sacrifice national promotion through historical pageantry, he would gain recognition for acquiring much-needed monetary returns for the Indian Affairs Branch.

Handicraft Sales as Government Income at the Royal Easter Show

Alberta was hit particularly hard during the Great Depression. In the late 1930s, the wheat industry collapsed due to unstable weather patterns. The second of two severe droughts in the prairies occurred in 1937.[72] Millions of Canadians were on relief. More specifically, between 1938 and 1939, annual relief monies paid to First Nations communities reached a peak expenditure of over one million dollars. This amount was far beyond the original totals for treaty payments and band funds.[73] Consequently, it became the Indian Affairs Branch's goal to recoup some of this debt.

In 1937 the Indian Affairs Branch created a "Welfare and Training Division," under the supervision of R.A. Hoey, to initiate a variety of vocational programs.[74] One of these was a marketing agenda for "Indian" handicraft work. The expansion of commercial production was the primary focus of this subdivision until the 1960s. The preservation of techniques, and/or designs of cultural and historic importance had little significance.[75] Ottawa assisted in the acquisition of supplies and indicated the types and styles of articles that should be made for sale. Most were utilitarian items and small novelty items intended for sale at very low prices. The subsequent wages given to the craftspeople were reduced in order to compete with foreign markets, meet retailer's wholesale objectives, and allow the Indian Affairs Branch to make a profit. First Nations families who participated received a small percentage of the gross sales and had to produce hundreds of items per month. For an example, "fully quilled round boxes were worth $3.60 to $12.00 per dozen; and plain woven sweet grass sewing baskets were worth $1.60 to $5.00 per dozen."[76] They were encouraged to make items that would sell on the retail market for under a dollar.

When the RAS asked for a supply of "Indian" handicrafts, Schmidt jumped at the chance to become part of this project. He immediately contacted Hoey to say that he would be responsible for gathering a shipment of approximately one thousand dollars worth of goods to send over to Australia. His plan was to buy small items for minimal prices so that the Indian Affairs Branch could profit from the proceeds. Unfortunately, in November 1938, when he contacted the Indian agents in Alberta, they all stated that they did not have any items available. The season was over, supplies such as deer hide were scarce, and local artists knew they could get much higher prices from tourists at sports days, fairs and local exhibitions. Schmidt said that when he asked one First Nations man what a fair price for a pair of gloves was, he answered, "[a]bout $2.25 today, but I would not sell them now[:] Wait until the tourists (Americans) come in the Summer[;] then you can get $5.00 easy."[77] After over two months of searching, Schmidt eventually acquired "270 articles, for which [he] paid $729.75."[78] Some of the pieces came from as far away as British Columbia.[79]

Just prior to their departure on 11 February 1938, a *Calgary Daily Herald* article described all eight First Nations cowboys as "Descendants of the nomads of the Western Plains [who] are becoming ambassadors of commerce."[80] It claimed that they were "Open[ing] Up Fresh Markets for Canadian Handicraft."[81] This promotional ploy was obviously instigated by Schmidt, Hoey and the Welfare and Training Division. The men themselves had nothing to do with the acquisition of handicrafts. Phrases such as "[t]hey hope their visit will create a market for tribal handicrafts", "[t]hey foresee a definite export trade developing", and "[i]f their dream comes true, it may mean the revival of an industry that in later years has shown signs of gradually becoming a lost art,"[82] were scattered throughout the article. This "trial shipment of nearly half a ton" of beaded work was described as "unique fashion accessories" that would enhance any wardrobe and develop an intense trade with the Australians.[83] A similar article was published in *The Sun*, in Sydney, after the arrival of the Canadian troupe (see Fig. 14). It was titled "Straight from the Canadian Indians: Colourful Handicrafts for Show," and contained the same bylines and photographs, suggesting that Schmidt sent the Canadian article to Sydney in order to encourage sales. This twin commentary repeated the notion that "[t]he Indians foresee a definite export trade."[84] It also explained that the shipment was worth twenty-five hundred Australian pounds.[85]

Ironically, the *Calgary Daily Herald* article also described the involvement of the Indian Affairs Branch in the acquisition of these handicrafts. It described C. Pant Schmidt as having "a wide knowledge of Indian handiwork,"[86] and noted his subsequent rejection of all pieces that did not meet the department's high standards, both in design and quality of materials. Each piece that passed was given an official tag, which "designated it as a genuine specimen of Canadian Indian craftsmanship."[87] Once they were all gathered, Schmidt had apparently increased the prices for selling purposes.[88]

The aforementioned demonstrates that the business of collecting and marketing First Nations items for the Royal Easter Show in Sydney was solely under the control of Schmidt and the Indian Affairs Branch, and is a testament to their creativity in dealing with "Indian problems." These articles also provide

Fig. 14: "Straight From the Canadian Indians." *The Sun* (Sydney), 15 March 1939.

another example of the use of First Nations culture in the promotion of Canada as a modern nation. Laying aside the discrepancies between fact and fantasy, this media discourse signaled to the Canadian public, and the Australian public, that Canada was an independent nation in the process of developing distinct export trading markets. Unfortunately, due to the additional 70 per cent duty charged

Fig. 15: "Canadian Pavilion at the Empire Exhibit in Glasgow, Scotland." As seen in James G. Parmelee, "Canada on Parade in Glasgow," Canadian Geographic Journal XVI (June 1938) Ottawa, p. 311.

by the Australian government, few crafts were sold in Sydney. Most of the stock was sent back.[89] The returned items were eventually sent to an exhibition held in Toronto for resale.[90]

Conclusions

In 1938 and 1939 Canada participated in two World's Fairs, one in Glasgow and one in New York. At both, displays reflected an ultra-modern national image. They were based on the promotion of Canada as an industrial nation searching for independence through global trade. The promotion of modernity, at this time, was an essential aspect of global consumer competition.

In 1938 Canada presented a lavish display at the Glasgow Empire Exhibition. Accompanying New Zealand, Australia, South Africa and the Irish Free State, Canada's display was located on "Dominions Avenue." At one end was the "Palace of Industry," and at the other was the "Palace of Engineering." These two signifiers sum up the external image that the Canadian government sought to

Fig. 16: "Water Power Statue, Canadian Pavilion, New York World's Fair." As seen in J.G. Parmelee, "Canada's Participation in the World's Fair," *Canadian Geographic Journal*, XIX (July 1939), Ottawa, p. 88.

present. Architecturally, Canada's pavilion was considered novel and in keeping with the scheme of the whole exhibition.[91] Inside, a large mural, a giant copper map, and twelve dioramas promoted various aspects of industry, sport, and education (see Fig. 15). The main purpose of these displays, as described by Deputy Minister James G. Parmelee of Trade and Commerce, was the promotion of export trade.[92]

On 30 April 1939, the New York World's Fair was opening its gate at the same time that Canada's troupe of rodeo riders were sailing home. The theme of this fair was "Building the World of Tomorrow." Words such as "stupendous," "unparalleled" and "perfect" were used to describe this event, which was supposed to create new hope during a decade of the worst economic depression ever experienced in North America.[93] James G. Parmelle again hailed Canada's pavilion as a testament to its status in "world trade, its unlimited resources, thriving industries and outstanding tourist appeal."[94] Government officials and artists selected the design for this huge, attractive building through an open competition. Giant murals and photographic collages depicted Canada as an ideal vacationland. Massive sculptures and dioramas illustrated hydropower, agriculture and transportation (see Fig. 16). Folksy, traditional types of displays were replaced with those representing an overt drive for "progress," newness and dynamic forms of modernism. First Nations culture was included in the form of two seventeen-foot totem poles carved and designed by Mungo Martin; however, their placement was in keeping with the "Streamlined Moderne"[95] that dominated this fair (see Fig. 17).[96]

The fact that this emphasis on modernity ran in tandem with the RAS production in Sydney is puzzling. Why did the Canadian government insist on an elaborate "Colourful Indian camp"[97] display if national identity was no longer focused on signifiers of race? The lack of First Nations symbolism at the Empire Exhibit, and the minimal amount of it at the New York World's Fair, does not mean that Canada had stopped representing itself through the use of First Nations culture. It simply means that for these two instances the direct advertisement of modernity was considered more effective in attracting international attention. Also, Canada had to keep in line with the general themes of both fairs, which unequivocally underscored modernity, technology and the desire for prosperity.

More importantly, the RAS proposal seemed like an effective way to alleviate financial distress, even if only hypothetically. Schmidt imagined that the department would net an easy one thousand dollars from the sales of handicrafts, and most likely receive further sales in the future. The Australian request offered an opportunity that Schmidt could tailor to benefit the department in many ways. By simply reverting to the tried and true formula that had been used in international display since the 1850s, Schmidt assumed he was guaranteed international trade and international recognition.

Schmidt's, and consequently the Canadian government's view of these First Nations cowboys was that they were pawns in the production of positive national identity and colonial ideals. Making money and gaining political recognition through racial ordering and subjugation was a well-known reality in the larger imperial project, including popular culture venues.[98] Unfortunately, even though the promotion of the 1939 performances was magnified due to its transnational nature, its economic impact was not. In the end only eight First Nations men benefited financially from the trip. The hopes of a burgeoning international trade market in handicrafts were eliminated with the onset of World War II only four months after they returned home.

3

Canadian Indian Cowboys at the Royal Easter Show in Sydney: Celebrities, Citizens & Wards

If you never see people as historical actors, then history becomes something that happened to them rather than something they created.[1]

He knew what he could do, he was a good cowboy. So, he was anxious to compete on behalf of his country.[2]

ON 15 FEBRUARY 1939, Joe Crowfoot and Joe Bear Robe from the Blackfoot Reserve, Frank Many Fingers and Joe Young Pine from the Blood Reserve, Edward One Spot and Jim Starlight from the Sarcee Reserve, and Johnny Left Hand and Douglas Kootenay from the Stoney Reserve began their trip to Australia. They were all middle-aged adults at the time, with the exception of twenty-three-year-old Kootenay. They were all seasoned rodeo performers with years of experience in Alberta's professional circuits. For them the challenge of travelling such a great distance was superseded by the opportunity to compete internationally as Canadian athletes and to demonstrate the distinct qualities of their traditions. A desire for adventure, money and prestige was secondary, even though these men were legally considered wards of the state and restricted in most aspects of their daily lives.

Scholars have previously acknowledged that Alberta was a place of contradictions for First Nations people in the 1930s. Legally, they had no rights other than those surreptitiously allowed by the Indian agents.[3] Economically, most were dependent on government welfare allowances. Ideologically, the mainstream non-Aboriginal population firmly believed they were a dying race. However, First Nations people of the time were comparatively well organized politically due to the establishment of the Indian Association of Alberta (IAA).[4] Ranching and rodeo became ways for individuals to transcend poverty and escape the confines of reserve life.[5] Public competitions also provided a place for promoting cultural identity, challenging white stereotypes, and symbolically (and personally) declaring regional citizenship. The eight men who travelled to Sydney in 1939 represented Canada as national competitors and, therefore, established a visible place for First Nations inclusion within the multicultural character of Canada's national citizenry.

The legacy of First Nations cowboys goes back to the mid-1800s. In fact, it has been suggested that casual sporting events using horses (often described as "early rodeo" in reference to non-Aboriginal events) became popular in First Nations communities much earlier than they did in white communities. It is generally believed that horses (and "early rodeo") arrived in North America in the mid-1600s with Spanish explorers and were quickly adopted by the Blackfoot, Stoney, Sarcee and Blood peoples in the mid-1700s.[6] The introduction of cattle came much later. Although First Nations communities began raising cattle in the 1830s, an economy based on cattle ranching was not well established until the late nineteenth century.[7] Wagered horse races and other equestrian competitions, which had been part of First Nations culture prior to cattle ranching, increased in popularity due to it, and also became part of this economy. A horse's value increased with its ability to win races, as did prestige for its owner, trainer and rider.[8]

Between the late nineteenth century and the early twentieth century, popular culture generally positioned the Indian in direct opposition to the cowboy. Although cowboys were rough and often lawless men, they were also heroes responsible for taming the Wild West. As in most other cowboy cultures throughout the Americas, the mythological cowboy constituted a tame but masculine citizen-subject in the Canadian west. Indians, on the other hand, signified wild savages who needed to be tamed or eliminated in order to facilitate the expansion of civilization and the project of nation building.[9] It is important to remember that while Buffalo Bill and all other Wild West promoters were establishing this dichotomy, many First Nations people had distinct lifestyles created in conjunction with rodeo and ranching culture. They simply described themselves as "Indian cowboys."[10] In many ways, rodeo filled a gap that had been created by colonialism and gave them a public venue where they could demonstrate their uniquely competitive skills as horsemen.

Fig. 18: Joe Crowfoot at the Calgary Stampede, 1939. Glenbow Archives, NA-1241-12. Photographer: F. Gully.

The eight Indian cowboys from Alberta who travelled to Sydney had different regional, cultural and economic lifestyles, yet were all regular competitors at the Calgary Stampede and smaller local rodeos. They were chosen during consultations between Joe Crowfoot, Stampede officials and various Indian agents. Horsemanship skills accompanied by celebrity status were the primary criteria in this selection process.[11]

Joe Crowfoot was born in 1892 near Gleichen, Alberta on the Blackfoot Reserve. He was the son of Bear Ghost and Susie Without a Doubt Bear. He was

Fig. 19: Joe Bear Robe at the Calgary Stampede, 1940. Glenbow Archives, NA-1241-69.

also the grandson of the famous Chief Crowfoot. In 1921 he married Maggie Spotted Eagle. He was a well-liked member of his community, a very successful farmer and rancher, and a professional rodeo competitor. In the early 1930s Crowfoot was made chief of the Blackfoot people. Although he lost this position in the forties, he regained it in 1953.[12] Mr. Crowfoot also held the position of foreman of the Indian

Fig. 20: Left, Ted Brave Rock; right, Joe Young Pine; woman and child unidentified, 1920. Glenbow Archives, NA-3284-7.

Round-up on the Calgary Stampede Board, and he was politically involved with the Indian Association of Alberta (IAA). He died in 1976.

Joe Bear Robe was born in 1901. He was a member of the Blackfoot Reserve. Well known in Alberta for his calf roping expertise,[13] in later life he became a well-respected Siksika elder.[14]

Frank Many Fingers was born in 1915 at the Belly Buttes on the Blood Reserve in Alberta. His clan was the Mamioyiiksi, and his parents were Morris Many Fingers, the famous and long-time chief of the Kainai Nation, and Annie Pace. Many Fingers attended the old Roman Catholic School in Standoff. In 1933 he focused on developing his ranching and rodeo skills. Many Fingers was a very successful rodeo competitor in both Canada and the US, and he won the Canadian All-Round Championship at the Calgary Stampede in 1940. He was also instrumental in organizing the Lazy B Ranch Association, the first Indian rodeo on the Blood Reserve, and the Indian Rodeo Cowboy Association. After his marriage in 1937 he had twelve children. Many Fingers died in 1996.[15]

Joe Young Pine was born in 1899 and was a member of the Blood Reserve. He was an excellent chuckwagon driver and was asked to attend the Royal Easter Show in 1939 by the Stampede Board because of his superior rodeo skills.[16] J.E. Pugh, Indian agent for the Blood Reserve, described him as an excellent handler of horses, an all round good hand, and the best chuckwagon driver of the group sent to Sydney.[17]

Johnny Left Hand was born in 1912, when he became a member of the Stoney Reserve. He had the reputation of being a good cowboy.[18] He was also well known as a leader in his community.

Douglas Kootenay was born in 1916 on the Stoney Reserve. He was the youngest of the group who travelled to Sydney. Constable Leach described him as "the smallest of the group," and the "little Stoney bachelor."[19]

Jim Starlight of the Sarcee Reserve was born in 1904. His grandfather was a chief and his father, James Starlight, was a scout for the RCMP. James was also an honorary member of the Pioneers of Alberta. Jim himself became a chief on the Sarcee Reserve in the 1950s and 1960s.[20] Starlight was well known on the rodeo circuit for his bronco riding skills.[21]

Eddie One Spot was a member of the Sarcee Reserve. He was born on 13 June 1906, and by the late 1920s had become a very well-known singer, dancer, rodeo-rider, movie actor and stunt man. In 1939 he was chosen to represent Canada in Sydney, and also served as an ambassador to touring British royalty. Throughout

Fig. 21: Chief Jim Starlight, 1965. Glenbow Archives, NA-1562-1. Photo in the *Calgary Herald*.

his lifetime he performed at many western Canadian fairs, and he regularly opened the Calgary Stampede by singing "Oh Canada."[22] He travelled to Hollywood to perform as a motion picture actor in *Saskatchewan, Broken Arrow* and *River of No Return*, all filmed in the 1950s.[23] One Spot was also a delegate for the IAA in 1950 and chief of the Sarcee in the 1960s. He was married twice and had seven children prior to his death in 1994.

Life on the Reserves in Alberta, 1930s

The creation of the Indian Act in 1876 began the process of cultural regulation for First Nations. By the 1930s, three generations had been forced to live under its often contradictory provisions. Secretary T.R.L. MacInnes of the Indian Affairs Branch described the Indian Act in 1939 as a policy that managed reserves, land, money, relief, education, medical services, agriculture and industry for First Nations protection and advancement. Its ultimate goal, according to his perspective, was the enfranchisement and assimilation of all First Nations people, which would turn them into responsible citizens of Canada.[24] MacInnes' attitude was common among many government officials of the time. Indian agents saw themselves as the purveyors of complete cultural and political assimilation and as essential instruments of civilization. Until 1960, First Nations in Canada were still legally considered wards of the state and, therefore, it was impossible for them to be considered "Indians" and citizens at the same time.[25]

In the 1930s, most First Nations, particularly those in western Canada, lived on reserves where their lifestyles never satisfied the imagined Euro-Canadian standards of civilization. Most were on relief due to the depression and all food rations were strictly controlled. In a CBC broadcast aired in 1939, Teddy Yellowfly described living conditions as deplorable.[26] Half of the population was living in tiny, wooden shacks with no insulation, no furniture and rarely even a door. The lack of sufficient nutrition and shelter facilitated the spread of infectious disease. Medical statistics indicated that ten times as many First Nations children died within their first year and twenty-eight times more First Nations people died of tuberculosis than whites in the 1930s.[27]

The Indian Affairs Branch established a "pass system" to make sure that no one left the reserves without permission. Fears of an uprising were the unspoken reason for such drastic tactics. There is evidence that in Alberta this "pass system," which was later referred to as a "permit system," was in place from 1885 until the late 1930s. This non-legislated system was implemented by the Indian

Fig. 22: Eddie One Spot at the Calgary Stampede, 1941. Glenbow Archives, NA-1241-58. Photographer: F. Gully.

Affairs Branch as a means for keeping its wards away from alcohol, prostitution and other "evils of the city."[28] This particular government policy was innately counterproductive, considering that the goal was to assimilate and "modernize"

First Nations people; the permit system only kept them as isolated as possible from the rest of Canadian society. The multiple hypocrisies of this government department's restrictions, best exemplified by the permit system, were of course resisted in many different ways.

Participation in festivals, fairs, rodeo and other exhibitions was one way for individuals to overcome segregation practices. Often great distances were travelled in efforts to participate in self-generated events such as Treaty Days, government-sponsored events such as agricultural fairs, and those controlled and organized by white show promoters such as the Calgary Stampede. In Alberta, First Nations have a long history of participation in Treaty Days festivities, which were three to four day festivals where bands would gather, feast, dance, sing, and race horses in order to commemorate the anniversary of treaty signings. These festivals renewed family ties and cross-community alliances.[29] Initially, Treaty Days seemed innocent enough to the Indian agents in charge, even though they perpetuated elements of pre-contact or traditional lifestyles, which were supposed to be eradicated. As time went on, these types of ceremonies were determined to be one of the main reasons why First Nations were not assimilating fast enough into white society.[30]

As mentioned in the last chapter, restrictions in the Indian Act specific to performance began in 1914. This legislation barred all First Nations people from performing off-reserve while dressed in traditional clothing without the permission of either the superintendent of Indian Affairs or the local agent. In 1939, an amended ruling was still in place. It stipulated that any participation in a public performance, not only those involving traditional clothing, was punishable by a fine and/or jail sentence.[31] Although this ruling did not curtail events such as Treaty Days, it did give Indian agents the right to intervene whenever they felt it was appropriate.

The restrictive nature of reserve life, in general, fostered resistance tactics and generated various types of organized political activity. Throughout the 1920s and the 1930s, the League of Indians of Canada, based in Alberta, provided First Nations communities with a structure for tackling their grievances. Opposition to the Indian Act, lack of social welfare benefits and low economic status, despite the prosperity of the province due to the development of oil and gas resources, were all issues dealt with in this forum.[32] By 1939, a draft of the Indian Association of Alberta's constitution was completed and the Bloods, the Blackfoot, the Stoneys and the Sarcee gained political leverage in the promotion of their "unique rights and interests."[33] Across Canada the development of this association played a hand in altering the landscape of First Nations politics,[34] besides giving many First Nations in Alberta a clear notion of what their rights were and how they could go about getting them.

In relation to the events of 1939, Constable Leach noted in an article in the *RCMP Quarterly* that one of the men (he did not give a name) had met with a lawyer to discern the limits of Leach's control once they were travelling off-shore. This member of the troupe explained he had been advised that Leach had "no legal power outside of Canadian Territory and once beyond the three mile limit of Canadian waters they [the First Nation men] could enjoy the same liberties as any white man."[35] Leach claimed that all the men "knew their way about" because of their participation in rodeo activities.[36] As mentioned earlier, rodeo offered travel, money and the development of freedom and self-esteem.[37] In Alberta, many of the First Nations men involved in rodeo were also involved in politics. All of the men who travelled to Sydney knew each other; many were either chiefs or members of their band councils. Rodeo became an important social arena where First Nations in Alberta solidified political connections during the 1930s.[38] It was also a space in which reputations were created through acts of competition that required skill, experience, courage, perseverance and talent.

Life as an Indian Cowboy

Wild West shows, as a form of popular entertainment, reached their peak between 1900 and 1917. By this time hundreds of First Nations people in Canada and the United States had participated as performers. Modern rodeo developed alongside Wild West shows, but eventually divorced itself from this venue's circus and carnival elements. It took over as a preferred form of entertainment and sport in the 1920s, both on a local level and as a tourist attraction.[39] Rodeo was a public form of social and cultural representation that became an integral component in the lifestyles of cattle ranchers, and it appealed more broadly to rural communities for a variety of reasons. In 1929, the Rodeo Association of America standardized all events, rules and judging, and turned rodeo into a professional sport. By the 1930s, it was a profitable business, often staged in larger centres where it became an elaborate and successful commercial venture on many levels, including sales of cowboy paraphernalia and items of clothing.[40] Prior to World War II rodeo assumed new dimensions as a form of international competition, primarily in Canada, the US, Australia, Venezuela and Mexico.[41]

During this expansion little was done to protect the cowboy's rights. They paid all their own expenses while on the road and were forced to pay high entry fees for each event. Even if they were lucky and won, their prize money barely covered their fees and rarely their travel and sundry expenses. Greedy judges and promoters kept most of the profits, sometimes "skipping town" without paying out prize monies. In the US, the Turtle Cowboy Association was founded in 1939. In Canada, a similar professional union called the Cowboy Protection Association was formed in 1944.[42] Both organizations helped resolve some of these issues, but few of these improvements extended to First Nations cowboys or other minorities represented in the sport.[43] Unless an individual was exceptionally talented, willing to persevere, and possessed emotional and financial backing, it was tough to participate regularly in larger professionally arenas.[44]

Tom Three Persons shattered the "Indian/cowboy" dichotomy with his 1912 performance, which subsequently allowed Indian cowboys to enter the professional rodeo circuit. He was a Blood Indian from Standoff, Alberta, and the uncle of both Joe Crowfoot and Frank Many Fingers. For ten years he worked as a ranch hand in the Fort Macleod district and was considered an excellent horseman.[45] He was the only Canadian to make it to the finals at the first Calgary Stampede in 1912, where he won the World's Bronco Riding title by taming the legendary "Cyclone," a horse claimed to have bucked off nearly two thousand cowboys.[46] This was the first of many successful competitions. Three Persons was also a smart businessman; he profited from cattle ranching, horse ranching and horse racing. He provided financially backing, encouragement and training to many of his relatives and others interested in the sport. This included sponsoring Frank Many Fingers and Joe Crowfoot in their travels to Sydney. Although the RAS paid their travel expenses and wages, the men needed appropriate clothing, suitcases, and riding gear as well. By the 1930s, First Nations competitive presence at professional rodeo events in Canada and the United States was substantial and "Indian/Cowboys" were no longer simply considered "feathered features" for white audiences to gaze at as they did at Wild West shows.[47]

Tom Three Persons' success symbolically represents a defining moment in understanding how the Indian cowboy challenged western Canadian mythology. Indian rodeo performances, prominent accomplishments such as those of Tom Three Persons in particular, symbolically re-made Indians into cowboys. They also disrupted the notion of First Nations people as a vanishing race, which was invisible and incomparable to white western society.[48] By occupying the space of the cowboy, First Nation men brought themselves culturally and politically to the forefront. They allowed their audiences the opportunity to visualize a different First Nation citizen-subject, a future when white cowboys and Indian cowboys could compete equally.

The beginning of First Nations-run community rodeos is unclear because horse racing and similar rodeo events were always popular at community-based celebrations in Alberta.[49] By the 1930s small local rodeo competitions were organized in all reserve communities. While larger professional venues such as the Calgary Stampede provided a space for the public reproduction of traditional culture, these local venues offered more intimate places where the display of traditional costume, storytelling, dancing and singing could take place. They also created economic opportunities where horse trading and selling could transpire.[50] Regarded by Indian agents as somewhat innocuous, these events became popular venues where First Nations legitimately gathered to reinforce community alliances.[51]

For those First Nations men who persisted in competing professionally the mainstream rodeo circuit was strenuous. It involved extensive travel every weekend between June and October to participate in approximately twenty different events. Floyd Many Fingers recalls how his brother, Frank, along with two or three of his friends, would hook up a team of horses to a buckboard, tie on a tent, load their gear and head off to a rodeo (see Fig. 23). By the late 1930s, Morris Many Fingers, Frank's father, had bought a car and acquired a horse trailer.[52] Although a widespread lack of motorized transportation was not uncommon in the 1930s, it was undoubtedly less common within First Nations communities. Discrepancies in judging were another challenge. First Nations riders were consistently marked lower in all events, and an individual had to be an excellent trainer and athlete to win and make money.[53] The only other way to continue competing was to have a secondary career such as cattle ranching or as an entertainer at the shows. These drawbacks attest to the persistence, determination and love of the sport that First Nation cowboys had.

On a more practical level, ranching and rodeo became ways for individuals to transcend poverty, escape the confines of reserve life and solidify First Nations political ties. Although Indians agents did not encourage professional rodeo as a valuable competitive practice, it was a by-product of ranching and did bring supplementary incomes to the families involved. Not only did local on-reserve rodeos offer a space where outside relationships were renewed and reinforced,

Fig. 23: Photograph of Frank Many Fingers at the Calgary Stampede, Calgary, Alberta, 1955. Courtesy of the Many Fingers family, private collection.

but also a place where leadership abilities equated with competition were demonstrated. Skills associated with horsemanship and horse training increased an individual's status and respect within the community. As well-liked public figures, rodeo heroes and their families gained prominence and mobility within band politics and First Nations provincial political circles.[54]

As mentioned earlier, five out of the eight First Nations cowboys who travelled to Sydney were either politicians or had numerous politically involved family members. Joe Crowfoot was a chief and band council member for many years between 1933 and 1960. Frank Many Fingers' father, Morris, was a chief, and his brother, Albert, was a delegate for the IAA in 1950. Jim Starlight's grandfather was a chief; his father was a scout for the RCMP and also an honorary member of the Pioneers of Alberta. Jim himself was a chief in the 1950s and 1960s. Joe Bear Robe became a revered elder in his community in the 1960s. And finally, Eddie One Spot was a delegate for the IAA in 1950 and a chief of the Sarcee in the 1960s.[55]

These men knew more than just "their way about." As a group they represented four of the most prosperous and politically active reserves in Canada. Individually, they were well educated and connected politically, and they all engaged in entrepreneurial activities. Although the professional rodeo circuit did offer travel, money and the development of freedom and self-esteem, it also increased their political mobility and motivation. On this trip in 1939, sporting prowess was combined with political intention to characterize this group's diplomatic presence in Australia. International travel deepened the political importance of rodeo and offered them the opportunity to represent First Nations in Canada to an international audience. The rodeo events at the Royal Easter Show became a political space where they attempted to alter outsiders' notions about Canada's colonial heritage through their competitive presence.

The Trip to Australia in 1939

With the exception of historical work concerning Buffalo Bill and Wild West shows, little has been written about international Aboriginal performance. Periodically, scholars have attempted to discern why individuals or small groups travel great distances to demonstrate their culture to others, especially considering that these audiences often have a limited understanding, which is steeped in stereotypes. The standard reasons gleaned from these reports are money, adventure and cultural promotion. This trip in 1939 offered two avenues for performance: rodeo, being the first, and a make-shift "Indian Village," being the second. The "Indian Village" provided a space where First Nations cultural identity could be displayed to an international audience, and although the men were used to this type of performance at home, evidence suggests that it was not their preferred scenario. Throughout the interviews there was no

Fig. 24: Left, Joe Crowfoot; right Duck Chief, prior to leaving for Australia, February 1939, Calgary. Glenbow Archives, NA-1241-171. Photographer: F. Gully.

emphasis placed on the importance of the "Indian Village" itself, or on the sale of handicrafts that took place there. Cecil Crowfoot and Floyd Many Fingers only spoke about their father and brother's desire to compete as athletes and represent "Indian rodeo."[56]

When asked why Frank Many Fingers wanted to go, his brother Floyd focused on the prestige of competing internationally. He elaborated on his family's history of participation in rodeo and Frank's outstanding natural abilities, which were obvious from a very early age. Like any other athlete, Frank was anxious to go to Australia for the thrill, the competition and the opportunity to represent his country.[57]

When asked why Joe Crowfoot wanted to go, his son Cecil said bluntly, "He didn't really want to go."[58] Cecil claimed that the Stampede Board picked him because he was the foreman of the Indian Round-up.[59] Joe Crowfoot felt that it was his duty as a First Nations representative and a leader of the Blackfoot people to go. He was forty-two years old at the time and had not competed seriously for ten years. Afterwards he did mention that he was looking forward to the adventure.

On this three-month adventure the men experienced and instigated varied reactions to their presence, whether it was aboard ships, practicing at MacFarlane's ranch outside of Sydney, or performing at the Royal Easter Show. On the passage over they were treated with respect by the captain of the *SS Niagara* and the other passengers. Although they performed briefly in their traditional costumes on one occasion, they spent most of their time participating in usual activities such as dances, movies, a masquerade party and on-board sports competitions. At each port along the way local officials treated them like privileged guests. For example, in Honolulu the press greeted them as they docked. They were then taken on a sightseeing tour, which was followed by dinner and a movie.[60] Their first two weeks in Australia were spent training at Merriwa. Here, frequent socializing became an important aspect of this trip, where relationships were formed or re-established with the white cowboys from Canada and the United States, who were also competing. While in Sydney at the Royal Easter Show, they were consistently mobbed by autograph seekers and the press. Their presence was perceived with the excitement and curiosity commonly expressed towards Wild West performers. Overall, the genuine respect, camaraderie and prestige they experienced was consistently intermingled with racial prejudice, harassment and restrictions. The men themselves constantly challenged this unfairness in attempts to neutralize negative stereotypical attitudes and to maintain the level of respect they felt they deserved.

Indian Cowboys as Celebrities

The trip to Australia in 1939 inspired varying degrees of celebrity status, both at home in Canadian newspapers, and abroad in Australian newspapers. Skidmore and MacFarlane's notion that they would provide an exotic attraction for the Australian public was overshadowed by the genuine interest and regard the men said they received. The excitement and importance of this trip, for the general public in western Canada, unfortunately remained short-lived, considering the fact that, to my knowledge, these men comprise the only First Nations team of athletes who have ever represented Canada in an international sporting competition. However, the stories of these men's successes in Australia are still well known within their communities.

The trip to the Royal Easter Show has remained a very important moment in the family stories of the men involved. A great deal of pride was associated with this event. Souvenirs that were brought back and clothing that was worn have all been saved and remain precious reminders of a "trip of a lifetime."[61] For the Many Fingers family, the trophies Frank won for all-round cowboy during the show and all-round athlete on the ship are treasured heirlooms that they hope will be part of a museum display one day. Comments from Cecil Crowfoot express the pride of knowing that his father was considered the leader of the group, serving as their spokesman at all public occasions and consistently being positioned in the foreground of all photo opportunities.[62] Both family members were proud of the fact that the Australians had been so enthusiastic and receptive, and that their kinsmen had represented their country overseas.

Several Canadian newspaper articles, both prior to their departure and after their return, focused on creating enthusiasm about the trip by describing the men as celebrities. The first article, in the *Calgary Daily Herald*, described them as "top-ranking Indian cowboys from Alberta," and the first "Canadian Indians to cross the Pacific." The article further claimed that it would be the first opportunity for Australians to witness "the colourful rangeland sports of Western Canada and Indian ceremonial dances."[63] Two other articles, printed in January and February of 1939, focused on promoting the men as entrepreneurs "going into the export business."[64] Here, the fact that they were rodeo performers was secondary to the notion that they were turning a local tourist industry into an international export market. In this journalistic exaggeration they were hailed as "ambassadors of commerce" seeking to "Open Up Fresh Markets for Canadian Handicraft"[65] (as was discussed in the last chapter). An article in the

Fig. 25: Troupe Leaving for Australia. Vancouver, February 1939. Glenbow Archives, NA-481-10. Titled: Group of young First Nations people leaving for Australia. Photographer: F. Gully. Same photo also seen in "Cowboys and Indians Sail for Sydney." *The Daily Province* (Vancouver), 8 March 1939.

Vancouver Sun on the day of their departure simply described the "husky and good-looking" men as "resplendent in cowboy hats, flaming silk shirts and high boots."[66] It focused on the fact that they were enthusiastically leaving for an exotic adventure in Australia (Fig. 25).

During the voyage to Australia, Joe Crowfoot in particular was shown special attention, first by the captain of the *SS Niagara*, and then by the Australian press. This was based on the fact that his grandfather was the famous Chief Crowfoot, a signatory to Treaty 7, and that Joe himself was a well known member and leader of the Blackfoot people. He was invited on several occasions to dine in the captain's private cabin. The *Niagara's* captain even asked him if he wanted to be "the first Indian" to navigate a ship across the equator. Joe, of course, said yes. Once at the helm he asked what he should do. "Just go any place, any where, just don't turn around backwards," replied the captain.[67] Joe asked, "What if I hit a rock?" The captain reassured him, "You can't hit any thing out here; you are in

Fig. 26: Troupe's arrival in Open Cars with Flags Titled, 'Pontiac Welcomes the Red Indians.' Sydney, 13 March 1939. Courtesy Peggy Maxwell, private collection.

the deepest part, which is seven miles."[68] So Joe played around with the wheel, steering in a zigzag fashion for a while, until the captain finally told him, "Now you are going across the equator."[69] When Cecil Crowfoot finished relating this story in an interview, he stated proudly that his father "was the first Indian to drive across the equator."[70]

The troupe arrived in Sydney on 11 March dressed in traditional attire.[71] Skidmore and MacFarlane greeted them at the docks. Elaborate publicity photographs were first taken on the deck of the *Niagara* before they even had a chance to disembark. The streets were lined with thousands of Australians as the men drove by in open cars decorated with flying pennants that read, "Pontiac Welcomes the Red Indians" (see Fig. 26). Initially they were driven to City Hall for a civic reception (see Fig. 27), and afterwards they were escorted to a picture show while Constable Leach, Joe Crowfoot and Joe Bear Robe were interviewed over the radio.[72] On the second day, the whole Canadian troupe was paraded for the press and two motion picture companies at the RAS show grounds (see Fig. 28 and 29), before being taken on a sightseeing tour of Sydney. During their entire

Fig. 27: Troupe Walking up Stairs at City Hall Upon Arrival. Sydney, 13 March 1939. Courtesy Peggy Maxwell, private collection.

stay, which lasted approximately five weeks, they continually attended lavish banquets and went on various types of sightseeing tours. In some instances these day trips were publicity stunts organized by the RAS, but wherever the Canadians went, the Australian public's admiration, combined with curiosity and fascination, was made evident.

In Constable Leach's article written for the *RCMP Quarterly*, and in his RCMP report, he repeatedly commented on the fact that huge crowds mobbed them constantly. He explained, "crowd[s] entered their teepees without an invitation [and] young boys clambered up the outside, tearing them in places."[73] These violations finally stopped, three days into the show, when the RAS built a fence around the encampment.[74] He also acknowledged that wherever they went autograph hunters approached them, people wanted to feel his uniform, touch the First Nations men's costumes and shake their hands. He remained surprised at the patience and good grace that his companions maintained throughout the show in spite of this excessive and often aggressive mobbing. Floyd Many Fingers confirmed the fact that his brother and the other men enjoyed the celebrity status shown by the Australian public, obviously much more than Constable Leach did.[75]

Fig. 28: Troupe posing at Moore Park for the press. Sydney, 14 March 1939. Courtesy Peggy Maxwell, private collection. Constable S.J. Leach of the RCMP with, standing left to right: Joe Young Pine (Blood), 40; Joe Crowfoot (Blackfoot), 38; Jim Starlight (Sarcee), 35; Joe Bear Robe (Blackfoot), 38; John Lefthand (Stoney), 27; Frank Many Fingers (Blood), 30; sitting left to right: Douglas Kootenay (Stoney), 24; Edward Onespott (Sarcee), 25.

When asked how the Australian audience treated the men, the unanimous answer was, "good." Floyd focused on the fact that the Australian crowds "liked them" and "were for them."[76] He said that initially there were some war-whoops and ignorant questions about tipis; however, such attitudes changed after they saw how talented the men were.[77] As Cecil Crowfoot said years later, "They really wanted to see them and they really took them in."[78] By this he was referring to the dinners and dances held in honor of the visitors prior to the Royal Easter Show. When asked to describe the difference between audiences in Australia and audiences in Alberta, he pointedly stated, "They don't like Indians in Alberta."[79] Deanna Crowfoot expanded on the fact that Canadians hate it when others mistreat or look down on "their Indians," yet at home negative treatment is just taken for granted, or ignored.[80] Interestingly, the men recalled feeling a sense of respect and appreciation in Australia, something that they seldom experienced at larger Canadian rodeos such as the Calgary Stampede.

Fig. 29: Eddie One Spot, Sarcee, Tsuu T'ina, in Australia. Sydney, April 1939. Glenbow Archives, NA-3256-3. Photographer: E. C. Barnes.

Floyd and Cecil also recalled the celebrity status that their brother and father received when they returned home. They both described community celebrations, which they called "honor dances," where the community gathered to hear about the trip and celebrated the men's achievements. Gifts were also distributed from the many souvenirs brought home from Australia. Cecil remembers being very happy that he and his sister were given time off from the residential school they were attending so that they could reunite with their father and the rest of their family.[81] Floyd recalled proudly watching his brother demonstrate the right way to throw a boomerang.[82]

Joe Crowfoot, Frank Many Fingers, Joe Bear Robe, Joe Young Pine, Edward One Spot, Jim Starlight, Johnny Left Hand and Douglas Kootenay were simultaneously considered to be both wards of the state and celebrities. This arrangement attests to the power of perspective and the social processes through which individuals achieve celebrity status. The celebrity status gained from having a member of one's family or community travel abroad to compete internationally is easily understandable, and a common enough response, which cannot be considered culturally dependent.[83] The Australian public's reaction is easily definable once it is aligned to the global popularity of Wild West shows and Western movies discussed previously. However, the celebrity status afforded the men by the Canadian press is debatable. The journalistic comments, which promoted the men as accomplished cowboys, expresses regional pride. The comments that described the men as exporters of beaded clothing were simply not true. These comments attempted to fabricate celebrity status for the benefit of the Canadian government, and particularly the Indian Affairs Branch, rather than for the individual men involved.

Indian Cowboys as Wards of the State

In 1939 First Nations in Canada were legally considered wards of the state. The Indian Affairs Branch, a subdivision of the Department of Mines and Resources, strictly controlled jurisdiction over this status. Constable Leach acted as an agent for this department during the trip to Australia, and his presence was considered imperative. In a letter to Skidmore, Schmidt stated that Leach would be in charge of "The Indian Party," controlling them "financially, physically and morally."[84] His job would involve controlling all monies, both earned and spent, keeping watch over them at all times in order to monitor their behavior, and most importantly, making sure they did not drink any alcohol. The severity of these restrictions attests to the paternalism followed by Indian Affairs Branch officials in their interpretation of the Indian Act at this time.

Constable Leach's role as an all-pervasive controller was never fully met, and his relationship with the men included elements of camaraderie mixed with authority. For the most part it was RAS officials who unmistakably treated

Canada's First Nation cowboys with the indignity afforded wards of the state. Stories told by Floyd Many Fingers and Constable Leach attest to the fact that RAS officials cheated during rodeo competitions, stole the men's horses, and posed serious threats of expulsion for minor infractions.

When the men arrived in Sydney they were under the impression that they would be competing in fair, open competitions with all of the white Canadian, American and Australian cowboys. They quickly learned that the RAS had planned to segregate them into specific races, two of which were "The 'Taronga Zoological Park' Red Indian Bareback Race" and the "Red Indian Bareback Race."[85] Here they would compete against each other as a sideshow attraction only. They were not allowed to participate in the two main events, "The International Buckjumping Contest" and "The International Bulldogging Contest." Dissatisfied with these arrangements, they asked Constable Leach to speak to Skidmore and MacFarlane on their behalf. Although Leach petitioned for changes to the rodeo schedule, the RAS never budged on the decision to exclude the men from these two main events.[86] Although racist attitudes were certainly a factor, their exclusion from the main races was perhaps precipitated by a fear that if they participated they might win. Skidmore and MacFarlane would have been well aware of their skills and competence as rodeo competitors. In the end they did compete internationally in the "The 'City Fashions' International Wild Cow Milking Championship," "Quadrilles on Horseback," "The 'Atlantic' Steer Riding Open Competition" and, of course, "The 'Clements Tonic' International Chuck Wagon Races."[87]

Floyd Many Fingers retold his brother's story of the trip to MacFarlane's ranch in Merriwa, located approximately 250 miles from Sydney. All of the men stayed there for approximately two weeks in order to train for the show. Most of the horses were polo ponies. They were small and fast for short distance sprints, and they were also good for rodeo because they took instruction well. Frank picked a grey horse that he felt would be easy to train. Joe Young Pine, described as an excellent trainer and the only chuckwagon driver of the group, picked four of the larger horses to train specifically for these races. It is difficult to train horses for chuckwagon races and, in this case, it was even more difficult due to the limited amount of time Young Pine was allowed to accomplish the task. In order to guide the other horses through specific tasks at high speeds the two lead horses needed to be perfectly synchronized. Joe Young Pine was successful at training these four and by the end of two weeks felt assured of winning. When they got to Sydney, however, RAS officials took these four horses from him and gave them to the

Australian team. This severely limited Young Pine's ability to compete, but he still placed second in two of the races. The Australian team, who had little prior experience with chuckwagon racing, came in first overall. Floyd ended this story with a touch of sadness, frustration and complacency: "Well, when they came to Alberta they took chuck wagon drivers, not Indians."[88]

Floyd also explained that an RAS official told Frank that he would have to share his horse with the Australian riders. Obviously they had been made aware of the fact that Frank Many Fingers was an excellent trainer. When it came time to compete, Frank's horse was tired and could not perform well.[89] This type of foul play was not uncommon, and was also confirmed in Constable Leach's reports.

Consequently, Joe Crowfoot, Frank Many Fingers, Joe Bear Robe, Joe Young Pine, Edward One Spot, Jim Starlight, Johnny Left Hand and Douglas Kootenay often ended up riding untrained horses, which caused a litany of accidents, far more than they would have experienced at home. While injuries are not uncommon occurrences for rodeo competitors, they do not frequently happen with experienced riders who are performing on horses they own and have trained.[90] This was not the case in Australia. On the first day of the show, a horse kicked Joe Young Pine. Joe Crowfoot's usual horse was taken away from him and he developed a sprained neck while riding a new horse he was unfamiliar with. Jim Starlight bruised his shoulder and Eddie One Spot developed chest pains.[91] There were multiple sprained ankles, shoulders, wrists and necks throughout. The two most serious accidents happened on opening day when John Left Hand broke his arm and a horse rolled onto Joe Bear Robe. Left Hand spent the rest of the week in the hospital, while Bear Robe apparently experienced no injuries because "the ground was soft and spongy."[92]

The correspondence between the RAS and the Indian Affairs Branch, as well as the comments in Constable Leach's notes, reveals many occasions when racial prejudice was made obvious. Although a contemporary reaction to the oppressive nature of these comments can be tempered by a contextual analysis of hegemonic ideas concerning modernism, social sciences and colonialism in the 1930s, they were still striking. Interestingly, the oppression and prejudice experienced by these men was not a predominant memory for their families. The overall tone of the stories pertaining to the trip of 1939 was very positive and seemed free from concerns about racial difference. For example, the men were subjected to three medical exams throughout, which attempted repeatedly to determine whether they had contracted tuberculosis and/or venereal disease. These incidents, which would now be considered invasive, were not remembered at all by the families, and presumably did not pose an issue for the men themselves. In this sense, the notion of being a ward of the state can be considered dependent on the treatment received by others as well as one's own perspective.

It was unclear from the personal interviews with Floyd Many Fingers and Cecil Crowfoot if their father or brother felt like wards of the state while travelling to and around Australia. Any reference to injustices suffered on the trip due to cheating were seen as being far less important than the fact that family members were competing for their country and representing their culture. Constable Leach's attempts to control the men were often seen as laughable. In general they described him as someone who did not try to control them or outrank them. This internal perspective and the subsequent external, collective memories related to it created a powerful form of resistance to colonial hegemony.

Indian Cowboys as Equals

In many respects, the First Nations performers were treated as equals throughout this experience. They had close relationships with some of the white cowboys from Canada and the US who also travelled to Sydney. They became friendly with Constable Leach and his wife during the trip. When confronted with stereotypical attitudes or comments, they frequently made attempts to reinforce their equality by contradicting misrepresentations. Central to this discussion, as it is concerned with the importance of international competition, was the fact that on several occasions they publicly used the word "citizen" to describe themselves while travelling outside Canada. These instances, in particular, reinforce the importance of perspective, or "perception as resistance." They demonstrate purposeful attempts to alter perceptions concerning cultural and, arguably, political status, while presenting themselves through a counter-hegemonic perspective. In this way, symbolic disturbances to the notion of the western Canadian citizen-subject that occurred at the Calgary Stampede, through successful Indian cowboy competitions,[93] were deepened through international exposure.

Other scholars referencing counterhegemonic views have not, as yet, used the term "perception as resistance." Leerom Medovoi, however, explains how Gramscian theory can be used in a "double sense" when applied to issues of gender and race, which fits appropriately with this concept. When "counterhegemony," the "formation of a political adversary to an existing hegemony," is furthered to recognize that locally it performs as a "hegemony in its own right, with its own means of 'manufacturing consent' for the sake of collective struggle,"[95] then it follows that this counter-perspective can be presented as separate and distinct from over-arching national or colonial hegemonies. The ease of such presentations is in many ways prompted and facilitated by an international audience, which is generally considered more objective and, therefore, more receptive. In conjunction, the term "cultural citizenship," which has been promoted by Renato Rosaldo, focuses on "difference" and the creation of "new" identities that allow minority groups the ability to claim cultural and social rights. Once clearly defined, cultural identities allow for community affirmation, as well as political empowerment.[95]

Following their extensive tour of North America, Skidmore and MacFarlane also hired a small group of white cowboys and cowgirls to perform at the Royal Easter Show.[96] Of this group of thirty-four, two men, Jerry Amble and Jack Wade, were from Alberta. Floyd Many Fingers said that his brother Frank was very friendly with both of these men and had a long-term relationship with them that lasted most of his life.[97] Cecil said his father was also extremely close with Wade and Ambler. They remained friends for many years even after they all stopped competing in the rodeo circuit.[98]

During the 1939 trip, which lasted three months, Constable Leach and Mrs. Leach were in constant daily contact with all the men. Although their relationships never became completely equal, they developed a closeness that was remembered very positively. Both Floyd and Cecil attested to this fact. They claimed that Leach was friendly to all the men and did not treat any of them in a condescending manner. Ironically, Cecil remembered his father telling him that Leach used to take off his uniform and go out drinking with the men. He would not drink himself; however, he did escort them, making sure they could have a good time without getting into too much trouble. Cecil further explained that although he was there to protect them, he did not outrank them in any way. He said, "[Leach] was there for the show too, because everybody liked that."[99]

Geraldine Many Fingers, Frank's daughter, explained how the men occasionally liked to play practical jokes on Leach.[100] As an aside, Floyd Many Fingers told a story about one such joke:

> While they were under the grandstand waiting, all in a line for their grand entry, Joe Young Pine told my brother Frank, "Here, look at my glove," and

Frank said he wondered what he was up to, so he grabbed his glove and then felt that there was a bottle in there, a mickey. I don't know if Frank took a drink, but when he gave the mickey back to Joe, the fringes of his glove went under Leach's horse's tail and the horse bolted. It threw Leach off. When he got back up on his horse Leach looked at Joe Young Pine and said, "What happened, what happened?" And Joe said, "Well, there's a flea under his tail."[101]

All the men apparently had a good laugh about that. Leach did not mention this incident in his notes, and it is doubtful that he found it as humorous.

Due to the fact that there was such a powerful emphasis in Australia at this time on American popular culture and well-defined stereotypes concerning North American Plains Indians, it is only logical that eight Canadian First Nations cowboys would come in contact with racial prejudice pertaining to these stereotypes. Floyd recalled his brother saying that the Australian crowds would make war-whoops when they entered the show ring. However, once their talents as horsemen were demonstrated, the crowds reacted differently.[102] In his article for the *RCMP Quarterly*, Leach mentioned a few incidents when the men took control of situations involving stereotypes in order to reverse this emphasis. The first took place during a radio interview on the evening of their arrival in Sydney. Constable Leach, Joe Crowfoot, and Joe Bear Robe were all in attendance, and apparently the interview was proceeding quite well until Joe Bear Robe was asked a question.

> ANNOUNCER: "Did you ever shoot any big game?"
> BEAR ROBE: "Naw."
> ANNOUNCER: "No Moose or Deer?"
> BEAR ROBE: "Naw."
> ANNOUNCER: "Have you ever done any trapping?"
> BEAR ROBE: "No."
> ANNOUNCER: "Do you ever use bows and arrows?"
> BEAR ROBE: "No."
> ANNOUNCER: "Do you ever make those yodelling whoops that we've heard so much about lately?"
> BEAR ROBE: "No, the first time I heard that was in Auckland."[103]

Joe Bear Robe's final comment apparently flabbergasted the announcer, who quickly ended the interview. Bear Robe had taken advantage of the situation to publicly ridicule widespread Australian ignorance concerning the actual nature of First Nations culture.

Another incident took place on the return trip home. It demonstrated the importance of physical appearance and costuming as a way to transform identity in order to resist. Instead of the First Nations men participating in the costume ball held for the ship's passengers (which all the men had participated in on the voyage over), their traditional costumes were lent to two American performers. Leach claimed he was "suddenly surprised by one of the men coming up to [him] and saying 'Leach – come here quick – Indian at the bar drinking'." He ran over and there was Jasbo the Clown, dressed like an Indian, having a drink. Then another one of the men "drew him confidently aside" and said, "Leach, there's an Indian on the deck pretty tight." Although he was a little suspicious he went out to look and found Bill McMackin dressed in a traditional costume, "squatting on the deck, whooping and clapping his hands." Leach described these incidents with a mild sense of humor, "[t]he Indians [apparently] were laughing uproariously."[104] This particular situation demonstrated a symbolic attack on Canadian colonial authority and furthered the sense of camaraderie experienced by all the men involved, including Leach.

There are two recorded incidents when members of this First Nations troupe publicly described themselves as Canadian citizens. The first took place on the voyage home. In Leach's account, Frank Many Fingers went to the ship's bar "dressed in his civilian suit and fedora hat guzzling beer."[105]

> "This man came to the bar," said the tender, and asked for a glass of beer.
> "I'm sorry, I can't serve you," said the bartender.
> "Why not?" said Many Fingers, "I'm a Canadian Citizen and you've got to serve me."
> "But you are an Indian from Canada", replied the bartender.[107]

The second such incident was found in a quote from Joe Crowfoot in the *Sydney Morning Herald*. Here he stated, "Nowadays the Red Indian is a peace-loving and good citizen of the country."[107] These public declarations contradicted the legal, colonial status that had been assigned to them by the Canadian government. By describing themselves to a foreign audience as citizens, they

Fig. 30: Cowboys in Grand Parade at the Royal Easter Show. Sydney, April 1939. Courtesy Royal Agricultural Society of New South Wales, private collection.

were clearly asserting their disregard for this categorization, preferring equality to dependency.

Conclusions

The Royal Easter Show in Sydney has always been famous for its Grand Parade. This impressive and traditional display "showcases the champion animals from the various sections of the show,"[108] as well as all equestrian competitors. In 1939 this parade took place at least once, and sometimes twice a day. It was headed by Constable Leach on horseback, followed by approximately forty white cowboys and cowgirls from North America, who were then followed by Canada's team of First Nations cowboys. Each rider carried a flag. Leach carried a very large Union Jack. The white cowboys and cowgirls carried a mixture of national flags and flags displaying their family names along with the name of their city and/or state or province of affiliation. The First Nations cowboys carried flags depicting their family names and band names (see Fig. 30). They were also dressed in full traditional regalia made by family members.[109]

Flags are one of the most commonly used symbols of nationalism and their carriers are automatically identified as citizens. The Olympics are a good example of an international sporting event where traditional costumes are incorporated with flags, anthems and emblems to demonstrate national affinity. These First Nations cowboys were demonstrating through visual spectacle how national identity and cultural citizenship are linked at the local level. They were relying on a bottom-up approach to articulate their position in Canadian society as both citizens and as culturally distinctive people.[110] The flags, created for local rodeos, were brought out of that colonial space into a larger place where the divide between the colonized and the colonizer was melded together in a single arena. Proficiency in sport, as a vehicle for the achievement of inner stability and external status, was shared and displayed to an international audience. In this way, these eight First Nations men definitively articulated their perceived position in Canadian society. Due to their combined heritage and careers as cattle-ranchers and cowboys, accompanied by severe government restrictions on ownership and land use, this perception privileged the association of land and culture, not the association of state and culture.[111]

Their performances at the Royal Easter Show were a combination of two primary objectives: to compete and represent their country internationally, and to represent their cultures internationally. They provide a unique instance when publicly performed cultural citizenship was combined with athletic competition. Sport has two primary roles in international relations: public diplomacy and the production of national identity.[112] What Floyd Many Fingers and Cecil Crowfoot described as a sense of pride and duty can be extended and understood as an important, early twentieth-century demonstration of distinct national identity. At a time when First Nations people in Canada were suffering severe political, economic and social restrictions, these eight First Nations cowboys embraced an opportunity to demonstrate the strength of their communities through demonstrating their individual skills as horsemen.

The Many Fingers' and the Crowfoot's family stories and memories connect the past with the present, and continue to construct meanings that define a distinct cultural nationalism. Rodeo, as a forum for the retention of cultural distinctiveness and the establishment of internal stability, has continued to have a profound impact on their communities. By the 1950s, First Nations performers in Alberta were still experiencing discrimination at professional rodeos. They were tired of competing in top-notch form while receiving low marks from white judges. In the late 1950s,

Frank Many Fingers started the All Indian Rodeo Cowboys Association in order to break away from the Canadian Professional Rodeo Association. At present this organization continues to hold international competitions for Indian (and now Metis) people in the United States and Canada. Local Indian rodeos continue to provide places where cultural heritage, ownership of land, determination, skill and integrity are all demonstrated. The same flag that Frank Many Fingers carried in the Grand Parade at the 1939 Royal Easter Show in Sydney was carried in 1997 by Buck Many Fingers, a close relative, in a parade preceding the Many Fingers Ranch annual rodeo.[113]

4

Constable Leach at the Royal Easter Show in Sydney: Tourist, Amateur Anthropologist & Chaperone

> The Show opened officially on April the 5th, the Governor-General of Australia, Lord Gowrie, performed the ceremony, and I was presented to him during the Grande Parade. As I was riding out of the ring, a photographer approached me and asked me to make the horse rear up on its hind feet. A little surprised I nevertheless had no reason to refuse so simple a request. However I was considerable startled when I opened one of the local papers one day and saw a picture of myself on the horse which was poised on one hind foot, and underneath read the following, "Constable Leach of the Nor'West Mounted Salutes the Governor-General. He is one of the competitive riders from America."[1]

IN 1939 THE DAILY PARADE FEATURED at the Royal Agricultural Easter Show was enhanced by the inclusion of a Royal Canadian Mounted Police (RCMP) officer, in full uniform, riding a white horse. A crowd of 55,000 people lined the stadium to view the "Grand Parade." Bands played and flags flew as the largest procession Sydney had ever seen marched by. Constable Samuel J. Leach was described as "the finest figure of all the horsemen in the show."[2] For the Australian audience, Leach's presence was as fascinating, if not more, as the cowboys who followed him (see Fig. 31). This chapter will analyze his impressions of the trip, while providing insights into the often contradictory relationship between a white Euro-Canadian RCMP officer and the eight Canadian First Nations cowboys he was charged to observe and control. Leach's role as chaperone placed him in a position of colonial authority; however, this authority shifted dramatically when

Fig. 31: Constable Leach Leading Grand Parade. Sydney, April 1939. Courtesy Royal Agricultural Society of New South Wales, private collection.

he came in contact with Australian colonial attitudes. It also shifted through the shared experience of travel.

Samuel Leach was thirty years old in 1939, and had been a member of the force for eight years. Born in Moose Jaw, Saskatchewan, he had spent his RCMP career to that point stationed in the northern detachment at Prince Albert. Family members believe he was asked to go to Australia for a variety of reasons. He had already been working closely with First Nations people in remote locations, he was one of the men chosen to go to Vimy Ridge to represent Canada, and his new wife was Dorothy E.H. Westgate, the daughter of T.B.R. Westgate, a well-known Anglican Minister.[3] Dorothy was a nurse, and she'd had a great deal of experience working in First Nations communities as well. Her services were actually critical for this trip. In addition, her father was a close friend of Col. Mitchell, one of the original members of the North West Mounted Police (the 153rd man to enlist). Mitchell was an honored guest and the best man at the Leach's wedding. His influence was believed to have precipitated the decision to hire Leach as an escort for this trip.[4] Leach was charming, photogenic, and good looking; his working

Constable Leach at the Royal Easter Show in Sydney   89

Fig. 32: Constable Leach Prior to Leaving. Sydney, February 1939. Glenbow Archives, NA-1241-172. Titled: Natives of Alberta, leaving for Australia. Photographer: F. Gully.

record was impeccable. All of these factors made him an ideal model to maintain the exemplary reputation of Canada's internationally known police force (see Fig. 32).

This trip was an excellent opportunity for a young RCMP officer to promote a reputation based on skills related to international diplomacy. In this respect Leach's responsibilities were extremely complex because he was representing Canada, as a nation, and also the Indian Affairs Branch, an important colonial institution. The pressures intrinsic to this role would have been omnipresent. Added to these were the day-to-day stresses of travelling in close daily contact with nine other people for three months, performing as a group for an international audience, and negotiating regularly between the RAS and the First Nations men. Leach's mythic role demanded that he remain fearless and bold, while simultaneously exhibiting unfailing courteousness. More realistically, his attention to details, flexibility, and organizational skills were the keys to his success.

Constable Leach was also a prolific writer, taking extensive notes from the minute he was asked to go, on 19 January 1939, until the day they all returned home, 5 May 1939. This chapter will be based on two primary documents, his official RCMP report and an article published two months following the trip in the *RCMP Quarterly*. Both differ dramatically from the information presented by the families of Frank Many Fingers and Joe Crowfoot, which is understandable considering the audience Leach was writing for. The RCMP report was comprised of a detailed diary of daily events describing his care and control of the eight First Nations men, as well as accounts of any "official" incidents related to the RAS. Chronicling such details was a mandated activity for any similarly employed RCMP officer, but Leach also added many personal perceptions concerning his travel companions. The *RCMP Quarterly* was first published in 1933, and was designed to provide historical and educational information to members of the force and the general public. Leach's comments in this article were more jovial than those in the official report, and included personal characterizations of his experience.

Leach's commentary was coloured throughout by a personal desire to prove that he was a good citizen and a good officer. Cultural meanings focused on a Canadian version of what it meant to do the right thing or "Maintain the Right," which was the slogan that he promoted in Australia. Descriptions of his actions followed the mythic image of a quiet, calm, stolid, yet commanding figure. Leach's commentary in respect to the First Nations men included stereotypical racial attitudes common to government officials, as well as to mainstream, North American popular culture at this time. He did not mention feeling a sense of equality with the First Nations men, nor did he mention the social excursions described by Cecil Crowfoot. Primarily,

Leach's writing must be viewed as an official record of this trip, which would have been necessarily rendered by its author in a manner socially and politically acceptable to the Canadian government and the Indian Affairs Branch. Its overall tone was paternalistic in nature.

However, more intimate perspectives can be read between the lines of this official view. Here a form of positive paternalism, one which was protective and sympathetic, was directed at correcting the unfair treatment the men received during the show. Leach was also very concerned with details of the physical injuries they suffered and recorded every incident. His prize-winning article in the *RCMP Quarterly* titled, "Redskins and Redcoat Visit the Antipodes," reflects his curiosity and sense of humor. His multiple references to himself, his wife and the eight First Nations cowboys as "we" suggested that he also felt a personal connection that transcended his role as an authority figure.

Following introductory comments regarding the mythic relationship between Canada's RCMP and First Nations people, this chapter will develop three themes drawn from an analysis of Leach's writing. In this way the contradictions inherent in his descriptions of this trip can be examined. It will not dwell on the actual events of the trip, which were summarized in the introduction, but will instead analyze three different roles Leach depicted concerning this journey. These subsections include: the apparent paradoxes associated with Leach's role as an RCMP officer and his experiences as a tourist; comments about the First Nations men that reflect stereotypical social beliefs of this time period; and Leach's more personal perceptions of his role as a chaperone, protector and representative of Canada. Each theme or role will follow the storyline in a chronological order, building in complexity on ideas related to racial prejudices during this time.

The Unique Relationship between First Nations and the RCMP

Canada is one of the world's only nations to recognize a police force as a national symbol.[5] The creation of order and peace in wilderness areas is considered to be the central achievement of the RCMP. Their accomplishments are expounded on in specific references to western and northern Canada and include the acquisition of sovereignty over the land by their mere presence. In Euro-Canadian popular mythology, RCMP officers had a particular knack for subduing undesirable and savage Indians.[6] The decision to have eight First Nations men accompanied by an RCMP officer was never questioned by the Royal Agricultural Society (RAS), nor was it debated by the Indian Affairs Branch.

The notion of a close and amicable relationship between the RCMP and First Nations in Canada also has a long history in the cultural mythology of the west. Prior to 1980 almost every author on the subject provided this quote from Chief Crowfoot, Joe Crowfoot's grandfather, to explain this relationship:

> If the Police had not come to the country, where would we all be now? Bad men and whiskey were killing us so fast that very few indeed of us would have been left today. The Police protected us as the feathers of the bird protect it from the frosts of winter. I wish them all good, and trust that all our hearts will increase in kindness from this time forward. I am satisfied. I will sign the treaty.[7]

This quote has been used to suggest that the RCMP were responsible for saving all Plains Indians from certain destruction, and that their kindness convinced all First Nations people living in southern Alberta to surrender their lands. As described by Stan Horrall, "The key to the successful signing of treaty [7] was the bond of trust, which developed between RCMP Commissioner MacLeod and two chiefs, Crowfoot and Red Crow."[8] While mainstream cultural memory and historical writing suggests that it was MacLeod's honesty and sincerity that won their respect,[9] other historians have suggested that in actuality the RCMP were only sympathetic to the needs of First Nations until 1886,[10] just prior to the treaty signing.

Teddy Yellowfly used this cultural mythology in 1939 on behalf of the Blood, Blackfoot, Sarcee and Stoney chiefs in a letter that he wrote to S.T. Woods, the commissioner of the RCMP. The letter voiced concerns about the welfare of the First Nations men who were travelling to the Royal Easter Show. Yellowfly mentioned Corporal D. Ashby of the Gleichen Detachment as the best man for the job because he was one of the only remaining old types of "Red Coats" that the Indians named "NE TA PI NA KE," or "Real Police." According to Yellowfly, these RCMP understood Indians on an intimate level and did not act as a "law enforcement officer, but a protector, a doctor, advisor and a friend in need, all molded into one person."[11] The chiefs' concern was that an officer who did not understand the cultural needs of the men who were going would not be able to care for them properly, or be an appropriate cultural interpreter for an Australian audience. In fact, they hoped that the man picked for the job would literally be a "human encyclopedia" on the social, economic and political life of the groups from Alberta he was representing. Yellowfly closed his letter by expanding on the importance of the chiefs' position and stated, "The Indians of all Canada will expect your representative to give the people of Australia a true picture of the Indians here in Canada."[12]

This attempt to influence Woods' decision was disregarded. Constable Leach, not Corporal Ashby, was hired as the chaperone for this trip. Leach's role, both metaphorically and realistically, placed him between the Canadian government, four of the largest First Nations communities in Canada, and the RAS in Australia. The Canadian government expected him to maintain complete control over the men at all times, as did the RAS. For the Australian audience, the image of an RMCP officer in full uniform leading eight First Nations cowboys on horses would send a clear, symbolic message concerning Canada's colonial success in taming its savage west. The chiefs of the Blood, Blackfoot, Sarcee and Stoney bands hoped that the presence of an RCMP officer would guarantee the safety and fair treatment of their well-respected members. Possibly, for the Indians of Canada, as suggested by Yellowfly, the RCMP officer's presence would also provide some sort of distinctive cultural representation. Leach became the mediator within this web of expectations; he was supposed to make sure everyone's needs, preferences and ideological concerns were met. His correspondence and reports reveal a man struggling under the burdens of these sometimes contradictory responsibilities while simultaneously trying to understand his own experience of the trip (see Fig. 33).

Constable Leach and a Touristic View

For Constable Leach this trip was also a trip of a lifetime. His family remembers repeatedly hearing stories about Australia, the Indian cowboys, and the Royal Easter Show. He kept a scrapbook of all the newspaper clippings, programs, and photographs. It could be argued that Leach experienced as much, if not more, celebrity status than did the First Nations cowboys. In his memoirs, he fondly recalled being introduced to Lord Gowrie in the show ring before thousands of Australians (see Fig. 34), and being swarmed by the crowds for a chance to touch his coat. "Do Mounties always get their man?" Even this often-repeated stereotypical question was remembered with humor. However, reports at the time, the article in the *RCMP Quarterly*, and Leach's official RCMP diary told a much more convoluted story. Throughout, the joys of travelling to Australia were intermingled with multiple challenges and frustrations.

Fig. 33: "Lance Corporal Leach with his charges at Sydney, N.S.W." Samuel J. Leach. "Redskins and Redcoats Visit the Antipodes." *RCMP Quarterly* 7, no. 1 (July 1939): 59.

Leach's comments in his RCMP report do not suggest that he perceived himself as a tourist during this trip. Nor do they mention the presence of his wife. Nonetheless, comments in "Redskins and Redcoat Visit the Antipodes" add a romantic and touristic view of the events of 1939. In the opening sentence he establishes his excitement about touring Australia by claiming to be looking forward to "[k]angaroo hunts, Koala bears, Aborigines with boomerangs, surfing at sunny beaches, the Southern Cross."[13] Throughout he alternates between describing himself, his wife, and the First Nations men as a cohesive group through the use of the term "we," and singling out the First Nations men as separate entities through use of the term "the Indian Party." Leach also alternates between glamorous travelogue-type descriptions based on emphasizing the exotic nature of the places they were seeing with comments about the First Nations men's unsophisticated or ignorant reaction to these places. The striking dynamic between these two types of comments is confusing as it alternates between notions of inclusion and exclusion.

An excellent example occurs in his description of Honolulu, the first stop on their voyage to Australia. His comments resembled a travelogue about exoticized destinations where palm trees, a lovely harbor, the tanned bodies of Hawaiian divers and swimmers, and "the romantic music of the Royal Hawaiian Band"[14] greeted them. He explained that after the SS *Niagara* docked, "[We] all wanted

Fig. 34: "Lord Gowrie with 'Mountie'." *The Sydney Morning Herald*, 6 April 1939.

to see as much as we could of this glamorous island, so we hurried ashore where Hoola Hoola girls clamoured around us selling beautiful flowered leis. We engaged cars and the drivers took us to vantage points where we could watch the long and spectacular parade, which commemorated this historic day."[15] It was Washington's Birthday and, ironically, the parade commemorating this event, which the Canadian group witnessed, included "six imitation mounted RCM Police, headed by a group of cowboys."[16] The coincidental nature of this sight amazed Leach.

This glamorous description, complete with background music, was abruptly disrupted by comments within the same paragraph referring to the ignorance of "the Indian Party." After lunch while shopping, Leach claimed that his "hair nearly stood on end" when he saw four of the men "standing in the middle of a thoroughfare nonchalantly taking snapshots." He guided them back to the ship with "a mingled feeling of regret and relief."[17] In his RCMP notes he emphasized that "the Indians appeared to be very indifferent to the city traffic," and that he had made a strong effort "to impress upon them the danger and the need for alertness."[18] His shift from using the term "we" to clearly delineating "the Indian Party" as primitives, who did not respond appropriately to dangerous city traffic, demonstrated the duality of his experience as both an individual, and as an RCMP officer responsible for the men's safety.

A similar, yet less elaborate, set of comments were used to describe the city of Auckland in New Zealand, their final stop before arriving in Sydney. The word "we" was also used throughout: "we visited the Auckland zoo" and "we had a commanding view of Auckland" were two examples. Here Leach seemed very comfortable identifying himself as part of a group. He also referred to the First Nations men as "the boys," indicating a familial-type of relationship, as well as connotations of paternalism and condescension.[19] His RCMP notes differed. Here he stated, "the Auckland Zoo … proved very interesting to the Indian Party."[20] This statement suggested that Leach himself was not sightseeing, but only accompanying "the Indian Party," which was.

Comments concerning "we" continued throughout their experience in Australia, primarily whenever they were sightseeing. However, "we" was not used in reference to incidents that occurred during the Royal Easter Show. In these descriptions Leach separated the actions of the First Nations men from his role as chaperone. On 13 March, three days after their arrival, they travelled to Merriwa, approximately 245 miles from Sydney, and his description of this trip was peppered with statements such as "we boarded the train," "we had to change trains," and "we had lunch."[21] As well, touristic comments referring to the beauty of the Australian countryside were all focused on the perspective of this ten-person troupe.

Saloni Mathur explores the notion of nationhood as a category for "otherness" in an example from the Colonial and Indian Exhibition of 1886 in London. Due to the caste system in India, a man of stature, upper-caste and educated, would never have taken any interest in lower class craftsmen, and he would never have gone near prisoners. One day Makharji, an upper-caste gentleman and the key figure in Mathur's historic study, went to the exhibition and happened upon demonstrations of Indian craftsmen at work. He focused on the fact that the primarily European audiences were looking at and evaluating these men's bodies only. The crowd's piercing stare disgusted Mukharji, as they seemed to look upon these other Indian men as if they were animals.[22] Mathur explained how the idea of "we" changed for Makharji from identification with class to identification with nationality only. Makharji became totally disenchanted with life in London and claimed that the racism these men experienced at the exhibition was cruel and of the type "that a European only is capable of."[23]

This sensibility can be aligned to the ways Leach described the party he was travelling with. It also explains his prevalent use of the word "we" in Honolulu, Suva and Australia, as these would have been the places where he most felt like an outsider. "We" in this sense becomes a descriptive noun of inclusion that identifies Constable Leach, his wife, and the eight First Nations men as a cohesive unit of Canadians, or perhaps western Canadians. Their solidarity was created through travelling and juxtaposed against all other people they met.

In Leach's article, comments concerning "we" were not used in descriptions of the return trip home. For this section he chose only to include "several little incidents," which "stood out, apart from [our] ports of call."[24] In these descriptions he again moved back to focus on "the Indian Party" as a separate entity. The First Nations men were referred to here as ignorant and rebellious charges, whose behavior Leach did not understand. Some degree of separation potentially needed to be acknowledged before Constable Leach returned to Canada and resumed his role as RCMP chaperone.

Homi Bhabha and other scholars have suggested that the generalized colonial process of "othering" is based on the dramatic and oppositional responses of fear and fascination.[25] Such distinction is not apparent in Leach's writing. Descriptions of "the Indian Party" were more modest. Annoyance at times replaced fear, and curiosity replaced fascination. Leach was frustrated with his charges when they challenged his authority or otherwise acted in ways he did not understand. He was also genuinely interested in their reactions to things and places, which were different from his own. Although many of his comments indicated an awareness of his public role as an educator, Leach's interest in First Nations culture went beyond this role. His curiosity mimicked that of an amateur anthropologist, which was supported by prolific anthropological commentary common to a variety of popular culture venues emerging in Canada at this time.

Primitivism Discourse within Constable Leach's Commentary

In Canada during the late 1930s, contradictory ideas circulated in regards to First Nations people and culture. On one hand, anthropology was promoting a new wave of sympathy based on what is now called the "Salvage Paradigm." This paradigm stated that "traditional" societies were rapidly disappearing and had been corrupted by modernity. It was assumed that surviving First Nations had abandoned their old traditions to embrace modern, white culture and mainstream social mores. Therefore, it was the responsibility of anthropologists to salvage any information and/or physical examples of their authentic past before it was obliterated.[26] This theory precipitated a certain amount of colonial guilt, which in turn created sympathy for the few surviving "Indians."

On the other hand, discourses about primitivism were also very popular. These ideas were dependent on racial evolutionist theories. Primitives were alive and well. These uncivilized groups were childlike, free, natural and innocent. They were also simultaneously irrational, violent and dangerous. Notions of the primitive were positioned against notions of modernity to define the latter as rational, logical, practical, advanced, complicated and civilized.[27] Although primitive peoples could elevate their civility, the erasure of their fundamental ignorance required a great deal of education and sophistication. This ideology created either a sympathetic attitude or a discriminatory attitude towards all indigenous people.

These social perspectives would have undoubtedly influenced Constable Leach's views concerning "Indians" in general. However, as an RCMP officer working in northern Saskatchewan, he would have been well aware of the practical problems faced by First Nations communities struggling to survive the depression. Mrs. Leach's work as a nurse also would have deepened the couple's awareness of the oppressive domestic, economic and political situations confronting these communities. Even so, any sympathies would have been combined with paternalistic ideas that were supported by government policies towards First Nations. In the 1930s these attitudes were also aligned with those of church officials, which strictly emphasized the importance of assimilation as the only way to relieve economic dependency and move First Nations people into mainstream society.[28] T.B.R. Westgate, Leach's father-in-law, was a particularly vocal advocate for the residential school system, which he viewed as a positive way to bring the First Nations population closer to full Canadian citizenship. Amongst his contemporaries Westgate was considered a very sympathetic and far-sighted supporter of cultural difference. Moreover, in the later part of the 1930s, a variety of popular culture media, including the *Canadian Geographical Journal*, CBC radio and amateur anthropological tales, all championed the need for quick and painless assimilation.[29]

There was a second level of contradictions apparent in regards to primitivist discourses, which veered between sympathy and discrimination. In some instances Leach projected racial prejudice, and in other instances he projected sympathy. Such an ambiguous understanding of cultural difference would be expected considering the social influences of the time.

Leach's initial description of "the Indian Party" was based on physical appearance accompanied by assumptions about their character. On 31 February, after meeting Douglas Kootenay he stated, "He appeared to be of small build, he could speak English, was well mannered and quite keen on the trip."[30] In comparison he described Johnny Left Hand as, "more intelligent than Kootenay, but not as trustworthy."[31] This suggests that an intelligent "Indian" was not to be trusted, which followed stereotypical beliefs associated to savagism. When Leach met Joe Crowfoot he stated that he appeared to be "a well built, fine looking Indian" and that "he seemed to be quite intelligent and keen on the trip."[32] This comment conversely suggested that good looks elevated intelligence and erased untrustworthiness. Joe Crowfoot's stature and professional demeanour perhaps reminded Leach of the classic motion picture image of the "noble savage," which may have coloured his attitude towards Crowfoot's character (see Fig. 35).

Throughout his writings Leach seemed captivated by moments when he imagined that modern technology or foreign landscapes fascinated the eight First Nations men he was travelling with. On the train ride from Calgary to Vancouver, he stated that "the Indian Party" had never travelled "further West than Banff," and that they were "amazed at the length of the tunnels."[33] His article for the *RCMP Quarterly* reiterated this impression by noting, "[All] were impressed by the grandeur of the Rockies and fascinated by the numerous tunnels through which we passed and tallied these up until darkness and drowsiness overcame

Fig. 35: Crowfoot and Leach in Sydney. Sydney Harbour, 1939. Courtesy of the State Library of New South Wales. Titled: "Arrival of Red Indians by 'Niagara'." *The Hood Collection: Part 1.* Frame Order # Home and Away – 19310.

them."[34] Upon boarding the *Niagara* in Vancouver, he claimed that the ship was just an "old tub"; however, "the Indians were amazed at the size of it."[35] A few days later Leach mentioned the astonishment of "The Indian Party" when he took them down to see the ship's engines; he maintained that they were all "amazed at the immense size of them."[36] At Koala Park in Sydney, Leach stated that "[A]ll the Indian Party were fascinated by an Aborigine's throwing of a boomerang."[37] In his article for the *RCMP Quarterly* he elaborated on this experience as one of the Indians' "greatest thrills."[38] These comments position the First Nations men as innocent and childlike, thus representing the sympathetic form of stereotypical ideas associated with primitiveness. Conversely, these comments allowed Leach to express emotion while maintaining professionalism in an article written for his peers.

There were several occasions when Leach highlighted the men's ignorance of modern technology. Two incidents were described in the article written for the *RCMP Quarterly*. The first occurred when they crossed the equator. Leach claimed that the Indians were completely mystified at the fact that a day was lost because they had traversed the 180th meridian.[39] The second described in detail a conversation Mrs. Leach had with one of the men (the name "Joe" was used, but it was not specified whether it was Joe Crowfoot, Joe Bear Robe or Joe Young Pine) while shopping in Sydney:

> MRS. LEACH: "Joe, what do you want to buy now?"
> JOE: "Suitcase."
> MRS. LEACH: "What kind of suitcase and how much do you want to pay for it?"
> JOE: "I dunno, I haven't any money."
> MRS. LEACH: "But Joe what did you do with your money?"
> JOE: "It ran out."

They went into the suitcase department of a large store and after the clerk showed numerous suitcases of various sizes and prices, he made his choice and asked Mrs. Leach if she would pay for it and he'd repay her later. Mrs. Leach asked the clerk if it would be in order to send it out COD. The clerk replied on affirmation.

> JOE: "You not going to pay Mrs. Leach?"
> MRS. LEACH: "Not now Joe, I'll pay for it when we get it tomorrow."
> JOE: "You no pay now I don't want suitcases."
> MRS. LEACH: "I can pay for it Joe, but it would be more convenient tomorrow."
> JOE: "I won't take suitcase."

Despite Mrs. Leach's assurances that COD was in order, he remained adamant and refused to have anything to do with that particular suitcase. However he bought a similar one a few days later when he was out again with Mrs. Leach.[40]

The length of this description attests to its derogatory and denigrating nature. It solely focused on foolishness and ignorance, negative qualities inherent in primitivist discourse. This description provides a very intense example of how deeply these ideas shaped non-Aboriginal perceptions about First Nations people.

Leach's focus on "the Indian Party's" presupposed innocence and ignorance demonstrated the incorporation of primitivist discourse into his personal belief system. These attitudes severely contradicted any close identification he may have had of the First Nations men as his friends or associates. These attitudes helped Leach re-establish perceived understandings of racial superiority with his readership of white Canadians. By keeping racial hierarchy in the forefront as a delineated boundary, Leach's attitude did not fit with the mythological relationship between the RCMP and the First Nations expressed by non-Aboriginal Canadian historians. Belittling comments destroyed the popular notion of friendship and instead confirmed the proliferation of mainstream racial prejudice of the 1930s.

Ironically, Constable Leach's racist comments can be considered moderate when compared to day-to-day white attitudes that First Nations people experienced in Alberta. Open hostility was rare only because contact was avoided whenever possible. Most believed that "Indians" were thieves and beggars, "a lazy lot, shiftless ... careless with property."[41] Hanks and Hanks claimed that positive contact only occurred during the tourist season, when "Indians" became an attraction that whites responded to with "mild interest in barbaric splendor mingled with amusement at their 'childish' ways."[42] The rest of the time contact could prove very antagonistic. For example, "[a] white in a soft-drink establishment, unable to contain his anger when an Indian accidentally prevented him from glancing at the newspaper, cursed and threatened the offending Indian who 'did not know his place.'"[43] Frequently the RCMP officer's job was to mediate between the two groups and therefore, within these scenarios, they did become protectors, friends and, sometimes, advisors. For First Nations people, who were obviously a minority, an RCMP presence was often welcomed and needed.[44]

Constable Leach as Chaperone and Representative of Canada

As a symbol of authority and order, the RCMP's imagined role as the protector of First Nations followed the doctrine of paternalism common to church and state authorities of the time. Paternalism is described as a form of governance that mimics the type of authority a father would have over his children. As with the tenets of primitivism, there are positive and negative variants of paternalism. Negative paternalism emphases the right of total control over another's behavior. The positive focuses on caring. Both are positioned on the idea of protection.

However, when applied within a colonial mindset, both variants become negative. Both are based on the belief that First Nations people do not possess an adequate level of intelligence and, therefore are a danger to themselves. Prior to the 1960s, church and state authorities in Canada argued that it was their moral duty to deprive all First Nations of their liberties because they lacked sufficient mental capacities to make sound moral judgments.[45] While the Canadian government publicly acknowledged the detrimental effects of this attitude and apologized for its implications in 1998, roots of this idea continue today in policy-making and generalized attitudes towards First Nations.[46]

It was under this rhetoric of paternalism that the Indian Affairs Branch decided it was imperative for the RAS to hire an RCMP officer to accompany "the Indians" to Australia (see Fig. 36). Leach was responsible for all travel arrangements and other logistical concerns in Australia, including the distribution and sale of a thousand pounds of beaded handiwork, the erection of eight tipis, and servicing all rodeo equipment. He was also responsible for "the Indian Party's" health, multiple medical exams, and the distribution of their wages. However, according to Schmidt in his letter to Skidmore, Leach's primary job was to make sure that the men did not sulk, drink alcohol, or spend all of their money. Alcohol consumption was considered such a serious problem that Schmidt was doubtful Leach could handle it on his own. He recommended that,

> [I]n regards to liquor (spirits, wines and beer): This is the one thing the Indian cannot handle. In Canada it is a serious offence to supply an Indian with same. I would ask you to kindly give Constable Leach police assistance in this respect, because if one of the Indians gets a drink or two, he will be unable to perform properly, and may "go wild." It has been known that other competitors (White people) have used liquor to disable an Indian in a hard-fought competition for prize money.[47]

It can be argued that Leach's interpretation of the Canadian government's expectations in respect to control, were connected to his personal sense of duty, his sense of morality, and his imagined responsibilities as an RCMP officer. While keeping the First Nations men away from alcohol was one of his primary concerns, Leach himself did not express any belief in the idea that they would "go wild" if they had one drink. As the trip progressed, isolation became the primary tactic Leach used to prevent access to alcohol, which he claimed was being continually

Fig. 36: Constable Leach, Col. Somerville and A.W. Skidmore on the deck of the SS *Niagara*. Courtesy State Library of New South Wales. Titled: "Arrival of Red Indians by 'Niagara'." *The Hood Collection: Part 1*. Frame Order # Home and Away – 19312.

given to them by the Australian crowds. There were many occasions when he had to challenge the integrity of the RAS in terms of their treatment of the First Nations cowboys because it frequently differed from the treatment experienced by the other rodeo performers. His determined efforts to attain equitable treatment for the men was based on his own sense of fairness accompanied by an enhanced sense of protectiveness procured through the shared experience of travelling together.

A statistical overview of all of the comments Leach made in reference to the First Nations men primarily described them as co-operative.[48] This was particularly true during the voyage to Australia. There was only one minor incident when two of the men "slipped off" in Auckland to get liquor, but they apparently did not procure very much of it.[49] Other than the odd health problem, he continually used phrases such as the "Indian Party was fine," "all was well," "nothing unusual occurred," or "nothing serious occurred."[50] From this perspective the voyage to Sydney seemed like a chaperone's dream. On a daily basis Leach described "the Indian Party's" participation in such on-board events as watching movies, engaging in deck games, dancing, and writing letters. Throughout they were described as happy, calm, and co-operative; they also took part in all activities and got "along very well with the rest of the passengers."[51] Leach emphasized his pride in the men's behavior during this portion of the trip.

The situation seemed to change once the troupe reached MacFarlane's ranch in Merriwa and came in contact with the rest of the Canadian and American rodeo performers. During this segment of the journey incidents of "bad behavior" escalated and Leach's comments began to focus on incidents related to alcohol and misdemeanors. From Leach's point of view, the primary problem was the fact that other people – cowgirls, cowboys, and stable hands – were continually trying to get the men intoxicated.

Leach's RCMP report outlined two specific incidents in detail. In the first instance, all of the Canadian and US cowboys and cowgirls were taken to the ranch of Sir Frederick McMaster. Liberal amounts of alcohol were served, but not to the First Nations cowboys, who were offered only soft drinks. Apparently they sulked, though there were no other repercussions.[52] The second instance was much more problematic. On 23 March, there was a party for all of the rodeo participants at MacFarlane's ranch, and this time "the Indian Party" became more resentful of the discrimination they experienced with regard to alcohol. A few of them arranged for drinks to be surreptitiously passed to them throughout the night. Leach claimed he escorted them to the boarding house they were staying at after he noticed they were drunk. They escaped his custody for the remainder of the evening and spent it socializing with some of the other guests.[53] The next day Leach interrogated the men before taking them to the local police station, where Sgt. Fairlamb of the New South Wales Police interrogated them again. Fairlamb also threatened to lock them up if they behaved similarly in Sydney.[54]

Leach's reaction to Fairlamb's criticism was somewhat similar to that of a possessive parent. He blamed T.B. MacFarlane for having liquor at his party. He reminded Fairlamb that if "the Indians" were put in jail, it would arouse much unfavorable press, which neither of them wanted. That evening Leach lectured the men on the dangers of alcohol and venereal disease. He also reminded them of "their responsibility not only to themselves, but to their tribes, Canada and the RAS."[55]

After this incident, Leach focused on isolating the men from almost everyone. He claimed that the biggest obstacle to achieving this was the Australian public. The aggressive crowds of thousands constantly mobbed them and asked for autographs. The showgoers were also giving the men alcohol. Apparently it was difficult escorting "the Indian Party" from the stables to the showground, while making sure they did not obtain a drink. "When the Indians were looking for liquor and the Australians notoriously anxious to display 'Hospitality' by giving it, it was practically impossible to keep it strictly from them."[56] Due to Leach's vigilance, there were only two incidents in which the RAS decided to intervene; both of these involved women.

The first was on 28 March, when Jim Starlight went out for the evening with one of the cowgirls, Ivadel Jacobs, "but returned at 10:30 p.m. in a sober condition."[57] Col. Somerville took Leach aside and stated that the RAS would not tolerate such behavior, and that they would all be sent back to Canada if it happened again. Leach's response was to blame the RAS for initially "sending the Indian Party into such close contact with the Cowgirls at Merriwa."[58] To avoid further problems he decided to erect a tent beside the Indian Village where he slept for the duration of the show.

The second occasion occurred on 6 April, during the Royal Easter Show, when Joe Young Pine brought a young girl into his tipi to show her his horse. According to Leach's report the horse bucked and frightened the girl. Mr. Joel, an RAS official, aggressively reprimanded Young Pine, who "became very abusive to him." There were no immediate repercussions due to the size of the crowd that gathered to witness the incident, but Leach was warned that they would all be sent back to Canada if this happened again. Alcohol consumption was suspected.[59] On 7 April,

Young Pine obtained alcohol from a stable hand, but was caught and placed under police guard. He was caught drinking alcohol again on the 8th, and placed in jail for two days.[60] Sadly, these incidents preceded Leach's decision to prohibit the whole group from attending the farewell party organized at the Hotel Grand Central by the RAS.[61]

The trip home proved to be even more difficult for Leach as a chaperone. From his descriptions it seemed that the men were tired of co-operating and wanted to have some freedom before the trip was over. Still, he blamed every incident simply on their desire to obtain alcohol. Consequently, the tension between the two parties increased dramatically, as did Leach's efforts to isolate certain individuals. A few of the men escaped on 17 April while the group was shopping in Auckland. A similar incident occurred the next day while they were eating breakfast. On 21 April, in Suva, Fiji, Leach was determined that no one would escape again. He enlisted the help of Jack Wade and Jerry Ambler (the white Canadian cowboys who were friends with the men) to escort four of them shopping while he and Mrs. Leach escorted the other four. Leach described in detail a dramatic scene on the gangplank of the ship when two of the men refused to leave the ship under these arrangements. The Suva police were called in, and the rebellious men were detained for the remainder of their stay. In Honolulu there were apparently no such problems.

The *RMMS Aorangi* docked in Vancouver on 5 May at 9:45 pm. All of the passengers immediately left except for the eight First Nations cowboys, who were forced to spend the night on board. They were detained by Corporal Floyd of the RCMP, immigration authorities, and the ship's purser, all acting under Leach's recommendations. In his official report, he stated that although the men were unhappy about this, it was necessary because two of them were overheard saying "that they were going to get drunk as soon as they landed."[62] Leach glossed over this decision in his comments for the *RCMP Quarterly*, where he described the landing quite differently:

> When we arrived in Canada it seemed as if home were almost in sight. A general air of excitement pervaded the Indian party and this increased as we approached Calgary. At Calgary the party broke up and all joyfully returned to their homes. I, too, was delighted to be home and breathed a deep sigh of relief as I handed my charges back to Inspector Schmidt of the Department of Indian Affairs – intact.[63]

It would seem as though he did not want the public or his fellow officers to know about the problems on the voyage home.

A modern analysis of Constable Leach's commentary might conclude that his concerns regarding alcohol were obsessive. However, social and legal histories easily explain why this concern was always in the forefront. The RCMP actually cancelled their contract and stopped providing a police service to Alberta between 1916 and 1932. This was due to the fact that enforcing prohibitory legislation was such a hazardous occupation.[64] Bootlegging and the traffic of illegal alcohol across the Canada/US border ran rampant in western Canada. As well, the firewater myth, which suggests that First Nations "lose all control over their behavior when they drink,"[65] was widely believed to be true at the time. Under the Indian Act, First Nations were legally forbidden to drink alcohol until 1965. In the 1920s and 1930s, alcohol was blamed for most problems faced by First Nations people, and it was also believed that alcohol could easily lead to their demise.[66] This idea, as demonstrated in the continued production of Chief Crowfoot's claim that "[b]ad men and whiskey were killing us so fast that very few indeed of us would have been left today"[67] was still prevalent in the late 1970s. The powerful colonial connections between alcohol and First Nations people will not be developed here, except to emphasize that their prevalence legitimated Leach's concern, which was usual rather than obsessive. Indeed, it was remarkable that he would have endeavored to take the men out for an occasional drink, as suggested by Cecil Crowfoot. If in fact this did actually happen it would attest to Leach's sense of fairness and his ability to see beyond legal and social precepts of the time.

Leach was also greatly concerned with the treatment the men received from the RAS. The First Nations cowboys, as mentioned in Chapter Three, held grievances concerning horses, cheating judges, and segregated races. These problems caused a high percentage of physical injuries and emotional distress for the men. Leach's report explained in detail his altercations with RAS officials concerning these problems. It is obvious that these incidents also caused him a great deal of distress. He positioned himself as the men's protector and challenged RAS show organizers on several occasions. His approach was either to attack the RAS for contributing to the problems, or to negotiate with them by comparing the treatment given to the other cowboys with the treatment given to the First Nations men.

The initial RAS reactions to all incidents of "bad behavior" were threats to incarcerate the First Nations cowboys or send them back home to Canada. Leach was consistently "disappointed in the lack of understanding and co-operation"[68] he received. On several occasions he countered their attacks by blaming the RAS for instigating what they referred to as "bad behavior." As mentioned earlier, Leach blamed MacFarlane for the alcohol incident at his ranch.[69] On 29 March, the day after Jim Starlight went out with Ivadel Jacobs, the RAS threatened to send the whole troupe back to Canada. Leach reciprocated with a counter-threat to "pack up and leave[70] if the RAS did not take control of the cowgirls. When the men were caught with alcohol, he blamed the RAS for not erecting a fence to protect them from aggressive crowds.[71] Throughout, Leach's role was to bridge the cultural gaps and moderate the anger and/or ignorance exhibited by RAS officials towards Joe Crowfoot, Frank Many Fingers, Joe Bear Robe, Joe Young Pine, Edward One Spot, Jim Starlight, Johnny Left Hand and Douglas Kootenay. These gaps were often very wide due to a general lack of respect for the men's professional abilities, and the primary RAS wish to promote them as a sideshow attraction only.

From the onset, as was made evident in the correspondence between Schmidt and Skidmore, the RAS did not view the First Nations cowboys as equal to the other performers. Leach fought against this unfairness. He repeatedly followed up on his promises to make sure the First Nations men were allowed to participate in all of the rodeo events, but unfortunately he was ignored. He also challenged the RAS concerning extra prize monies owed to the men, which they tried to reduce from eighty-five pounds to sixty-two pounds. Through lengthy negotiations he managed to recoup the full amount. To his dismay, Leach later found out that all the other cowboys were getting an extra ten-pound bonus. He did not reopen the discussion because Skidmore indicated that it was futile, considering that the RAS had "already spent the allotted amount on the Indian Party."[72] Even though overall fairness was never fully attained, Leach took every opportunity to challenge the RAS on these issues.

It could be argued that Leach's interference undermined the personal agency of these men; however, he did consult them prior to all meetings with RAS officials. On many occasions he was asked to negotiate for them. Each time, RAS officials promised to rectify any grievances as long as the First Nations cowboys became more co-operative.[73] Unfortunately, they never seemed to become quite co-operative enough to appease RAS officials. Incidents of normal behavior were often exaggerated into incidents of "bad behavior." RAS officials continued to discriminate against the men throughout the show and, therefore, Leach's role as a mediator became imperative for their well being.

On a more personal level, Leach frequently mentioned being concerned about the men's welfare in a variety of other ways. He found the extremely hot weather and large (up to 180,000), aggressive crowds very difficult to handle. Although he described the men as showing "great courtesy and patience in dealing with the throng,"[74] he also asked for police help in protecting them on numerous occasions. On 17 March, Leach specifically obtained fresh fruit and vegetables for the men, as these were difficult to find due to an ongoing drought. He showed consistent concern for their health, as evidenced by daily reports of minor injuries and the acquisition of prudent medical care. He also demonstrated genuine pride in the men's abilities to compete and to present themselves in a professional manner. For example, he stated that a number of passengers on the *Niagara* "commented very favorable on their good manners and general behavior."[75] Moreover, he was proud of the fact that Frank Many Fingers won multiple sports competitions played on the ship.[76]

Leach's own reports and those of Joe Crowfoot and Frank Many Fingers reveal a caring individual, but his role as chaperone must be viewed in light of the exploitive treatment First Nations experienced in the 1930s. In many ways Constable Leach's determined confinement and restraint of the eight cowboys in his charge, whether it was to protect them from the Australian public or RAS officials, to protect them from themselves, or to protect the Canadian government from embarrassment, was unnecessary and unfair. While discrepancies in his reports blur colonial boundaries, Leach's role as a chaperone must be closely aligned with government rhetoric based on paternalism. Comparatively speaking, Leach did treat the men as human beings and not simply as objects to be manipulated, which was Schmidt's suggestion. His personal perceptions reveal a man genuinely interested in the welfare of his charges, which may have been an important aspect of "real" relationships other RCMP officers had with First Nations individuals.

Conclusions

On the trip over to Australia, the whole troupe participated in a costume ball. Johnny Left Hand won a prize for his costume, as did Constable Leach.[77] However, the First Nations men did not participate in the costume ball held during the return voyage. Mr. and Mrs. Leach did. They "went as [s]heriff and [c]riminal respectively and won a prize for the most original costume."[78] Leach claimed that "the evening was a great success,"[79] yet did not mention that this choice of costumes effectively relegated him to the role of a jailer. This telling performance typifies what was probably the most difficult aspect of Leach's job, both for himself and for Joe Crowfoot, Frank Many Fingers, Joe Bear Robe, Joe Young Pine, Edward One Spot, Jim Starlight, Johnny Left Hand and Douglas Kootenay. Constable Leach acted as these men's jailer and, conversely, he was personally confined by the requirements of his role as an RCMP officer and as a representative of Canada.

Leach's flexibility and ability to shift his point of view depending on the situation was probably his greatest personal attribute for this unique appointment. Nevertheless, his multiple roles and public presence restricted his decision-making processes in many respects. He did not seem to really enjoy the excitement or spontaneity of being a tourist because that would have been unprofessional. He did not seem to become close friends or be overtly social with the men because of his role and the paternalistic attitudes associated with it. In addition, he did not seem to fully enjoy his responsibilities as a chaperone because that meant completely curtailing the freedom of eight men. As it was, he disallowed them from going to the farewell dinner, kept them from going out at night with friends, and even forbid them from going to a restaurant by themselves. Ironically, even though he was their constant jailer in many ways, Leach also contributed greatly to the respect they received as rodeo competitors and as First Nations performers.

For the purpose of understanding colonial relations, particularly those between First Nations and the RCMP, Leach's negotiation processes with the RAS were most telling. Although the Australian show promoters and Leach would have been considered equals, their differing views concerning fair play and racial hierarchy frequently turned them into adversaries. This suggests that colonial ties were not as important as national ties. When push came to shove, and when Leach had to make a moral decision based on fairness and rightness as he knew it, he generally chose to support the needs of "the Indian party." This fact also suggests that racial and colonial boundaries were blurred by the close contact experienced while travelling. Although Leach did not veer away from his role as a colonial authority figure, there was proof in his notes that his experience altered many of his preconceived stereotypical ideas about "Indians."

Fig. 37: "Alberta Indians and Cowboys Return from Australia." *Calgary Herald*, 5 May 1939. Glenbow Archives, NA-1241-169. Photographer: F. Gully.

Perhaps the biggest challenge for Constable Leach throughout this experience was the comprehension of his personal relationship with these First Nations men. Under the rubric of popular culture he was supposed to have an amicable, supportive connection based on care and understanding (see Figs. 28 and 37). Following the tenets of government authority permitted by his position, he was supposed to view the men with a highly paternal attitude in a relationship based on power and control. However, as a man travelling with his wife and eight other men from Canada, he developed a bond of shared intimacy that positioned them all as citizens of the same nation. Unfortunately, there were too many variables based on false or missed understandings to allow for clear definitions to emerge. Constable Leach instead improvised and recreated the tenets of this relationship whenever he needed to. While in Australia Leach helped the First Nations cowboys become more publicly represented as competitors, but his writings often promoted derogatory perceptions that did nothing to accurately or positively represent them.

Moreover, Leach's writings stress the fluidity of identity recreated through notions of "others" and "self" which occurs during the experience of travel and performance. Both provide the ability to transcend and open up alternative realities and perspectives. The tourist experience specifically takes individuals away from their usual realities and connects them in a combined mythic/realistic way with the other people they meet and are travelling with.[80] Transcultural experiences renegotiate cultural/colonial boundaries by incorporating multiple perspectives. The international character of this event aided in creating new, hybrid social meanings, and added fluidity to the relationships of the individuals involved. Leach did not necessarily recognize the ambiguous nature of his perspectives as evidenced in his writings, because they were created in combination with preconceived insights and new meanings he developed while travelling. One of the outcomes of this unique experience was that possessiveness and paternalism conversely became the motivators that aided in assisting eight First Nations cowboys to participate as equals in an international competition.

Although he claimed to be very proud of his efforts and ability to care for and protect these men, Constable Leach also sighed deeply with relief as he "handed [his] charges back to Inspector Schmidt of the Department of Indian Affairs – intact."[81] In a humorous closing statement he again emphasized race in descriptions of the fluidity of identity that can occur while travelling:

> We often thought of our friends at home stoking up furnaces and ploughing through snowdrifts as we lay basking on deck in the tropical sun or swimming in the salt water pool. In fact so successful were my sun baths that one of the Swift Current members said, "I knew you had slept, eaten and lived with the Indians, but I didn't think you would change colour to that of a Redskin."[82]

Even though racial and colonial boundaries may have been blurred while Leach was touring Australia, they were immediately re-established for him once he returned home.

5

The Australian Audience's Reaction to their Canadian Visitors

SHOW INDIANS TOO FAR FROM HOME
Indians at the Show are homesick they say.
"This is fine country, but its long way from wife and mother-in-law."
    Said Frank Many Fingers yesterday.
The others grunted approval.
All are married except Douglas Kootenay.
"Me? I love my mother," said Douglas. "Me no squaw yet."[1]

CANADA'S EIGHT FIRST NATIONS COWBOYS were showered with attention from the minute they docked in Sydney. First a photo shoot was arranged on the deck of the SS *Niagara* (see Fig. 38). Then, after they were allowed off the ship, large crowds gathered around them. The streets were lined with thousands of Australians as the men drove to City Hall where they were greeted at an official civic reception.[2] Descriptions of the various Australian responses to the visitors varied depending on the source. Constable Leach found the massive crowds too aggressive and felt that the men repeatedly underwent excessive mobbing. The First Nations cowboys did not mind the attention they received, which they felt was all positive and aimed only at demonstrating appreciation.

    Understanding the Australian public's reaction is critical because stereotypes are made real through cultural practices when images and concepts oscillate between the actors and the audience. According to Gillian Poulter, "[W]hen the individual performance is made available as a public performance, the identity is further confirmed through the recognition it receives from the audience's reaction. In fact, the audience authorizes and constrains the performance because the limits of what is acceptable behavior are established by the audience's reaction."[3] This chapter will seek to better understand the

Fig. 38: "Making Real 'Whoopee'." *The Sun* (Sydney), 11 March 1939.

perspectives underlying the Australian public's persistent attempts to get close to these exotic Canadian visitors. This analysis will be primarily based on Australian press reports. While journalists' comments are often influenced by and sometimes tailored to the ideologies of elite groups in society, they are just as deeply shaped by public opinion.[4] Stories, topics, and styles all conform to specific attitudes. Commercial publications must reflect the needs, values, and desires of its readers so that they can provide a suitable product for public sale and consumption. Realistically, most newspapers are tailored to specific groups with similar social class and ethnic backgrounds. "Them" versus "us" conflicts based on stereotypes are common in the production of ideologies because they are well understood by the general public. The reproduction of racist stereotypes in the press is a give-and-take process, whereby journalists' comments support elite views of national ideologies. In an adjunct manner, public response often serves to supports these views.

Articles written about the Royal Easter Show were based on the cultural stereotypes of a particular colonial experience. This Australian emphasis, which historically has positioned "Aborigines" at the bottom of a racial hierarchical scale, does not allow for the North American/European dichotomous "savage/noble savage" designation. Therefore, public press responses did not place these

Canadian First Nations cowboys in this category either, but instead focused on a similarly dichotomous "primitive/ordinary" form of representation.[5] A few articles were scathingly racist. However, most simply glorified the men's costumes, or focused on the fact that they were approachable people with wives and children back home. Noble characteristics were more often associated with Constable Leach and his presence at the show. For the Australian audience there was a much more obvious connection between Canada as a nation and the RCMP, than between Canada as a nation and its First Nations population.

"Noble Savage" and Savage Ideology in North America and Australia

Canada's predominant use of First Nations cultural objects as national symbols spilled over into a multitude of venues. Audiences familiar with depictions of North American Plains Indians as seen in Wild West shows and read about in dime novels were again bombarded with these images when motion pictures gained popularity after the turn of the twentieth century.[6] Plains Indian imagery was also used in Canada and the United States to represent national and regional distinction on items such as stamps, coins, postcards, and sporting logos.[7] "Indians" made ideal subjects and fascinated white viewers who imagined them as exotic, dangerous, and mysterious beings. Two specific themes prevailed within the multitude of symbolic representations of First Nations people in Canada: savagery and nobility. The emphasis on each fluctuated depending on shifts in ideologies, but the use of both continued and was popular in many cultural venues. Ters Ellingson claims that an emphasis on the use of the term "noble savage" originally began in Canada with Marc Lescarbot's 1609 invention of the concept in reference to First Nations living in Quebec.[8]

This dualistic dramatization positioned First Nations in both Canada and the United States as "noble savages," savages, or a combination of both. According to Robert Berkhofer, "Indians lacked certain or all aspects of White civilization [and] could be viewed as bad or good depending upon the reader's feelings about his own society and the use to which he wanted to put the image."[9] Hoxie Fairchild described the metaphoric "noble savage" as "any free and wild being who draws directly from nature's virtues, which raise doubts as to the value of civilization."[10] Although Fairchild's definition was specific to Rousseau, the mid-eighteenth century and the Romantic era, it still remains applicable to twentieth- and twenty-first-century interpretations.

Canadian scholars have provided two general theories to explain why "noble savage" ideology became particularly popular in the visual culture of the 1930s and the 1940s.[11] Both can be related to the "salvage paradigm" mentioned earlier, yet differ in their views of how it was applied. The first theory is aligned to the generalized emphasis on ideas concerning vanishing frontiers and a nostalgic feeling for this loss. During this period it was imagined that colonization was complete; European civilization dominated the globe and imperialism seemed legitimized. Idealizing Aboriginal culture in Canada became more acceptable because First Nations were no longer considered a threat.[12] The second theory focuses on modernism and industrialization. Artists such as Emily Carr lamented the fate of the vanishing Indian, elevating First Nations culture for ecological reasons, idealizing traditional, environmentally safe ways of living off the land. In Carr's view, "the noble Indian [as] forest philosopher, stands by while the forces of civilization invade and disrupt his land."[13] Her significant position in Canadian culture coincided with her determined effort to differentiate Canada as an independent nation through visual representation.[14] Although similar expressions of First Nations culture had been used previously at various World's Fairs, this renewed emphasis was closely bound to landscape and an imagined wilderness ethos where imperial nostalgia was associated with modernity and powerful notions of "noble savagery" became synonymous with popular culture and national ideology.[15]

Historically the treatment of Australian "Aborigines" has lagged somewhat behind that of Canadian First Nations in terms of social attitudes, visual culture and government policy.[16] The predominant social attitudes of white Australians positioned "Aborigines" in 1939 at the very bottom of a Eurocentric racial hierarchy. This allocation was based on imagined physiology accompanied by visually determined aesthetic values in an attempt to rationalize brutal colonial tactics. T.H. Huxley, an apostle of Social Darwinism, brought issues of primitiveness to the forefront in 1887 when he compared a Neanderthal cranium to that of an Australian "Aborigine" and claimed that they were identical.[17] In the 1930s, colonial folklore continued to accentuate the belief that Australian "Aborigines" were inferior, "backward and lowly."[18] Popular visual images depicted them as impoverished, uneducated, and afflicted. Bare-breasted young girls, unkempt children, and families dressed in worn-out European clothes were commonly seen standing in front of dilapidated shacks.[19] Assimilationist government policies were focused on the premise that "blackness" and other biological tendencies could be "bred out" of all Aboriginal people. Here visual culture and photography also played a part in promoting the effects of "breeding in" whiteness.[20] Due to this omnipresent desire to keep "Aborigines" in a lowly position, there was a distinct delay in the conferring of citizenship rights to Australia's indigenous people (this did not begin until 1967, when Aborigines received voting rights), and an even greater delay in the legal attainment of property rights (this occurred in 1992).[21]

"Noble savage" imagery was only marginally present in white Australia's public representations of the 1930s due to a pervasive emphasis on the "Aborigines'" imagined primitive and savage qualities. The primary difference to be noted here is that Australian "Aborigines" were not mythologized at the turn of the century in the same way, or to the same extent, that North American First Nations were due to Wild West shows and similar productions. Regardless, an overview of popular visual culture does demonstrate how singular examples of romantic, noble depictions of "Aborigines" weave in and out of Australian history. Captain James Cook described the first Australian natives that he met in the 1770s as "noble savages." During this period, scientific draughtsmen were sent to capture images of Australia's natural environment in order to educate Europeans about this newly "discovered" land. These engravings entwined ideas of primitiveness and "noble savagery" that were short-lived after colonization began.[22] During a long period of denigration between 1790 and 1840, multiple wars took place between the settlers and the Aboriginal people as colonial imposition proceeded. During this era they were described as being even lower than savages. According to this view, "killing Aborigines was no worse than destroying wild dogs."[23] By the late nineteenth century, however, a few artists were developing a fine-art, portraiture style in their depictions of indigenous Australians. Margaret Maynard has stated that these individual works "imbue with dignity the 'fate' of a reputedly dying race."[24] Between 1900 and 1920, an abundance of photographic images were used on postcards to display shots of impoverished indigenous groups, while odd examples can be found of portraits evoking a "noble savage" sensibility.[25] Elizabeth Edwards claims that the invention of the "dying race theory" combined with ever-improving photographic techniques in the late nineteenth century precipitated this minor focus on romanticized images in Australia.[26]

The "dying race theory," along with the efforts of certain anthropologists, also had the effect of raising public awareness about problematic government policies and the status of Australian "Aborigines". In 1938, A.P. Elkins, Australia's first anthropologist, advocated for exhibitions of Aboriginal art in an effort to counter detrimental stereotypes. The gradual public acceptance of his ideas marked the beginning of an Aboriginal art movement that forever changed popular opinion and, eventually, influenced government policies. Ian Mclean maintains that this was the first time "Aborigines" were firmly imagined in a positive light by white Australians. Once cast as anti-modern and subhuman, they were instead progressively associated with virtuous ideas about place, landscape, and nation.[27] Although the links between nationalism, savagery, nobility and spirituality were seeded in the late 1930s, the actual use of Aboriginal cultural symbols, in the promotion of nationalism, did not begin until much later.

In 1988 Aboriginal cultural symbols proliferated in advertisements for bicentenary celebrations. This use was precipitated by the need for a new international touristic image,[28] which in turn popularized and promoted "noble savage" ideology. Once Aboriginal cultural symbols were connected to nationalism, they also became connected to notions of nobility. The public acceptance of these images became a significant way to separate modern Australia from its troubled colonial past.

This new visual expression of Australian nationalism was grounded in New Age spirituality, which was linked to landscape and Aboriginal heritage. Australian "Aborigines" were ideologically elevated from the position of lowly primitives to that of "noble savages." Australian scholars recognized and were critical of this application almost immediately. Although they did not directly connect it with the historic and global use of this category, the same tenets were used to discuss its introduction into Australian political ideology. As Andrew Lattas has noted, "This aestheticizing of Aborigines transforms them into the spiritual side of the western self, they become that which the West lacks and must recoup if it is to re-establish wholeness."[29] This direct link between Aboriginal culture and spiritualism became an influential national revelation with a widespread and poignant impact.[30]

The delayed recognition of imagined links between Australian Aboriginal culture and "noble savage" ideology explains why this category was not equated in 1939 press reports with Canada's First Nations rodeo performers. Although white Australians were thrilled to have "Red Indians"[31] reminiscent of Buffalo Bill's Wild West performers at their Royal Easter Show, the celebrity status of the eight men involved was based on stereotypical representations of a generalized North American frontier, as opposed to a specific Canadian identity. In this way, the men's personas were, in a sense, misread by the Australian audience. In place of a more typically Canadian "savage/noble savage" dichotomy, the Australian press drew on a more mundane "primitive/ordinary" emphasis for their descriptions of the First Nations cowboys. While racist comments were sometimes severe the men were generally recognized as family members and church-going people who could speak English. However, any ideas concerning "nobility" were more often reserved for dashing Constable Leach and his scarlet uniform.

Press Reports from Australia

There were no comments glorifying the horsemanship of the Canadian First Nations cowboys in Australian press reports. Neither was there any mention of their entrepreneurial spirit in selling handicrafts. Indeed, there were no comments praising their behavior in any way. Comments that described an appreciation for the beaded workmanship on their costumes, and comments which reinforced the fact that they were not like the fictitious "Indians" seen in the movies or read about in novels, were the only instances when these men were not described as primitives. This is where cultural differences between Canada and Australia became very obvious. As mentioned in Chapter Two, *The Calgary Herald* valorized these men as "ambassadors of commerce" who were intending to open up international markets for the sale of their traditional handicrafts.[32] Other Canadian articles focused on their careers as professional rodeo competitors.[33] The Australian press veered between the use of words such as "grunting" or "shuffling" to describe their behavior and comments referring to the ordinary qualities of their lives. It would seem that the sensationalism associated with North American Plains Indian stereotypes in motion pictures of the time was lost when it was applied to a reality-based situation, even though multiple advertisements still championed the men as "Something New at the Royal Show" (see Fig. 39).

One article in particular accentuated primitive stereotypes by using scathing remarks. It was printed in the *Sydney Daily Telegraph* and titled, "Meaty Men are these Braves of the Prairie.... 'Whoo'!" Text and photographs provided a clear insight into the unabashed racial prejudice of the time. It began by describing Johnny Left Hand's reaction to the reporter's questions:

SHOW WINDOW OF THE STATE

Always Something New at the ROYAL SHOW

The *... Show Window* will be more fascinating.... more ... better dressed than ever before. Greater, ... the finest methods of display. PLUS Ring ... of the World—famous for their daring ... keep our show the greatest on the Globe.

EXPECT THESE STIRRING RING EVENTS

THE DANCE OF THE RANGES QUADRILLES ON HORSEBACK
Indian Bareback Horse Races
AMERICAN COWGIRL TRICK RIDERS
CHUCK WAGGON RACES
RED INDIANS v AMERICA v CANADA v AUSTRALIA
INTERNATIONAL AND INTERSTATE HORSE EVENTS

Steer Riding... Wild Horse Races....Treefelling, Woodchopping, Sawing Championships.... Hunting, Trotting, Jumping Events .... a 1,001 Events to thrill you!

PLUS
A FAMOUS CANADIAN MOUNTIE AND
"JASBO," THE COWBOY CLOWN

NOTE THE DATES OF THE SHOW OF SHOWS

ROYAL EASTER SHOW
APRIL 1ST TO 12TH 1939 · 10 DAYS · 8 NIGHTS

Fig. 39: "Show Window of the State: Always Something New at the Royal Show." *The Sydney Herald*, April 1939. This advertisement was published numerous times throughout the show.

> Johnny Left-hand squatted on his hunches in the sun and listening with suspicious attention. Mahogany skinned, black-eyed, indifferent, he stared stonily away towards the entrance gates where his Indians friends would be seen returning soon. They were shopping or something, he didn't know.
>
> "But in your native state what do you eat?" And my voice was the voice of childhood. "The grub here perhaps is a bit odd and you long for.... for...." I stammered.
>
> *"MEAT!"* the word came out like a packet from a slot machine. *"Whoo!"*
>
> "That's all?" (reporter's question)
>
> "Meat, bacon and eggs, an't cornflakes."
>
> His black eyes hadn't moved.[34]

This reporter also described the men as "stringy, colourful, monosyllabic people,"[35] and translated all of their comments into broken English. For example, when asked what they did when the rain came into the hole at the top of their tipis, Johnny Left Hand apparently answered, "Rain No Matter." Later in the article this reporter described the First Nations men's entrance into a nursery school, which was part of a publicity stunt for the Royal Easter show.

> They shuffled shyly into a day nursery the other morning to thrill some children and a sweet little nurse in aseptic uniform asked them what they would eat with their morning tea.
>
> **Eight black heads bent swiftly together on the problem, and the spokesman grunted, "Beefsteak pie!"** (this comment originally was in bold type)
>
> The nurse is still recovering[36]

In general his comments conjured up images of Hollywood Indians, men of a prehistoric era, Neanderthal beings who "shuffled shyly," were unable to think as individuals, grunted rather than talked, and were always hungry, especially for meat.

Considering the stereotypical imagery associated with this type of commentary, it is surprising that this report was immediately followed by remarks describing what an Australian audience would consider to be "normal" aspects of these men's lives. The "primitive/ordinary" dichotomy was strongly reinforced through the listing of their religious affiliations: "Three are Anglican, three Catholics and two United Church adherents."[37] The reporter added their marital status to this list: "One [was] single, the rest [were] married and [had] children, one seven."[38] When combined with previous racist comments these observations seemed highly contradictory.[39]

Six photographs surrounded the textual description. Three of them were contemporary: one of Joe Crowfoot holding a small child, one of Constable Leach (the same picture is seen in Chapter Three (Fig. 27) with the "Red Indians" cut out), and one of a child crying as a woman tried to put a war-bonnet on his/her head (see Fig. 40). The other three pictures were obviously given to the RAS by the Canada government. They depicted isolated shots of First Nations people in traditional clothing and landscapes filled with tipis at the Banff Springs show grounds. These images resembled those common to postcards of the nineteenth century,[40] and immediately reinforced the touristic notion of a race frozen in time. They were included to confirm the authenticity of the group, which was essential for their use by the RAS as a show attraction. They did not complement or seem connected with the textually descriptions in any way.

The majority of Australian newspaper articles followed this "primitive/ordinary" view, although most were less focused on primitivism and more focused on representing the eight First Nations cowboys as "average" people. Therefore, I would argue that these reports were not representative of "true racism" in the press as outlined by Teun van Dijk. He states that the "major institutions and elite groups in society"[41] responsible for forming and reinforcing public opinions concerning ethnicity establish a "them" versus "us" conflict based on "concepts such as order, authority, loyalty, patriotism and 'freedom'."[42] In this case, another theme accompanied racist comments. It was based on notions of familiarity, which emphasized that these men did not look or act like the "Red Indians" seen in Hollywood westerns, but looked and acted more like "ordinary" (white?) people. This notion ties into a host's view where hospitality becomes tantamount to welcoming others and consequently imagining oneself to be a good and patriotic citizen.[43] It can be further argued that this imagined bond may have somewhat lessened colonial guilt surrounding racist acts perpetrated in Australia, while encouraging questions about stereotypes, thus giving these Canadian representatives the opportunity to dispel certain myths.[44]

Fig. 40: "Meaty Man are these Braves of the Prairie.....'Whoo'!" *Daily Telegraph Home Magazine*, (Sydney), 3 April 1939: 2.

One of the articles that performed this function specifically described the trip taken to a local nursery. It was entitled, "Wild West at Woolloomooloo: Eddie One-Spot Visits Day Nursery."[45] This article emphatically repeated that the young children at the nursery were either fascinated or frightened by the "Red Indians" they saw that day. Some were described as being dazzled and delighted by the men's traditional beaded costumes, while others trembled and ran behind their nurse's skirts. Their reaction was presented as humorous and immature, thus projecting typical racist attitudes, fear and fascination, to the realm of children's behavior. Comments made it clear that racist notions and stereotypes tied to US cultural representations were silly because these Canadian Aboriginal men were obviously just "ordinary people." The normalcy of Eddie One Spot's reaction to the babies in the nursery particularly demonstrated this fact, because he too was a father (see Fig. 41).[46]

The last section of this article was subtitled, "Genuine Friendliness." It emphasized that all the men were "[s]miling with genuine pleasure and friendliness,"[47] and that their obvious sociability encouraged the children to gather closely around them. Eddie One Spot sang a distinctly Canadian lullaby. Following this moment of serenity and intimacy, a small boy began drumming and the men became "very fierce and war-like"[48] as they performed a war dance while exiting the nursery. A reciprocal connection was highlighted by stating that "Eddie One Spot [would] go home to his people and tell them all about these children,"[49] and that the Sydney group (meaning the caregivers at the orphanage) would "wish them ('the Indians') all sorts of luck and remember the[ir] genuine interest in the children."[50] This example combines the idea of hospitality with the "primitive/ordinary" view in a marked Australian account of a one-on-one meeting with "Red Indians."

Several articles quoted the First Nations cowboys' answers to reporters' questions about stereotypes. In one instance a reporter asked Frank Many Fingers why they were not carrying tomahawks. Many Fingers explained, "We have given up tomahawks because we are now pretty good with our fists."[51] When asked about their lifestyle in Canada, Joe Crowfoot replied, "[N]owadays the Red Indian is a peace-loving and good citizen of the country. He lives on a reserve, has his own farm, and sells his product. He hunts his own birds and animals, from which he obtains the things necessary to make his tribal dress. The squaw makes his clothes."[52] Although this quote does not seem completely accurate, it does show how this type of questioning allowed the men to explain the realities

Wild West at Woolloomooloo

—Cinesound.
Admiration was mutual when Red Indians watched with interest the games of the little "Palefaces."

Eddie One-Spot Visits Day Nursery

WHAT would your child do if he were suddenly confronted by an Indian brave, feathers and all?

The reactions of the children at the Woolloomooloo Day Nursery one day last week were as amusing as they were varied. Of course they had often heard about Indians. Some of them had probably even seen them on a rare visit to a picture theatre. There was a fine colour-print in the play-room, too.... Nevertheless, a few of them were definitely startled!

Fig. 41: "Wild West at Woolloomooloo: Eddie One Spot Visits Day Nursery," *The Sydney Morning Herald: Women's Supplement*, 3 April 1939.

of their lives to an Australian audience. This example also demonstrates how Crowfoot seized the opportunity to reinforce the view of First Nations in Canada as purposeful citizens.

Reporters were also astonished at the fact that these men could speak English. An *Auckland Star* reporter claimed to have been expecting "taciturnity and ceremonious 'Hows'," and was very surprised when Joe Crowfoot cheerfully answered his questions in "good English."[53] Another article simply established the fact that "most of the Indians [spoke] fairly good English."[54] One Spot himself was quoted in a Canadian newspaper as stating that visitors at the exhibition were "surprised that we all spoke English, were educated and took an interest in the same things that they did."[55] In general, from all accounts, it seemed as though the men had a good deal of direct, individualized contact with the Australian public.[56] By making themselves available for this type of contact they encouraged the dissipation of stereotypes developed through American models of Wild West shows where "Indians" were untouchable actors, representative national icons far removed from real life.

The "primitive/ordinary" dichotomy was similarly represented in a small article titled, "Too Far From Home," which contained only five sentences:

> Indians at the Show are homesick they say.
> "This is fine country, but its long way from wife and mother-in-law," said Frank Many Fingers, yesterday.
> The others grunted in approval.
> All are married except Douglas Kootenay.
> "Me? I love my mother," said Douglas, "Me no squaw yet."[57]

These "full-blooded Red Indians"[58] grunted, yet were also extremely sympathetic characters. Their primitiveness seemed to have been superseded by their emotional responses to travel in a foreign country.

Australian newspaper articles repeatedly highlighted and listed the men's names, often including their place of residence. The word "picturesque" was frequently used to explain the unique and captivating quality of these names. In one article, when asked how he got his name, Johnny Left Hand was quoted as saying, "I suppose one of my ancestors was left-handed."[59] Although their names were viewed as a curiosity, they were at least identified as individuals instead of being lumped into broad racial categories such as "Redskins," "Red

Indians," or "the Indian Party." Most articles mentioned that the men were from Canada. Two articles listed their band affiliations with accuracy.[60] One article simply stated that they were from Saskatchewan, which was incorrect.[61] These examples demonstrated attempts to distinguish these eight men as individuals. This practice ran counter to popular representations, which relegated all North American First Nations to a collective realm that undermined an emphasis on individuality and, consequently, modernity.[62]

The level of interest the Australian press directed towards Canada's First Nations cowboys was moderate compared to the emphasis placed on Constable Leach's presence at the show. Leach was singled out as the sole controller of the "Red Indians." His physical presence and his character were consistently described as powerful, regal, modest, and brave (see Fig. 42). These are categories used in definitions of nobility and, similarly, in "noble savage" rhetoric.

One account of the "Grande Parade" described Constable Leach as "the finest figure of all the horsemen at the show."[63] Riding "a magnificent Grey and carrying aloft an immense Union Jack," he was repeatedly referred to as a "colourful figure." One article describes Leach's uniform in far greater detail than those of the "Indians." It stated that, although young boys would be excited to see the "Red Indians," it was their fathers who would relish the sight of "Constable S.J. Leach of the Royal Canadian Mounted Police in his scarlet jacket, bandolier, blue riding breeches with the yellow stripe, highly polished leggings and of course, the wide-rimmed felt hat."[64] This article stressed that the "Indians" were fierce, stoic, and unable to smile, whereas Leach was friendly, modest, and informative. It juxtaposed Leach's imagined nobility with the "Red Indians'" imagined primitiveness to emphasize colonial dominance.

All audiences at the Royal Easter Show saw Constable Leach leading the "Red Indians" and watching over them. As described in Chapter Three, he actually led all of the cowboys and cowgirls from Canada and the United States into the show ring during the daily "Grande Parade." The "Indian Village" was composed of eight tipis with a makeshift Sun Dance Lodge in the centre and Leach's bell-tent at the front by the entrance gate. On top of the bell-tent flew a large Union Jack flag. While describing this scene, one reporter stated that it was in keeping with Canadian tradition: "[W]herever the Indians are there also are the Royal Canadian Mounted Police."[65]

Mrs. Leach, who played a very important role in chaperoning and caring for the men, was given very little attention in the Australian press. She was not

Fig. 42: Constable Samuel Leach Raising Horse in Salute at the Royal Easter Show. Sydney Australia, 1939. Courtesy Peggy Maxwell, private collection. This photo was also published in the *Sydney Morning Herald*, 3 April 1939.

mentioned in any of the articles that described the Canadian troupe's presence at the show. Only one small article, "Canadian 'Mountie's Wife Among Niagara Arrivals," recognized her as a member of the group. Here she was described as "petite and fair."[66] In comparison to the "Red Indians," who shouted wildly while they performed a war dance, and her husband, who was described as a "colourful figure,"[67] there was no attempt to explain Dorothy Leach's contributions to this spectacle. The article simply mentioned that she was a nurse in Saskatchewan before she was married, that she lived in a drought zone where her husband was stationed, and that she was born in England. It identified Mrs. Leach as a typical wife, one who had come to Australia in support of her husband. Although an analysis of gender issues will not be undertaken in this book, this simple lack of interest in Dorothy further isolated Samuel Leach as the sole carrier of elite status within this Canadian troupe.

Depictions of Leach as the white, male patriarch of this Canadian group can easily be aligned to van Dijk's theory about how the press reinforces racial and ethnic differences through conflict, featuring "concepts such as order, authority, loyalty, patriotism and freedom."[68] As a symbol of loyalty and patriotism, Leach was expected to provide a visual presence that created order by limiting and monitoring the First Nations men's freedom at all times. This "Canadian tradition," as it was described in the Australian press, was easily read and understood by the Australian public. They had no doubts concerning Constable Leach's intentions and character because he was a Canadian "Mountie." Comments that may have defined Leach's character or lifestyle on a personal level were never published. His public persona remained elusive and untouchable. In this way Leach remained more mythic than the "Red Indians," which further enhanced his imagined nobility.

Conclusions

While this chapter emphasizes the representation of public views through press reports, it is also essential to consider the influence of specific groups and institutions. A large part of the public's social and cultural learning happens through the media; therefore, links between the reproductive and symbolic roles of the press and other powerful institutions of the state must also be recognized.[69] In this case, members of the RAS council, which consisted of a collection of politicians and intellectuals, undoubtedly had a significant influence on Australian journalists' reports about the show. A survey of RAS correspondence with Canadian government officials just prior to, during, and after the Royal Easter show demonstrates an interest in the First Nations cowboys' presence. However, the same correspondence heralds Constable Leach as the primary representative of Canada.

A.W. Skidmore sent three reports to C. Pant Schmidt: one upon the arrival of the Canadian troupe, the second on the day before the show opened, and the third after the men had left. Upon their arrival he wrote that "they were driven through the city streets in open cars with an escort of motorcycle Police"[70] to the steps of the Sydney Town Hall, where a huge crowd waited their arrival. In describing this civic reception he elaborated on the physical appearance of Constable Leach and his impressive character. His description of the "Indians" simply stated that "from all accounts the Indians behaved themselves particularly well on board."[71] He also reassured Schmidt that even though it was inevitable that thousands of people would "naturally congregate around" them during the show and probably offer them "hospitality" (meaning liquor), he would make sure they did not get any.[72] In Skidmore's comments just prior to the show he focused on the issue of handicraft sales. He stated that the "Indian Village" looked spectacular, and offered assurances that it would be the "centr[al] attraction for the tens of thousands of people"[73] passing through the show. Here, he did not specifically mention the First Nations cowboys at all.[74] Following the show, Skidmore repeatedly stated that it was an unqualified success and reiterated that "the Indians" behaved themselves very well. He also mentioned that Constable Leach had curtailed multiple opportunities to socialize while in Sydney and, therefore, the "Red Indians" had remained somewhat isolated, though comfortable, during their stay. Overall, his report suggested an overtly restricted, prison-like existence as opposed to one inspired by celebrity status. Regardless, the overall importance of the First Nations men as representatives of Canada was downplayed in favor of Leach, who was viewed as the central character.

This official perspective opposes the emphasis on Canada's "Red Indians" in accounts by Australian journalists. It instead recognized the colonial connection between the two countries. The unspoken RAS mandate to reinforce political alliances was suggested through this emphasis. This fact, combined with Leach's comments concerning incessant mobbing, confirms the theory that press reports about the show were more representative of a public view, based on an interest in Canada's First Nations cowboys, than of political propaganda.

Culturally speaking, the more important outcome came about due to personal interactions between the Australian public and the First Nations men. Due to their

A Paleface Listens

"But in the end our arrows found their mark and not a man escaped. My ancestors said . . . " Was it some breathless story of tribal feud on the wide prairie this Indian told yesterday at the Showground? His paleface audience of one was enthralled.

Fig. 43: "A Paleface Listens," *The Sun and The Guardian* (Sydney), 2 April 1939.

desire to meet real "Red Indians" in person, shake their hands, ask them questions, and get their autograph, a good deal of individual communication occurred (see Fig. 43). The Australian public admired Constable Leach; however, the average Australian spectator was more interested in interacting with Joe Crowfoot, Frank Many Fingers, Johnny Left Hand, Eddie One Spot, Douglas Kootenay, Jim Starlight, Joe Bear Robe and Joe Young Pine. Ironically, while a long history of myths perpetuated by international venues such as Wild West shows allowed the Australian public to view these men as approachable, the one-on-one interaction made possible at the Royal Easter Show provided an opportunity for these First Nations cowboys to dispel some of these myths. They had names, they could speak English, they had families, and they went to church. Although it seems surprising that these "ordinary" aspects of the men's lives would be interesting to an audience initially intent on seeing savage "Redskins," it was these "ordinary" qualities that ultimately endeared Canada's First Nations cowboys to Australian showgoers.

Perhaps the Australian public's response was indicative of attitudes concerning their own sense of themselves as colonial subjects. When compared to the harmful treatment doled out to "Aborigines," their desire to approach these indigenous Canadian visitors on more human terms was striking. Possibly the dramatic acts of resistance, which took place in Sydney during Australia's sesquicentenary celebrations on 26 January 1938 (approximately one year before the 1939 show), influenced their curiosity and sensibilities. The Aborigines Progressive Association hosted a conference and political protest, which simultaneously celebrated a "Day of Mourning." This event was designed to express Aboriginal sentiments towards 150 years of callous treatment by the Australian government, and was the first political protest of its kind in Australia. During the conference, which over two hundred Aboriginal people attended, there was a focus on the need for vast improvements in the areas of education and employment. Aborigines Progressive Association representatives also advocated for full citizenship rights for all Aboriginal people.[75] Although this compelling act did little to sway government policies, it is quite possible that it had a social impact on Sydney's white population. Perhaps this was one of the reasons they approached Canada's First Nations cowboys in a more humane manner.

Conclusion

> People fight to maintain control over their future by striving to maintain control over the multiple spaces that they can inhabit; that multiplicity is what confers the experience of freedom, movement, and indeed the power to create history.[1]

On 1 February 1939, before the First Nations cowboys had even begun their journey, C. Pant Schmidt and D.W. McGill started making plans for the arrival of King George IV and Queen Elizabeth in Calgary.[2] Correspondence between Schmidt, McGill, and the Indian agents in Alberta reflects the same type of objectification of First Nations people and culture as did the correspondence pertaining to the trip to Sydney. Initially, Schmidt wanted "some fifteen hundred Indians"[3] to create a huge camp with which to dazzle the royal party. Debates ensued about money, and it was obvious that the Indian Affairs Branch wanted to spend very little on this "Indian" display. There was also a letter from Principal S.H. Middleton of St. Paul's Residential School arguing that this type of display, with "Indians in war-paint and feathers," would undo thirty-four years of missionary work and millions of dollars worth of education. Middleton's compromise involved thrilling His Majesty with "depictions of ancient pageantry in all its eloquent symbolism" to represent the past. Then, to represent the present, he suggested dressing "their offspring" in Boy Scout, Girl Guide, and Army Cadet uniforms.[4] In the end, only sixty First Nations individuals (all chiefs and their wives) were formally asked to attend, and the original asked-for budget of $2,500 turned into $450.[5] Their transportation was paid and they were each given five dollars for personal expenses.[6] Ironically, $150 was allotted as prize money for the "best dressed Cowboy," "best dressed Cowgirl," and "best decorated house,"[7] suggesting that little expense was spared in other areas of this event.

In Schmidt's initial remarks, he explained what this royal visit would mean to "the Indians." These comments were intended to convince the Indian Affairs Branch to financially support his grandiose fantasy:

> I know the Indians will crowd in to see their King, the beloved Great White Mother's great grandson. Old and young on the reserves are already mentioning and longing for the visit, and are anxious to see his Majesty, and his Royal Consort, the young queen. This visit, following the departure of members of their bands for Australia – another of His Majesty's countries – to take part in the Royal Agricultural Show, makes the year 1939 a "high-light" in their lives; and with fine spring weather in May, green grass growing, foliage coming out and all the excitement of the forthcoming visit of their Majesties, how can we possibly hold the Indians back from making the trip; as, for many of them, similar occasion will never again present itself.[8]

However, this argument obviously did not have an impact. Pleasing "the Indians" or assisting in their participation was far less important than cutting costs. In the end, a large number of First Nations people did attend all the western stops on this tour, without any official support.[9]

Britain had made its opposition to Hitler's regime clear. The royal visit to North America was designed "to rally support for the Allied cause,"[10] in much the same way Skidmore and MacFarlane's tour of North America had been. The Indian Affairs Branch was eager to supply "Indians" as an attraction as long as it did not cost them any money. The First Nations people who participated did so for their own reasons. Making their traditional culture visible to British monarchs would have been a primary concern. They also benefited financially from the tour. Many received compensation for loaned horses, tipis, and tipi poles. Among this group were Joe Crowfoot, Teddy Yellowfly and Eddie One Spot, who demonstrated an entrepreneurial spirit.

The royal tour in Calgary can be viewed as a repeat performance of the same type of production that took place at the Royal Easter Show in Sydney. The producers of this popular public event wanted to use Canadian First Nations people as an attraction to solidify political alliances, but with minimal financial expense. The actors, who constituted a much larger group this time, agreed to participate for a variety of personal reasons, but their primary motivation was to renew and reaffirm their treaty partnerships with the Crown. The main difference between the two events was the composition of the audience, which in this case included First Nations Canadians, white Canadians from many ethnic backgrounds, King

George and his queen. Suffice it to say there would have been a great deal of variety and contradiction in terms of the multiple perspectives afforded by all those who observed or participated in this spectacle. The multicultural nature of this audience would have undoubtedly meant that each individual could have gleaned a different cultural meaning from this event.[11]

Without an analysis of the audience's responses, or the actors' perspectives, this story remains one in which government desires take precedence. The Indian Affairs Branch's objectification of First Nations people reminds us of injustices common to all forms of colonialism. It also relegates them to pawns in the production of a form of nationalism that does not include them as full citizens. The British monarchs' desire to see "Red Indians" relegates their presence to that of stereotypical figures, again reminiscent of Wild West imagery. They become the oppressed, without personal or collective agency and without the desire to represent themselves culturally. This one-sided story perpetuates an understanding of "domination [that] is universalized within [a] standard framework[s] of colonialism and imperialism."[12] First Nations people become "people without history,"[13] without cultural diversity, and without a social presence.

The account of the 1939 Sydney performances offered in this study has documented the reordering of stereotypes and the renegotiation of cultural/colonial boundaries by tracing the movements of individual people presenting distinct views of national identity. Through such an examination of multiple perspectives it is possible to see how cultural meanings are intertwined, and how new meanings take form. The international character of this event makes the shifting, fluid nature of cultural meaning more explicit. It also emphasizes the impact that individuals can have in alterations to ideological meanings based on national identity, particularly when a foreign audience's interpretation is taken into account.

Central to such an analysis of colonial relationships is the reconstruction of the past by exposing discourses, which often have alternative meanings or hidden agendas. The concept of "lived hegemony," as defined by Raymond Williams, is based on the notion that power is constantly being negotiated. Therefore, in historical writing the same amount of emphasis must be given to all sides, including the voices of those wielding political or ruling power and the individual voices of those who resist being controlled. The latter stresses the individuated capacity for creation and manipulation, which inevitably influences social change, yet works within traditional structures to negotiate cultural identity and new social meanings. Transcultural perspectives, which cross national boundaries, deepen and give more power to individual voices of dissent. Their comparative value aids in exposing aspects of cultural citizenship and in deconstructing stereotypes.

This 1939 story began with the RAS and its desire to reproduce well-known colonial frameworks of knowledge by enhancing notions of progress and modernity through the use of primitive imagery. It ended with Australian newspapers describing "Red Indians" as average individuals. Stereotypical attitudes appear to have shifted slightly. Mythologies were challenged; different realities were revealed. Yet, Skidmore and MacFarlane had no intention of promoting the real-life stories of eight First Nations cowboys. In fact, they were determined to do the exact opposite. So then, why did the outcome differ so greatly from the intent?

In fact, this outcome was greatly influenced by moments of connectedness that occurred through the act of travelling and performing. Transcultural representation magnified cultural differences and, conversely, cultural similarities. The sense of "we" that Samuel Leach described in his writing transcended social class, race, and legal authority. It spoke to an awareness of fairness and justice that challenged colonial hegemony. Leach's sense of national affiliation with the eight First Nations men he was travelling with motivated him to negotiate for fairer international competition, where they could demonstrate their distinct identities on a more level field. It also allowed him to rise above his restrictive role as chaperone on other occasions. His story is one of personal pride and determination, which was extended to the First Nation men he was travelling with. In this way, the Royal Easter Show provided a space where a Canadian sense of national identity transcended colonial legal and social categories and took on a more human face.

Frank Many Fingers and Joe Crowfoot described themselves as citizens of Canada, disrupting the popular pre-war notion that First Nations people were a vanishing race. As athletes, they brought themselves culturally and politically to the forefront, allowing their audiences the opportunity to visualize a future when white cowboys and Indian cowboys could compete equally. All eight First Nations men spent much of their lives fighting to control their own destinies and gain access to political and economic power for their families. This story demonstrates only one small example where they did effect change. It is not just a family story, which aids in remembering "the trip of a lifetime," but also a story about how these men ventured out into the world to declare their national and regional identity.

The "ordinary" category used in Australian newspaper accounts should not be minimized. It confirms a connection, in essence a connective view, which closely identifies one group with another. The gap between notions of "Red Indians" and the realities of "average, white Australians" is very wide, but somehow the First Nations cowboys crossed it in Sydney. The intended meanings of the RAS, saturated with well-understood racial and racist messages, were somewhat altered. The primitive became, at least to some degree, "just like" their Australian audience.

As a scholar, and as a storyteller, my efforts to expose instances where racist meanings and stereotypical beliefs were ignored are intended to deconstruct and renegotiate dominant hegemonic notions about colonialism. Histories in colonial societies are not one-sided stories. The colonized, too often presented as unfortunate victims, can become powerful creators within webs of meaning. State representatives do not always follow the mandated roles of oppression they are assigned. Individuals impact dominant hegemonic messages with their own attitudes and perspectives. Eight First Nations cowboys were able to effect change by using a popular public venue to make personal contact through interviews, autograph signings, and conversation. In this way, they represented themselves as ordinary people with ordinary feelings, lives, and attitudes. An RCMP officer was able to challenge state authority in order to dispute prejudiced attitudes, thus helping a group of colonized people gain respect and recognition. These acts of connection became acts of cultural representation that can also be considered powerful forms of resistance, powerful enough to affect larger mainstream ideologies.

Endnotes

Introduction

1 Greg Dening, "The Theatricality of History Making and the Paradoxes of Acting," *Cultural Anthropology* 8 (1993): 73–95, 85.
2 Cable quoted in a letter from A. T. Seaman, Assistant Commissioner for the Canadian Government Exhibition Commission to Dr. H. W. McGill, Director of the Indian Affairs Branch, Ottawa, 8 July 1938, Record Group 10 (RG10), Records Relating to Indian Affairs (RRIA), vol. 4010, file 253,430, National Archives of Canada (NAC).
3 The terminology used in the thesis will follow suggestions made by the National Aboriginal Health Organization in Canada, "Terminology Guide," National Aboriginal Health Organization (NAHO), <www.naho.ca> (accessed 30 May 2004) and the Applied History Research Group at the University of Calgary, "Alberta's First Nations: A Note on Terminology," The Applied History Group: University of Calgary, <www.ucalgary.ca/applied_history/tutor/calgary/nativeterm.html> (accessed 30 May 2004). Occasionally, I will use the term "Aboriginal" in reference to the team of cowboys that travelled to Sydney; however, most often I will use the term "First Nations." This term came into use in the 1970s to offset the offensive nature of the word "Indian," although "Indian cowboy" is the way both Floyd Many Fingers and Cecil Crowfoot referred to their brother and father. "Indian" will be used when referring to comments made in 1939 because this was the only title given to these men other than "Red Indians," which was predominantly used by Australians. The names of the First Nations communities have also changed since 1939 from Blackfoot, Blood, Stoney and Sarcee to Siksika, Kainai, Nakodabi and Tsuu T'ina respectively. The names that were common in 1939 will be the ones used throughout this book. The term "Aborigines" will be used in reference to white comments made about indigenous people living in Australia in 1939, although this term is currently used in tandem with the term "Aboriginal." For a discussion of Australia terminology see David Hollingsworth, "Guidelines for non-racist language use in Aboriginal Studies," College of Indigenous Education and Research, University of South Australia, <www.uniza.edu.au/unaipon/current/guidelines.htm> (accessed 31 May 2004).
4 Leslie Sara, "Display of Indian Craft Travels to Australia: May Open Up Fresh Export Markets," *Calgary Herald*, 11 February 1939, RG10, vol. 4010, file 253,430, NAC.
5 Ibid.

6 The bulk of these facts were taken from Constable Leach's daily RCMP report. See Corporal S. J. Leach, *RCMP Report*, January–April 1939 (Supplied by Peggy Maxwell, July 2003).
7 Marilyn Burgess looks historically at the way Indian cowboys have challenged symbolic meanings through visual representation in response to colonial hegemony. See Marilyn Burgess, "'Dark Devils in the Saddle': A Discursive Analysis of Tourist and Entertainment Formations Constituting Western Canadian Regional Identity" (PhD diss., Concordia University, 1992) and "Canadian 'Range Wars': Struggles over Indian Cowboys," *Canadian Journal of Communications* 18 (1993): 352–64. Elizabeth Furniss specifically analyzed the complexities of Canadian rodeo in consolidating local identity. Her contemporary study, *The Burden of History: Colonialism and the Frontier Myth in a Rural Canadian Community* (Vancouver, BC: UBC Press, 1999), focused on Williams Lake in British Columbia, and investigates issues surrounding the reproduction of stereotypes at this annual stampede. Sarah Carter actually provides a short overview of the 1939 trip to Sydney in a collection of essays focused on perspectives gleaned from the Canadian Cowboy Conference in 1997. See "'He Country in Pants' No Longer–Diversifying Ranching History," in *Cowboys, Ranchers and the Cattle Business*, ed. Sarah Carter, Simon Evans, and Bill Yeo, 162–65 (Calgary, AB: University of Calgary Press, 1999). Peter Iverson in *Riders of the West: Portraits of the Indian Rodeo* (Vancouver, BC: Greystone Books, 1999), and more currently Alison Fuss Mellis, *Riding Buffaloes and Broncos: Rodeo and Native Tradition in the Northern Great Plains* (Norman, OK: University of Oklahoma Press, 2003), both provide comparative models that look at American versus Canadian lifestyles. Morgan Baillargeon and Leslie Tepper, in *Legends of Our Times: Native Cowboy Life* (Vancouver, BC: UBC Press, 1999), focus exclusively on Indian rodeo in western Canada. Also, several authors have written short articles about Indian rodeo and in particular Tom Three Persons' famous ride in 1912. For examples see Glen Mikkelsen, "Indians and Rodeo," *Alberta History* 35 (1986): 13–19 and Hugh A. Dempsey, *Tom Three Persons: Legend of an Indian Cowboy* (Saskatoon, SK: Purich, 1997).
8 Raymond Williams, "Selections from Marxism and Literature," in *Culture/Power/History: A Reader in Contemporary Social Theory*, ed. Nicholas B. Dirks, Geoff Ely and Sherry B. Ortner (Princeton: Princeton University Press, 1994), 585–608, 598.
9 Dening, "The Theatricality of History Making," 85.
10 For a discussion of the importance of the audiences view see Gillian Poulter, *Becoming Native in a Foreign Land: Visual Culture, Sport and Spectacle in the Construction of National Identity in Montreal, 1840–1885* (PhD diss., York University, 1999), 9–10.
11 Samuel Hordern, society president, foreword, *Annual RAS Promotional Brochure, 1938–1939*, p.14, RAS Heritage Centre, Sydney.
12 The exaggerated advertisement of this event is curious considering that Aboriginal people in Australia had been involved in ranching and rodeo since the late nineteenth century. In the 1930s many worked as hired hands and some competed in local rodeo venues. For a discussion of the cattle industry see Richard Broome, *Aboriginal Australians: Black Responses to White Dominance, 1788–1994*, 2nd

ed. (Sydney, NSW: Allen & Unwin, 1994), 124–42. For comments pertaining to Aboriginal participation in rodeo see Broome, "Seeking Mulga Fred," *Aboriginal History* 22 (1998): 1–2.

13 Cable quoted in a letter from A.T. Seaman, Assistant Commissioner for the Canadian Government Exhibition Commission to Dr. H.W. McGill, Director of the Indian Affairs Branch, Ottawa, 8 July 1938, RG10, vol. 4010, file 253,430, NAC.

14 For a discussion concerning the fluidity of discourses surrounding colonial identities see Homi Bhabha, "The Other Question: Difference, Discrimination and the Discourse of Colonialism," in *Literature, Politics and Theory*, ed. Francis Barker (New York, NY: Methuen, 1986), 148–72; Stuart Hall, "Cultural Identity and Diaspora," in *Identity: Community, Culture, Difference*, ed. J. Rutherford (London, UK: Lawrence and Wishart, 1990), 222–37.

Chapter 1: The Australian Request

1 This is an excerpt from an ad for Clements Nerve Tonic, which appeared repeatedly in newspapers published during the 1939 Royal Easter Show. For one example of the ad see, "A New Thrill – Chuck Wagon Races at the Royal Show," *The Sun* (Sydney) 29 March 1939 (Fig. 12).

2 Samuel Hordern, society president, foreword, *Annual RAS Promotional Brochure, 1938–1939*, 3.

3 Ibid., 14.

4 Ibid., 13.

5 Keith Walden, *Becoming Modern in Toronto: The Industrial Exhibition and the Shaping of a Late Victorian Culture* (Toronto, ON: University of Toronto Press, 1997), xiv, 15.

6 For a detailed discussion of the politics concerning exhibitions in Canada, see E.A. Heaman, *The Inglorious Arts of Peace: Exhibitions in Canadian Society during the 19th Century* (Toronto, ON: University of Toronto Press, 1999).

7 Fred Kniffen, "The American Agricultural Fair: The Pattern," *Annals of the Association of the American Geographers* 39, no. 4 (Dec. 1949): 264–82. The Smithsonian's Research Guide No. 6 titled, *The Book of Fairs*, <http://microformguides.gale.com/Data/Introductions/10020FM.htm> (accessed 15 May 2005), explains that very few studies have discussed the connection between local agricultural fairs and colonial or nation-building projects. Here they claim that Robert Rydell's article, "Visions of Empire: International Expositions in Portland and Seattle, 1905–1909," *Pacific Historical Review* 52 (1983): 37–65, is the only instance where the "reciprocal relationship between local fairs and international expositions" has been noted. They also state that this connection deserves further consideration because it can "illuminate the process of cultural organization on local, national, and international levels."

8 For a critique of the Royal Easter Show see Kay Anderson, "White Natures: Sydney Royal Agricultural Show in Post-Humanist Perspective," *Transactions of the*

Institute of British Geographers 28, no. 4 (Dec. 2003): 422–42. She explains how white nation-building was produced symbolically through this type of colonial agricultural venue.

9 For a history of the creation of the Royal Agricultural Society of New South Wales that clearly explains the political importance of Royal Easter Show, and which mentions how colour pamphlets were new to this particular fair in 1938, see Brian Fletcher, *The Grand Parade: The History of the Royal Agricultural Society of New South Wales* (Sydney, NSW: The Society, 1988), 209.

10 Interestingly, the description of the Toronto Industrial Exhibition contained in Skidmore and MacFarlane's report of the trip to North America in 1938 clearly explains the components of a nation-building emphasis at this time. It focuses on the "greatness" of Toronto, "its adherence to the best and noblest traditions of the British Empire" in promoting "progress and development," and the global importance of its industrial and commercial advances. These comments include an abundance of historic and statistical details, which suggest they were supplied by official Canadian sources. See *Annual RAS Promotional Brochure, 1938–1939*, 6–7. The foreword in this same document, written by Society President Samuel Hordern, states that the RAS has been "vitally concerned in the many phases of Australia's national and educational development," "high standards," and "the nation's welfare" (p. 3).

11 Fletcher, *The Grand Parade*, 18–28.

12 Ibid., 181, 185–86.

13 Ibid., 195, 205–7.

14 Cable quoted in a letter from A.T. Seaman, Assistant Commissioner for the Canadian Government Exhibition Commission to Dr. H.W. McGill, Director of the Indian Affairs Branch, Ottawa, 8 July 1938, RG10, vol. 4010, file 253,430, NAC. Although Canadian Trade Commissioners were mandated to facilitate and develop the exporting of products, it seems as though they were also involved in organizing performers for overseas jobs. For an example of their public announcements see "The Work of These Men in Foreign Lands Should be Known to All Canada," *The Toronto Daily Star*, 30 August 1938, 7.

15 Cable quoted in a letter from A.T. Seaman, Assistant Commissioner for the Canadian Government Exhibition Commission to Dr. H.W. McGill, Director of the Indian Affairs Branch, Ottawa, 8 July 1938, RG10, vol. 4010, file 253,430, NAC.

16 "MacFarlane, Thomas, Brydone," in *Who's Who in Australia, 1944*, ed. Joseph, A. Alexander (Melbourne, VIC: The Herald and Weekly Times, 1944).

17 Campdrafting was the first rodeo event to become popular in Australia. The basic details of this activity are explained in the next paragraph.

18 James F. Hoy, "Americanization of the Outback," *Vision Splendid* (1995): 205–8.

19 For an in-depth discussion of the origins and rules of campdrafting see website: <http://www.campdrafting.com.au/history.htm> and Gene Makim-Willing, *Get Up on his Shoulder: A History of Campdrafting in Australia* (Toowoomba: Mrs. G. Makim, 1997).

20 Clifford Westermeier, *Man, Beast, Dust* (Denver, CO: World Press, 1947), 329–30. He makes this statement based on the notion that buckjumping and bullock-riding were rodeo events created in North America.

21 RAS, *Rodeo Programme: Royal Easter Show, 1939* (Sydney: W.T. Baker and Co., 1939), 3.

22 MacFarlane, T.B. "Rodeo Popular in Australia," *Hoofs and Horns* (Tucson, AZ), July 1940.

23 Chuckwagons were the American equivalent of the stagecoach. Chuckwagon racing in Canada can be aligned to campdrafting in Australia, as they are both the only internationally recognized rodeo events that did not originate in the United States or Spanish America. Chuckwagon races have been the highlight of the evening program at the Calgary Stampede, Canada's most famous rodeo show, for the last sixty years. Symbolically, they represent white cattle ranchers' first technological enhancement aimed at taming the Wild West. The initial public display of this truly Canadian event was devised by Guy Weadick, the originator of the Calgary Stampede, as a way to entice crowds in 1923. By the early 1930s, these races had become one of the Stampede's most exciting and competitive events. These races involved a great deal of skill and consequently supplied lots of spills and pile-ups for the audience. For an explanation of the history of chuckwagon racing in Canada see Art Belanger, *Chuckwagon Racing: Calgary Stampede's Half Mile of Hell* (Surrey, BC: Frontier Books, 1983), 13, 22.

24 "Skidmore, Alexander, William," *Who's Who in Australia, 1944*, ed. Joseph A. Alexander (Melbourne, VIC: The Herald and Weekly Times, 1944).

25 Fletcher, *The Grand Parade*, 233.

26 For discussions about the popularity of Plains Indian imagery see John F. Sears, "Beirstad, Buffalo Bill, and the Wild West in Europe," *Cultural Transmissions and Receptions: American Mass Culture in Europe*, ed. R. Kroes, R.W. Rydell and B.F.J. Bossher (Amsterdam, NL: VU University Press, 1993); Richard Slotkin, "Buffalo Bill's 'Wild West' and the Mythologization of the American Empire," *Culture of United States Imperialism*, ed. Amy Kaplan and Donald E. Pease (London, UK: Duke University Press, 1993); John Ewers, "Emergence of the Plains Indians as the Symbol of North American Indians" *The Smithsonian Report* (1984): 531–44; Fraser J. Pakes, "Seeing with the Stereotypic Eye: The Visual Image of the Plains Indian," *Native Studies Review* 1, no. 2 (1985): 1–31; Daniele Florentino, "'Those Redbrick Faces': European Press Reactions to the Indians of Buffalo Bill's Wild West Show," *Indians and Europe: An Interdisciplinary Collection of Essays*, ed. Christian Feest (Knogrebstr, NL: Roder Verlag, 1987), and William Brasner, "The Wild West Exhibition and the Drama of Civilization," in *Western Popular Theatre*, ed. David Mayer and Kenneth Richards (London, UK: Methuen, 1977).

27 For a discussion of the American invasion of Australian popular culture during this time period see Philip Bell and Roger Bell, *Implicated: The United States in Australia* (Melbourne, VIC: Oxford University Press, 1993), 65–87. They quote the US consul in 1926 as stating, "the motion picture business is in healthier condition in Australia than in any other country outside the U.S."

28 Radiogram, C.P. Schmidt to Secretary MacInnes of Indian Affairs, Calgary, 27 July 1938, RG10, vol. 4010, file 253,430, NAC.

29 Letter, C.P. Schmidt to Secretary MacInnes of Indian Affairs, Ottawa, 2 September 1938, RG10, vol. 4010, file 253,430, NAC.

30 Letter, A.W. Skidmore and T.B. MacFarlane to Inspector C.P. Schmidt, Indian Affairs, Alberta, 3 October 1938, RG10, vol. 4010, file 253,430, NAC.
31 Final contract between the Canadian Government and the RAS, 28 October 1938, RG10, vol. 4010, file 253,430, NAC.
32 Letter, A.W. Skidmore to Commissioner S.T. Woods, Royal Canadian Mounted Police, Ottawa, 13 October 1938, RG10, vol. 4010, file 253,430, NAC.
33 Final contract between the Canadian Government and the RAS.
34 *Annual RAS Promotional Brochure, 1938–1939*, 14.
35 RAS, *Rodeo Programme: Royal Easter Show, 1939*, 7.
36 Ibid., p. 4.
37 Ibid., p. 22. This advertisement contained an amusing byline that stated, "Thundering by with legs adangling, Red Men fly – their trappings jangling."
38 Ibid., 24
39 Ibid., 3.
40 *Annual RAS Promotional Brochure, 1938–1939*, 2.
41 In a letter to C. Pant Schmidt, Skidmore stated that J.E. Pugh gave him "a fine publication on the Blackfeet, together with coloured illustrations." This is the information that was used in the RAS brochure. See Letter to C.P. Schmidt from A.W. Skidmore, 19 December 1938, RG10, vol. 4010, file 253,430, NAC.
42 *Annual RAS Promotional Brochure, 1938–1939*, 15.
43 Ibid., 14.
44 Ibid.
45 Ibid.
46 The RAS website mentions Iron Eyes Cody (a famous American performer) who performed at the show in 1935, see *Sydney Royal Easter Show: The Great Muster Show*, website of the Royal Agricultural Society of New South Wales, <http://www.great australianmuster.com/aboutus/past.htm> (accessed 8 January 2004).
47 "Red Indians and Cowboys," *The Sydney Morning Herald*, 7 April 1911. A description of this trip can also be found in "Red Men Leave on Tour of Antipodes," *Victoria Daily Times* (Victoria, BC) 25 February 1911.
48 *Annual RAS Promotional Brochure, 1938–1939*, 14.
49 Ibid.
50 Ibid.
51 This comment is followed by the remark that the Canadian government's "work is succeeding," and that "the Red Indians are rapidly becoming self-supporting by raising cattle and crops." I would argue that this perception was gleaned directly from the various Indian agents that Skidmore and MacFarlane met while in Alberta.
52 For a detailed discussion of the history of First Nations farming in Alberta see Sarah Carter, *Lost Harvests: Prairie Indian Reserve Farmers and Government Policy* (Montreal, PQ & Kingston, ON: McGill-Queen's University Press, 1990).
53 *Annual RAS Promotional Brochure, 1938–1939*, 14.
54 Ironically, as will be discussed in Chapter Three, First Nations rodeo competitors in Canada had been competing in chuckwagon races since the turn of the century.
55 *Annual RAS Promotional Brochure, 1938–1939*, 14.

56 Ibid., 15. This phrase seems to have been taken from literature offered by the Canadian government as well. It was also the most popular phrase used by C.P. Schmidt to describe the type of display that he wished to provide.
57 Ibid.
58 Eight tipis were brought to Australia, but the First Nations men and their families provided them.
59 Ibid.
60 For a discussion of "Others" in textbooks specific to Alberta see M.R. Lupul, "The Portrayal of Canada's 'Other' Peoples in Senior High School and Social Studies Textbooks in Alberta, 1905 to the Present," *Alberta Journal of Educational Research* 22, no. 1 (March 1976): 1–33.
61 These statistics were taken from Patricia V. Ofner, "The Indian in Textbooks: A Content Analysis of History Books Authorized for Use in Ontario Schools" (master's thesis, Lakehead University, n.d.), Microfiche Set 1445 (Ottawa, ON: National Library of Canada, 1983). The textbook used in Ontario between 1928 and 1949 was Stewart W. Wallace's, *A First Book of Canadian History* (Toronto, ON: Macmillan, 1928).
62 *Annual RAS Promotional Brochure, 1938–1939*, 3.
63 In fact their trip did generate notoriety in a few North America newspapers. For an example see "Two Australians Visit City in Quest for Cowboy Riders," *The Detroit Free Press*, 3 October 1938, and "Sydney Fair Signs Rodeo," *The Chicago Daily Press*, 25 October 1938.
64 A.W. Skidmore and T.B. MacFarlane, *Final Report to the Royal Agricultural Society, re: trip to North America, 1938*, p. 1, RAS Heritage Centre, Sydney.
65 The Honourable Percy Pease, "Trade Relations Between Australia and Canada," *The Empire Club of Canada Speeches, 1936–1937* (Toronto, ON: The Empire Club of Canada, 1937), 223–37, from <http://www.empireclubfoundation.com/details.asp?SpeechID=158&FT=yes> (accessed 10 January 2004).
66 The Right Honourable J. A. Lyons, "An Address," *The Empire Club of Canada Speeches, 1935–1936* (Toronto, ON: Empire Club of Canada, 1936) 1–18, from <http://www.empireclub foundation.com/details.asp?SpeechID=305&FT=yes> (accessed 10 January 2004).
67 Pease, "Trade Relations Between Australia and Canada," 2–4 of 10.
68 Right Honourable Sir Earle Page, "Australia and the Empire," *The Empire Club of Canada Speeches, 1938–1939* (Toronto, ON: Empire Club of Canada, 1939), 1–18, from <http://www. empireclubfoundation.com/details.asp?SpeechID=922&FT=yes> (accessed 8 January 2004).
69 L.G. Churchward, *Australia and America, 1788–1972: An Alternative History* (Sydney, NSW: Alternative Publishing Cooperative, 1979), 133–35.
70 For a discussion of Australia's "White Policy," an immigration policy in place between 1901 and 1974 that fuelled illogical fears concerning an Asian invasion, see Robert A. Huttenback, *Racism and Empire: White Settlers and Coloured Immigrants in the British Self-governing Colonies, 1830–1910* (Ithaca, NY: Cornell University Press, 1976), 312–15; 324–26.
71 Bell and Bell, *Implicated: The United States in Australia*, 89.

72 Due to the depression of the 1930s, escalating tariffs, competitive devaluations, and protectionist strategies circulated globally. This period of economic conflict was accompanied by an obsession with material progress, and led to what has been described as "competitive nationalism." For a discussion of "competitive nationalism" as a form of nationalism oriented towards economic growth and the fiscal health of a nation, see Liah Greenfeld, *The Spirit of Capitalism* (Cambridge, MA: Harvard University Press, 2001) as cited by David Burrow, "Book Review: *The Spirit of Capitalism*," <http://www.nationalism project.org/books/bookrevs/greenfeld.html> (accessed 27 May 2005).

73 Richard White, *Inventing Australia: Images and Identity, 1688–1980* (Sydney, NSW: Allen and Unwin, 1981), 114.

74 Skidmore and MacFarlane, *Final Report to the Royal Agricultural Society*, 7.

75 This spectacle took place in 1938 while they were travelling in Australia.

76 Skidmore and MacFarlane, *Final Report to the Royal Agricultural Society*, 2.

77 Ibid., 4

78 Ibid., 4–5.

79 Fletcher, *The Grand Parade*, 212–13.

80 Ibid., 214. Fletcher takes these comments from the RAS annual report of 1941.

81 Anderson, "White Natures," 422–42, 425.

82 Cable quoted in letter, Assistant Commissioner A.T. Seaman, Canadian Government Exhibition Commission, to Dr. H.W. McGill, director of the Indian Affairs Branch, Ottawa, 8 July 1938 RG10, vol. 4010, file 253,430, NAC.

Chapter 2: The Canadian Response

1 Letter, C. Pant Schmidt to Major D.M. MacKay, Indian Commissioner, 17 August 1938, RG10, vol. 4010, file 253,430, NAC.

2 Letter, A.T. Seaman, Assistant Commissioner of the Canadian Government Exhibition Commission, Ottawa, to H.W. McGill, Director, Indian Affairs Branch, Ottawa, 8 July 1938, RG10, vol. 4010, file 253,430, NAC. Between 1925 and 1949 the Department of Indian Affairs was made into a branch of the Department of Mines and Resources. In 1938, H.W. McGill was the director of the Indian Affairs Branch.

3 Letter, Secretary T.R.L. MacInnes, Indian Affairs, to G.H. Gooderham, Gleichen, Alberta, 18 July 1938, RG10, vol. 4010, file 253,430, NAC.

4 Ibid.

5 For an example, see cable from Thomas Robertson, Regina, to Secretary MacInnes, Indian Affairs Branch, 22 July 1938, RG10, vol. 4010, file 253,430, NAC.

6 Following initial correspondences with Director McGill of the Indian Affairs Branch, T.R.L. MacInnes, the secretary of the department, took over and became Schmidt's primary contact person. In early letters MacInnes refers to himself as "Acting Director." His responsibilities as secretary seem flexible and include all decision-making concerning the trip to Australia.

7 Cable from Inspector Schmidt, Indian Agencies of Alberta, to Secretary MacInnes, Indian Affairs Branch, Ottawa, 27 July 1938, RG10, vol. 4010, file 253,430, NAC.
8 S.D. Grant explains in her abstract to "Indian Affairs Under Duncan Campbell Scott: The Plains Cree of Saskatchewan 1913–1931," *Journal of Canadian Studies* 18, no. 3 (1983): 21–39, that this was a common theme in the practices of the department.
9 Letter from C.P. Schmidt to T.R.L. MacInnes, acting director, Indian Affairs, Ottawa, 18 August 1938, RG10, vol. 4010, file 253,430, NAC.
10 Letter, D.M. MacKay to C.P. Schmidt, 25 August 1938, RG10, vol. 4010, file 253,430, NAC.
11 Report from Schmidt to MacInnes, 2 September 1938 RG10, vol. 4010, file 253,430, NAC.
12 Ibid.
13 Ibid.
14 Ibid.
15 David Glassberg describes the popularity of these events in the US in his book, *American Historical Pageantry: The Uses of Tradition in the Early Twentieth Century* (Chapel Hill, NC: University of North Carolina Press, 1990). One prominent twentieth-century Canadian example was *The Tercentenary of the Founding of Canada*, staged in Quebec City in 1901. It was comprised of multiple pageants in a lavish effort by the government to imbue patriotism in Quebec. See H.V. Nelles, *The Art of Nation Building: Pageantry and Spectacle at Quebec's Tercentenary* (Toronto, ON: University of Toronto Press, 1999).
16 Treaty 7 Tribal Council Homepage, as seen at <http://www.treaty7.org/> (accessed 16 December 2002). For more information on Treaty 7, see Treaty 7 Elders and Tribal Council with Walter Hildebrandt, Sarah Carter and Dorothy First-Rider, *True Spirit and Original Intent of Treaty 7* (Montreal, PQ: McGill-Queen's University Press, 1996) and John Leonard Taylor, "Two Views on the Meaning of Treaties Six and Seven," in *The Spirit of the Alberta Indian Treaties*, ed. Richard Price (Edmonton, AB: Pica Pica Press, 1987).
17 See Keith Regular, "On Public Display," *Alberta History* 34, no. 1 (Winter 1986): 1–10 and Jon Whyte, *Indians in the Rockies* (Banff, AB: Altitude Publishing, 1985).
18 There is a well-known scholarly critique concerning the history and the development of "people shows" or "human zoos." For some examples see Robert W. Rydell, *All the World's a Fair: Visions of Empire at America's International Expositions, 1867–1916* (Chicago, IL: University of Chicago Press, 1984); Paul Greenhalgh, *Ephemeral Vistas: The Exhibition Universelle: Great Exhibitions and World's Fairs, 1851–1937* (Manchester, UK: Manchester University Press, 1988); Curtis M. Hinsley, "The World as Marketplace: Commodification of the Exotic at the World's Columbia Exposition, Chicago, 1893," in *Exhibiting Cultures, the Poetics and Politics of Museum Display*, ed. Ivan Karp and Stephen D. Lavine (Washington, DC: Smithsonian, 1991), 345; Jonathan C.H. King, "A Century of Indian Shows: Canadian and United States Exhibitions in London 1825–1925," *European Review of Native American Studies* 31 (1991): 35–42; Benedict Burton, "Rituals of Representation: Ethnic Stereotypes and Colonized Peoples at World's

Fairs," in *Fair Representations*, ed. Robert Rydell and Nancy Guinn (Amsterdam, NL: Amsterdam University Press, 1994), 54; Raymond Corbey, "Ethnographic Showcases, 1870–1930," *Cultural Anthropology* 8, no. 3 (Aug. 1993): 338–69; Bernth Lindfors, "Ethnological Show Business: Footlighting the Dark Continent," in *Freakery: Cultural Spectacles of the Extraordinary Body*, ed. Rosemarie Garland Thomas (London, UK & New York, NY: New York University Press, 1996); William Schneider, "Race and Empire: The Rise of Popular Ethnography in the Late 19th Century," *Journal of Popular Culture* 11 (1997): 98–109; Peter Hoffenberg, *An Empire on Display: English, Indian and Australian Exhibitions From the Crystal Palace to the Great War* (Berkeley, CA: University of California Press, 2000), and Saloni Mathur, "Living Ethnological Exhibits: The Case of 1886," *Cultural Anthropology* 15, no. 4 (2000): 492–525.

19 Burton, "Rituals of Representation," 30.
20 Corbey, "Ethnographic Showcases," 341. Also mentioned in Alison Griffiths, *Wondrous Difference: Cinema, Anthropology and Turn-of-the-century Visual Culture* (New York, NY: Columbia University Press, 2002), 59–60.
21 Corbey, "Ethnographic Showcases," 341.
22 Benedict Burton, *The Anthropology of World's Fairs* (London, UK & Berkeley, CA: Lowie Museum of Anthropology and Scolar Press, 1983), 45.
23 E.A. Heaman, *The Inglorious Arts of Peace: Exhibitions in Canadian Society during the 19th Century* (Toronto, ON: University of Toronto Press, 1999).
24 Letter from J.E. Pugh, Indian agent, to Secretary McInnes, Indian Affairs Branch, Ottawa, 26 July 1938, RG10, vol. 4010, file 253,430, NAC.
25 Ibid.
26 Ibid.
27 Chapter Three will include specific comments about the extent of control Indian agents had during this time period.
28 Letter from W.B. Murray, Indian agent, Morley, Alberta, to Secretary MacInnes, Indian Affairs Branch, Ottawa, 24 July 1938, RG10, vol. 4010, file 253,430, NAC.
29 Grant, "Indian Affairs Under Duncan Campbell Scott," 32.
30 For historical overviews of this practice see Katherine Pettipas, *Severing the Ties That Bind: Government Repression of Indigenous Religious Ceremonies on the Prairies* (Winnipeg, MB: University of Manitoba Press, 1994), 93–97, and Christopher Bracken, *The Potlatch Papers: A Colonial Case History* (Chicago, IL: University of Chicago Press, 1997).
31 Pettipas, *Severing the Ties That Bind*, 148–49.
32 For a detailed discussion of the conflicts between Indian agents and First Nations people in Alberta over local exhibitions between 1900 and 1912, see Keith Regular, "On Public Display," *Alberta History* 34, no. 1 (Winter 1986): 1–10.
33 Pettipas, *Severing the Ties That Bind*, 164.
34 Paige Raibmon, "Theatres of Contact: The Kwakwaka'wakw Meet Colonialism in British Columbia and the Chicago World's Fair," *The Canadian Historical Review* 81, no. 2 (2000): 157–90, 178.
35 Ibid., 179.

36 George Hunt (1854–1933) was an assistant to anthropologist Franz Boas, as well as a First Nations ethnographer/photographer in his own right. His focus on Kwakwaka'wakw ceremonialism is distinctive due to his sensitivity towards native categories and perspectives. Hunt's life-long goal was to record Kwakwaka'wakw cultural history. For a short bibliography see Ira Jacknis, "George Hunt, Kwakiutl Photographer," in *Anthropology and Photography: 1860–1920*, ed. Elizabeth Edwards, (New Haven, CT & London, UK: Yale University Press, 1992), 143–51.

37 Ibid., 157, 182–84.

38 Letter from L.O. Armstrong to Deputy Superintendent General Frank Pedley, Indian Affairs, Ottawa, 22 January 1904, and response, 27 January 1904 RG10, vol. 4010, file 253,430, NAC.

39 Letter from the Governor General of Canada to Geo. A. Dodge, 17 January 1905, RG10, vol. 4010, file 253,430, NAC.

40 Letter from Adolf Klinko to Indian Department, Regina, Saskatchewan, 21 May 1909, and response, 28 May 1909,

41 Letter from William George Fyfe to Superintendent General of the Department of Indian Affairs, 30 January 1911, and response, 2 February 1911, RG10, vol. 4010, file 253,430, NAC.

42 Evidence of this trip can be found in three newspaper articles: "Indian Leave for Antipodes," *Victoria Daily Times*, 25 January 1911; "Red Indians and Cowboys," *The Sydney Morning Herald* (classifieds), 7 April 1911; "Red Men Leave on Tour of Antipodes," *Victoria Daily Times*, 25 February 1911. All three can be found in RG10, vol. 4010, file 253,430, NAC.

43 The comments in his lengthy letter suggest that Sced had befriended the "Opitsit Indians," was made aware of their financial difficulties, and simply wanted to help them out by encouraging government officials to allow them to perform traditional dances for extra income.

44 Letter from Sgt. Benjamin F. Sced to Mr. Neil, Clayoquot, BC, 26 February 1933, RG10, vol. 4010, file 253,430, NAC.

45 Ibid. Also see the response in a letter from H.W. McGill to A.W. Neil, 9 March 1933, and a letter from C.C. Perry to McGill, 25 March 1939.

46 Ibid.

47 Letter from Kalervo Oberg to the Department of Indian Affairs, Ottawa, 5 May 1933, RG10, vol. 4010, file 253,430, NAC.

48 Letter from Fay-Cooper Cole to Secretary A. F. MacKenzie, Department of Indian Affairs, Ottawa, 11 May 1933, RG10, vol. 4010, file 253,430, NAC.

49 All requests for off-reserve performing after 1933 were granted quickly as long as the organizers agreed to pay expenses and wages; see all files between 1933 and 1938, RG10, vol. 4010, file 253,430, NAC.

50 For an early example of this debate, see Chauncey Yellow Robe, "The Menace of the Wild West Show," *Quarterly Journal of the Society of American Indians* (July–Sept. 1914): 225.

51 Elizabeth Furniss discusses this debate in a contemporary context in her book *The Burden of History: Colonialism and the Frontier Myth in a Rural Canadian Community* (Vancouver, BC: UBC Press, 1999), 182–85, and her article, "Cultural

Performance as Strategic Essentialism: Negotiating Indianness in a Western Canadian Rodeo Festival," *Humanities Research* 3 (1998): 23–40.

52 Furniss, "Cultural Performance as Strategic Essentialism," 25.

53 Letter from Schmidt to Secretary MacInnes of Indian Affairs, Ottawa, 2 September 1938, RG10, vol. 4010, file 253,430, NAC.

54 Michael Allen, *Rodeo Cowboys in the North American Imagination* (Reno/Las Vegas, NV: University of Nevada Press, 1998), 23.

55 Marilyn Burgess, "'Dark Devils in the Saddle': A Discursive Analysis of Tourist and Entertainment Formations Constituting Western Canadian Regional Identity" (PhD diss., Concordia University, 1992), 30.

56 Elizabeth Atwood Lawrence, *Rodeo: An Anthropologist Looks at the Wild and the Tame* (Knoxville, TN: University of Tennessee Press, 1982), 7.

57 This type of reference was continuously reiterated in correspondence between Indian agents in respect to this trip. It was usually accompanied by phrases such as "our boys" and "our Indians."

58 For detailed comments concerning the impact that the Calgary Stampede had on Indian agents' views about rodeo in the early twentieth century, see Katherine Pettipas, "Severing the Ties that Bind," 163–64.

59 Letter from Schmidt to Secretary of Indian Affairs MacInnes, Ottawa, 2 September 1938, RG10, vol. 4010, file 253,430, NAC.

60 Ibid.

61 References to these types of displays at the Vancouver Exhibition and the Calgary Stampede in the 1930s can be seen in RG10, vol. 7558, file 1167-1 and 1120-1, NAC.

62 For further confirmation of this fact, see Daniel Francis, *The Imaginary Indian: The Image of the Indian in Canadian Culture* (Vancouver, BC: Arsenal Pulp Press, 1992), 102–103.

63 Allen, *Rodeo Cowboys*, 28.

64 Letter, C.P. Schmidt to A.W. Skidmore, 13 February 1939, Blackfoot Indian Agency (BIA) files, Glenbow Foundation Archives (GFA), Calgary.

65 Joy Leland, *Firewater Myths: North American Indian Drinking and Alcohol Addiction* (New Brunswick, NJ: Publications Division, Rutgers Centre of Alcohol Studies, 1976).

66 Letter, C.P. Schmidt to A.W. Skidmore, 13 February 1939, BIA files, GFA.

67 Morgan Baillargeon and Leslie Tepper, *Legends of Our Times: Native Cowboy Life* (Vancouver, BC: UBC Press, 1998), 165–72.

68 For a thorough discussion of the theoretical aspects of Indian rodeo see Burgess, "Dark Devils in the Saddle," Marilyn Burgess, "Canadian 'Range Wars': Struggles over Indian Cowboys," *Canadian Journal of Communications* 18 (1993): 352–64.

69 Letter, Schmidt to MacInnes, 2 September 1938, RG10, vol. 4010, file 253,430, NAC.

70 Ibid. This was a decent wage in 1938, equal to that of a junior RCMP officer and half of the annual income of an average First Nations family in Alberta.

71 Ibid.

72 For a discussion of specific problems in the prairies experienced during the depression see Gerald Freisen, *The Canadian Prairies: A History* (Toronto, ON: University of Toronto Press, 1987).

Endnotes: Chapter 2

73 R.A. Hoey, "Economic Problems of the Canadian Indian," in *The North American Indian Today*, ed. C.T. Loram and T.F. McIlwraith (Toronto, ON: University of Toronto Press, 1943), 199–206.

74 Hoey, 204–205. Here he briefly discusses the wholesale and retail sales of Indian handicrafts, which had been taken over by the department.

75 For comments about the mass production of Indian arts and subsequent loss of authentic design see Gerald McMaster, "Tenuous Lines of Descent: Indian Art and Craft of the Reservation Period," *Canadian Journal of Native Studies* 9, no. 2 (1989): 205–36.

76 Trudy Nicks, "Indian Handicrafts: The Marketing of an Image," *Rotunda* (Summer 1990): 14–20. In 1939 Blackfoot people, considered one of the wealthiest bands in Canada, were thought to be gainfully employed if they made $300–400 per year. A mediocre income for white citizens was approximately double this amount. For details of the reserve economy of the Blackfoot see Lucien M. Hanks and Jane Richardson Hanks, *Tribe Under Trust: A Study of the Blackfoot Reserve of Alberta* (Toronto, ON: University of Toronto Press, 1950), 103–23.

77 Report from Schmidt to MacInnes, "Indian handicrafts for sale at the Royal Agricultural Show at Sydney, Australia," Calgary, 30 December 1938, RG10, vol. 4010, file 253,430, NAC.

78 Letter, Schmidt to McInnes, Calgary, 21 February 1939, RG10, vol. 4010, file 253,430, NAC.

79 Alice Lighthall also wrote several articles for the Canadian Handicraft Guild in support of commercializing First Nations work and was intensely involved with Hoey and Kathleen Moodie, the fieldworker for the Welfare and Training Division. See Alice M. Lighthall, "Report of the Indian Committee," *Annual Report of the Canadian Handicraft Guild* (Montreal, PQ: Canadian Handicraft Guild, 1938), 25–27; Alice Lighthall, "Indian Work," *Annual Report of the Canadian Handicraft Guild* (Montreal, PQ: Canadian Handicraft Guild, 1937), 21–23. Here she states that Hoey claimed there was "a real demand for native craft-work," which had kept "many families off relief."

80 Leslie Sara, "Display of Indian Craft Travels to Australia: My Open Up Fresh Export Markets," *Calgary Daily Herald*, 11 February 1939.

81 Ibid.

82 Ibid.

83 Ibid.

84 "Straight from the Canadian Indians: Colourful Handicrafts for Easter Show," *The Sun* (Sydney), 15 March 1939.

85 Ibid.

86 Sara, "Display of Indian Craft."

87 Ibid.

88 Letter, Schmidt to Hoey, Calgary, 22 March 1939, RG10, vol. 4010, file 253,430, NAC.

89 For a more thorough explanation of Schmidt's acquisition process see NA, RG 10, vol. 4010, file, 253,430, Letter from Schmidt to T.R.L. MacInnes, 30 December 1938 and 19 January 1939.

90 Letter, R.A. Hoey to Schmidt, Ottawa, 11 July 1939, RG10, vol. 4010, file 253,430, NAC.
91 W.H. Van Allen, "Canada and the Glasgow Exhibition," *Canadian Geographic Journal* 16, no. 3 (March 1938): 153–54.
92 James G. Parmelee, "Canada on Parade at Glasgow," *Canadian Geographic Journal* 16, no. 6 (June 1938): 306–12.
93 David Gelernter, *1939: The Lost World of the Fair* (New York, NY: The Free Press, 1995), 12, 18–19. Somewhat recently there have been a number of theses focused on this aspect of the fair. For examples see Thomas M. Barrington, "A Vision of a Modern Future: A Fantasy Theme and Rhetorical Vision Analysis of the New York World's Fair of 1939" (master's thesis: Southwest Texas State University, 1992); Joseph P. Cusker, "The World of Tomorrow: the 1939 New York World's Fair." (PhD diss., Rutgers University, 1990); Valerie Ann Frydrych, "Building the Consumer of Tomorrow: Social Messages of the Spectacle at the New York World's Fair" (PhD diss., University of Pennsylvania, 2000).
94 James G. Parmelee, "Canada's Participation in the World's Fair," *Canadian Geographic Journal* 19, no. 1 (July 1939): 85–100.
95 The prevalence of this type of architecture is analysed in Elspeth Cowell, "The Canadian Pavilion at the 1939 New York World's Fair," *SSAC Bulletin* 19, no. 1 (March 1994): 13–20. Here the author also provides a detailed analysis of the process involved throughout this competition and the importance of this pavilion in the development of modern architecture in Canada.
96 Leslie Dawn has discussed the application of Martin's work at the New York World's Fair in "Staging the Revival: Producing and Policing the Image of the 'People of the Potlatch'" (paper delivered at NAASA Conference, Salem, MA, 7 November 2003).
97 Report from Schmidt to MacInnes, 2 September 1938, RG10, vol. 4010, file 253,430, NAC.
98 David Theo Goldberg, *The Racial State* (Oxford, UK: Blackwell, 2002), 120–21.

Chapter 3: Canadian Indian Cowboys at the Royal Easter Show in Sydney

1 Betsy Jameson (lecture, Trent University, 20 November 2003).
2 Floyd Many Fingers, interview with the author, Cardston, AB, 21 October 2003.
3 See Katherine Pettipas, *Severing the Ties That Bind: Government Repression of Indigenous Religious Ceremonies on the Prairies* (Winnipeg, MB: University of Manitoba Press, 1994) for an overview of Canadian government policy during this time period.
4 For the history of this organization, which started in 1939, see Laurie Miejer Drees, *The Indian Association of Alberta: A History of Political Action* (Vancouver, BC: UBC Press, 2002).

5 Proof of the realities of economic independence can be found in Lucien M. Hanks and Jane Richardson Hanks, *Tribe Under Trust: A Study of the Blackfoot Reserve in Alberta* (Toronto, ON: University of Toronto Press, 1950); Sarah Carter, Simon Evans, and Bill Yeo, *Cowboys, Ranchers and the Cattle Business* (Calgary, AB: University of Calgary Press, 1999); Sarah Carter, *Lost Harvests: Prairie Indian Reserve Farmers and Government Policy* (Montreal, PQ & Kingston, ON: McGill-Queen's University Press, 1990); Peter Iverson, *Rider of the West: Portraits of the Indian Rodeo* (Vancouver, BC: Greystone Books, 1999); Peter Iverson, *The Plains Indians of the Twentieth Century* (Norman, OK: University of Oklahoma Press, 1985); Morgan Baillargeon and Leslie Tepper, *Legends of Our Times: Native Cowboy Life* (Vancouver, BC: UBC Press, 1998). See also Cecil Crowfoot, interview by Deanna Crowfoot, Edmonton, AB, October 2003, and Many Fingers interview.
6 See John Ewers, *The Horse in Blackfoot Indian Culture* (Washington, DC: United States Printing Office, 1955), 153–54, 226.
7 Peter Iverson, *The Plains Indians of the Twentieth Century*, 14.
8 Ibid. Also see Baillargeon and Tepper, *Legends of Our Times*, 91, and Glen Mikkelson, "Indians and Rodeo," *Alberta History* 35 (1986): 13–14.
9 Rob Shield eloquently explains this contradiction in "Imaging Sites," *Between Views* (Banff), 1991: 23. Although opposing stereotypes, including those associated with "noble savagery," are also seen in Wild West shows, they are not very common. For a discussion of "noble savage" imagery in Wild West posters see Joy Kasson, *Buffalo Bill's Wild West: Celebrity, Memory, and Popular History* (New York, NY: Hill and Wang, 2000), 198–211.
10 Many Fingers interview.
11 Crowfoot interview.
12 George H. Gooderham, "Joe Crowfoot," *Alberta History* 32, no. 4 (1984): 26–28.
13 Crowfoot interview.
14 Comments were made to this effect on the Glenbow Museum archival website; see <www.glenbow.org>.
15 Jim Striker (ed.), Lazy "B" 70 Memorial Rodeo Souvenir Program, Many Fingers Ranch, Blood Reserve, 27–28 June 1997, 3, 8.
16 Crowfoot interview.
17 Letter, J.E. Pugh to C. Pant Schmidt, 2 November 1938, *General Correspondence Regarding Indians Travelling to Various Exhibitions Around the World (New York, Paris and Sydney, Australia)* RG10, vol. 4010, reel C-10171, file 253,430, NAC
18 Crowfoot interview.
19 Corporal S.J. Leach, "Redskins and Redcoat Visit the Antipodes," *RCMP Quarterly* 7, no. 1 (July 1939): 52–60.
20 This information about the men's political careers was found on the Glenbow Museum archival website; see <www.glenbow.org>.
21 Crowfoot interview.
22 There are many photographs documenting aspects of One Spot's career as a performer on the Glenbow Museum archival website; see <www.glenbow.org>. Conversations with Erna Gingold, his widow, also confirmed his multiple talents and long career as an entertainer and professional rodeo competitor.

23 Victor Leach, telephone conversation with the author, August 2003.
24 T.R.L. MacInnes, "The History and Policies of Indian Administration in Canada," in *The North American Indian Today*, ed. C.T. Loram and T.F. McIlwraith (Toronto, ON: University of Toronto Press, 1943), 158, 163.
25 Claude Denis, "Indigenous Citizenship and History in Canada: Between Denial and Imposition," in *Contesting Canadian Citizenship: Historical Readings*, ed. Robert Adamoski, Dorothy E. Chunn, and Robert Menzies (Peterborough, ON: Broadview, 2002), 113.
26 Teddy Yellowfly's mother was Blackfoot and his father was Chinese. He lived on the Blackfoot Reserve all his life, attended Gleichen Agricultural College, and was an interpreter and office worker at the Indian Agency. In the 1930s he took charge of the Blackfoot coalmines and served on the band council. He was a very well-known spokesperson for First Nations rights until his death in 1950.
27 Chief Teddy Yellowfly, "The Red Man's Burden," part of *The Indians Speak to Canada*, a series of broadcasts sponsored by the Canadian Broadcasting Corporation, in co-operation with the Indian Affairs Branch, Department of Mines and Resources, Ottawa, 1939. For a thorough description (including statistics) of the economic trends and the social effect of these trends during this period for the Blackfoot people see Hanks and Hanks, *Tribes Under Trust*, 103–23.
28 F. Laurie Barron, "The Indian Pass System in the Canadian West, 1882–1935," *Prairie Forum* 13, no. 1 (Spring 1988): 30–31. For proof of the longevity of these policies in Alberta see Katherine Pettipas, *Severing the Ties that Bind*, 112.
29 Baillargeon and Tepper, *Legends of Our Times*, 165–67, 174. For a detailed description of the events of Treaty Days see William Graham, *Treaty Days: Reflections of an Indian Commissioner* (Calgary, AB: Glenbow Museum, 1991), 113–19.
30 For a detailed discussion of Indian agents views about local First Nations celebrations during this time period see Pettipas, *Severing the Ties that Bind*, 162–65.
31 Ibid., 164.
32 Meijer Drees, *The Indian Association of Alberta*, 6.
33 Ibid., 18.
34 Ibid., xix–xxi.
35 Leach, "Redskins and Redcoats Visit the Antipodes," 54.
36 Ibid.
37 The acquisition of pride and self-esteem was actually a concern for Indian agents. W.D. Murray, the Indian agent for the Stoneys, in his correspondence to Schmidt, stated that rodeo in general "glorified a part of Indian life which [was] a hindrance to their progress," and that following the trip to Australia they would "come back feeling too important to work." Ironically, he added that perhaps this would not prove to be "too great an evil if the financial return was considerable." See letter, W.D. Murray to C.P. Schmidt, 24 July 1938, RG10, vol. 4010, reel C-10171, file: 253,430, NAC.
38 Noel Dyck discusses how powwows have been used for the purpose of political promotion in the 1960s and the 1970s in "Political Powwow: The Rise and Fall of an Urban Native Festival," in *The Celebration of Society: Perspectives on Contemporary*

Cultural Performance, ed. Frank E. Manning (Bowling Green, OH: Bowling Green University Press, 1983), 165–85.

39 Kristine Frederiksson, *American Rodeo: From Buffalo Bill to Big Business* (College Station, TX: Texas A&M Press, 1985), 21. In western Canadian First Nations communities, rodeo began in the late 1890s, in conjunction with Treaty Days and Indian Days, as described by Baillargeon and Tepper, *Legends of Our Times*, 165–72.

40 Ted Barris, *The Rodeo Cowboys: The Last Heroes* (Edmonton, AB: Executive Sports Publications, 1981), 32.

41 For an overview of international rodeo events during this time period see Clifford Westermeier, *Man, Beast, Dust* (Denver, CO: World Press, 1947), 315–38.

42 Claire Eamer and Thirza Jones, *The Canadian Rodeo Book* (Saskatoon, SK: Western Producer Prairie Books, 1982), 22–23.

43 For a further discussion of discrimination and handicaps experienced by Indian cowboys in the US, see Silvester John Brito, "The Indian Cowboy in the Rodeo Circuit," *Journal of Ethnic Studies* 5, no. 1 (1977): 52–54. For a discussion of discrimination and handicaps cowgirls experienced in professional rodeo see Mary Lou LeCompte, "Wild West Frontier Days, Roundups, and Stampedes: Rodeo Before There was Rodeo," *Canadian Journal of History of Sport* 16, no. 2 (1985): 54–67.

44 Many Fingers interview.

45 Baillargeon and Tepper, *Legends of Our Times*, 187. For a full biography on Tom Three Persons, see Hugh A. Dempsey, *Tom Three Persons: Legend of an Indian Cowboy* (Saskatoon, SK: Purich, 1997). For an overview of Three Persons famous ride at the Calgary Stampede in 1912, see Mikkelson, "Indians and Rodeo," 14–15.

46 Allison Fuss Mellis, *Riding Buffaloes and Broncos: Rodeo and Native tradition in the Northern Great Plains* (Norman, OK: University of Oklahoma Press, 2003), 34.

47 Ibid., 62. In his article, "Indians and Rodeo," Glen Mikkelsen reiterates this comment and also provides a lengthy list of the victories of First Nations competitors at the Calgary Stampede during this time period. Johnny Left Hand is mentioned as winning the "wild cow milking championships" in 1932 and 1944. Joe Kootenay won a "steer riding championship" in 1936. See "Indians and Rodeo," 13–19.

48 Marilyn Burgess, "'Dark Devils in the Saddle': A Discursive Analysis of Tourist and Entertainment Formations Constituting Western Canadian Regional Identity" (PhD diss., Concordia University, 1992), 92–93.

49 Baillargeon and Tepper, *Legends in Our Times*, 165–79. The authors suggest that horse racing and betting was popular in the late 1800s in western Canada.

50 Ibid., 180, and Iverson, *Rider of the West*, 28–33.

51 Mellis, Riding Buffaloes and Broncos, 41.

52 Many Fingers interview.

53 Ibid. Jan Penrose explains that racial discrimination, and the desire to continue to provide a distinct "authentic Indian" presence at the Calgary Stampede, were the two primary reasons for unfair judging. He claims that Tom Three Persons advised others to participate only in timed events because "the clock could not be racist." See Jan Penrose, "When All the Cowboys Are Indians: The Nature of Race in All-

Indian Rodeo," *Annals of the Association of American Geographers* 93, no. 3 (2003): 687–705.

54 Iverson, *Rider of the West*, 33, 71. Dyck's discussion of dance competitions in powwow can be easily aligned to rodeo competition; see *The Celebration of Society*, 166, 170. Mellis focuses on the political importance of rodeo for the Crow and Lakota people in South Dakota in "Rodeo and Renewed Cultural Life during the New Deal," chapter three of *Riding Buffaloes and Broncos*, 81–120.

55 Erna Gingold, personal interview with the author, Sarcee Reserve, Alberta, 20 October 2003. Erna, his second wife, claimed that Eddie never missed an opportunity to perform, and described the trip to Sydney as the "time of his life". This information about the men's political careers was found on the Glenbow Museum archival website; see <www.glenbow.org>.

56 Although I use the term "First Nations rodeo or cowboys" in most of my references, "Indian cowboy" is the term that these family members used.

57 Many Fingers interview.

58 Crowfoot interview.

59 In his comments, Cecil Crowfoot explained that members of the Stampede Board went to the reserves to pick the men that they wanted to go, yet there is also proof in the RG10 files that the Indian agents involved were responsible for picking the men that went to Sydney. See letter, J.E. Pugh to C. Pant Schmidt, 2 November 1938, as well as letter, G.H. Gooderham to Schmidt, 3 November 1938, RG10, vol. 4010, file 253,430, NAC.

60 Corporal S.J. Leach, *RCMP Report, January 1939–April 1939* (copy supplied by Peggy Maxwell, July 2003), entry for 22 February 1939.

61 Both Cecil Crowfoot and Floyd Many Fingers used this phrase to describe how their father and brother felt about the trip.

62 Crowfoot interview.

63 "Eight Indian Riders, Ropers from Alberta Reservations Perform at Sydney Show," *Calgary Daily Herald*, 18 December 1938.

64 "Indians from Alberta's Reserves to Sell Relics at Australia Exhibition," *Calgary Daily Herald*, 19 January 1939.

65 Leslie Sara, "Display of Indian Craft Travels to Australia: My Open Up Fresh Export Markets," *Calgary Daily Herald*, 11 February 1939.

66 "Indian Cowboys Sail for Sydney" *The Daily Province* (Vancouver), 8 March 1939.

67 Crowfoot interview.

68 Ibid.

69 Ibid.

70 Ibid.

71 This was part of the contract. See letter, Schmidt to MacInnes, 2 September 1938, RG10, vol. 4010, file 253,430, NAC.

72 Leach, *RCMP Report*, 11 March 1939.

73 Leach, "Redskins and Redcoat Visit the Antipodes," 60.

74 Leach, *RCMP Report*, 2 April 1939.

75 Many Fingers interview.

76 Ibid.

77 Ibid.
78 Crowfoot interview.
79 Ibid.
80 Deanna Crowfoot, conversation with the author, 23 October 2003, Strathmore, AB.
81 Crowfoot interview.
82 Many Fingers interview.
83 John J. MacAloon, "Olympic Games and the Theory of Spectacle in Modern Societies," in *Rite, Drama, Festival and Space: Rehearsals Toward a Theory of Cultural Performance*, ed. John J. MacAloon (Philadelphia: Institute for the Study of Human Issues, 1984).
84 Letter, C. Pant Schmidt to A.W. Skidmore, 13 February 1939," Correspondence relating to an exhibition in Australia, including lists of handicrafts for display and sale and information about the Indians who accompanied the display, 1938–1939," Blackfoot Indian Agency (BIA) files, M. 1783, Glenbow Foundation Archives (GFA), Calgary.
85 Names of races taken from 1939 scorecards supplied by RAS Archives, Sydney, Australia.
86 Leach, *RCMP Report*, 31 March 1939. In Schmidt's letter he also explained the character of "our boys" and "Indians" in general. He described them as "slow," "difficult," "sulky" and "improvident." See Schmidt to Skidmore, 13 February 1939, BIA file, GFA.
87 Names of races taken from 1939 RAS scorecards.
88 Many Fingers interview.
89 Ibid.
90 Ibid.
91 Leach, *RCMP Report*, 1 April 1939.
92 Ibid., 4 April 1939.
93 Burgess, "Dark Devils in the Saddle," 89–94.
94 Leerom Medovoi, "Reading the Blackboard: Youth, Masculinity, and Racial Cross-Identification," in *Race and the Subject of Masculinities*, ed. Harry Stecopoulos and Michael Uebel (Durham, NC: Duke University Press, 1997), 138–68.
95 Although currently indigenous groups are using this platform politically in a global context to acquire equal rights, I would argue that the comments and actions of the men involved in this story similarly attempted to alter hegemonic attitudes by resisting them through ideas concerning citizenship, which are linked to pride, agency, and respect. For a more thorough discussion of "cultural citizenship" see Renato Rosaldo, "Social Justice and the Crisis of National Communities," in *Colonial Discourse, Postcolonial Theory*, ed. F. Barker, P. Hulme, and M. Iversen (Manchester, UK: Manchester University Press, 1994), 239–52, and Bryan S. Turner, "Outline of a General Theory of Cultural Citizenship," in *Culture and Citizenship*, ed. Nick Stevenson (London, UK: Sage, 2001).
96 The cowgirls were hired mainly as an attraction and competed separately in their own events. Alice Greenough, Tad Lucas, Ivadel Jacobs, Trixie McCormack, Doris Hayes, Alice Van, and Gene Creed were among those who went to Sydney in 1939. They were all famous American cowgirls. For details about their life see

Marylou LeCompte, *Cowgirls of the Rodeo: Pioneer Professional Athletes* (Chicago, IL: University of Illinois Press, 1993). The white cowboys who competed in Sydney were from both Canada and the United States. Westermeier, *Man, Beast, Dust*, 332, includes a full list of the thirty-two white cowboys and cowgirls who travelled to Australia. Research pertaining to these other performers was not undertaken for this book; however, there are a variety of sources describing the careers of these men. Some examples are Theodore Barris, *Rodeo Cowboys: The Last Heroes* (Edmonton, AB: Executive Sport Publications, 1981); Eamer Claire and Thirza Jones, *The Canadian Rodeo Book* (Saskatoon, SK: Western Producer Prairie Books, 1982); Art Belanger, *Chuckwagon Racing: Calgary Stampede's Half Mile of Hell* (Surrey, BC: Frontier Books, 1983); Kristine Frederiksson, *American Rodeo: From Buffalo Bill to Big Business* (College Station, TX: Texas A&M Press, 1985); Wayne S. Wooden, *Rodeo in America: Wranglers, Roughstock and Paydirt* (Lawrence, KS: University Press of Kansas, 1996); and David A. Poulsen, *Wild Ride!: Three Journeys Down the Rodeo Road* (Toronto, ON: Balmur, 2000). As well, Harald Gunderson wrote a biography of one of the cowboys from Canada titled, *The Linder Legend: The Story of Pro Rodeo and its Champion* (Calgary, AB: Sagebrush, 1996).

97 Many Fingers interview.
98 Crowfoot interview.
99 Ibid. Here he was referring to audiences enjoying seeing RCMP officers in full uniform.
100 Geraldine Many Fingers, conversation with the author, 21 October 2003, Cardston, AB.
101 Many Fingers interview.
102 Ibid.
103 Leach, "Redskins and Redcoat Visit the Antipodes," 58.
104 Ibid., 62.
105 Ibid., 61.
106 Ibid., 60–61.
107 "War Dance on Liner," *Sydney Morning Herald*, 13 March 1939.
108 Elizabeth Nannelli, (archivist for the RAS), email correspondence with author, 13 July 2003.
109 John J. MacAloon, "Olympic Games and the Theory of Spectacle in Modern Societies," 252, discusses the use of "flags, anthems, emblems and costumes of the[ir] motherlands" in the opening ceremonies of the Olympics, as an important part of the ritualization of identity that takes place at these international events.
110 In opposition to the top-down approach discussed by Anderson and Gellner, more recently scholars have focused on the bottom-up approach to explain how ordinary people express national sentiment. See Peter G. Mewett, "Fragments of a Composite Identity: Aspects of Australian Nationalism in a Sports Setting," *Australian Journal of Anthropology* 10, no. 3 (1999): 357–75, and Renato Rosaldo, "Introduction: The Borders of Belonging," in *Cultural Citizenship in Island Southeast Asia*, ed. Renato Rosaldo (Berkeley, CA: University of California Press, 2003), 7.

111 Since colonization, land rights have become a critical platform in the attainment of First Nations political agency in western Canada. Penrose claims that the focus on all-Indian rodeos in the 1950s marks a particularly determined attempt to challenge the Canadian government's promotion of agricultural activities. Here reserve land becomes a place of "freedom and influence, rather than enforced confinement and subordination." See "When All the Cowboys Are Indians," 699.

112 James H. Frey and D. Stanley Eitzen, "Sport and Society," *Annual Review of Sociology* 17 (1991): 503–21, 511–12.

113 Iverson, *The Plains Indians of the Twentieth Century*, 71.

Chapter 4: Constable Leach at the Royal Easter Show in Sydney

1 Corporal S.J. Leach, "Redskins and Redcoat Visit the Antipodes," *RCMP Quarterly* 7, no. 1 (July 1939): 54–62.

2 "Great Scenes at Show: Fine Pageantry," *Sydney Morning Herald*, 3 April 1939.

3 Peggy Maxwell, personal conversation with the author, Merrickville, ON, 22 August 2003.

4 Victor Leach, telephone interview with the author, 30 August 2003; also mentioned in Sam Leach, *Memoirs of Sam Leach* (Merrickville, ON, 1999).

5 Daniel Francis, *National Dreams: Myth, Memory, and Canadian History* (Vancouver, BC: Arsenal Pulp Press, 1997), 29.

6 Keith Walden, *Visions of Order* (Toronto, ON: Butterworths, 1982), 95–97, 100.

7 In Canadian history books there are multiple references to this quote, apparently made by Chief Crowfoot as part of his speech the day before signing Treaty No. 7, 21 September 1877. It is published either in its entirety or in segments in Richard L. Neuberger, *Royal Canadian Mounted Police* (New York, NY: Random House, 1953), 59; A.L. Haydon, *The Riders of the Plains: A Record of the Royal North-west Mounted Police of Canada, 1873–1910* (Edmonton, AB: Hurtig, 1971), 67; Ronald Atkin, *Maintain the Right: The Early History of the North West Mounted Police, 1873–1900* (Toronto, ON: Macmillan, 1973), 110; S.W. Horrall (RCMP historian), *The Pictorial History of the Royal Canadian Mounted Police* (Toronto, ON: McGraw-Hill Ryerson, 1973), 68; Molly Anne MacDonald, *The Royal Canadian Mounted Police* (Toronto, ON: Macmillan, 1973), 5; Bruce D. Sealey, *The Mounties and Law Enforcement* (Agincourt, ON: The Book Society of Canada, 1979), 21.

8 Horrall, *The Pictorial History of the Royal Canadian Mounted Police*, 68.

9 For a description of how literary constructions of this relationship created the popular myth see Keith Walden, "The Great March of the Mounted Police in Popular Literature, 1873–1973," Canadian Historical Association Historical Papers: A Selection of the Papers Presented at the Annual Meeting Held at Montreal, 1980, 33–54.

10 R.C. Macleod, "Canadianizing the West: The North-West Mounted Police as Agents of the National Policy, 1873–1905" in *Essays on Western History*, ed. Lewis H.

Thomas (Edmonton, AB: University of Alberta Press, 1976), 103–104.
11 Letter, Teddy Yellowfly to Commissioner Woods, RCMP, Ottawa, 21 November 1938, RG10. vol. 4010, reel C-10171, file 253,430, NAC.
12 Ibid.
13 Leach, "Redskins and Redcoat Visit the Antipodes," 54.
14 Ibid., 55.
15 Ibid., 56.
16 Ibid.
17 Ibid.
18 Corporal S.J. Leach, *RCMP Report, January* 1939 – *April* 1939 (supplied by Peggy Maxwell, July 2003), entry for 22 February 1939.
19 Leach, "Redskins and Redcoat Visit the Antipodes," 57.
20 Leach, *RCMP Report*, 7 March 1939.
21 Leach, "Redskins and Redcoat Visit the Antipodes," 58.
22 Saloni Mathur, "Living Ethnographic Exhibits: The Case of 1886," *Cultural Anthropology* 15, no. 4 (2001): 492–524.
23 Ibid., 509.
24 Leach, "Redskins and Redcoat Visit the Antipodes," 61. These incidents are outlined in detail in Chapter Three as acts of resistance, not misdemeanours.
25 Homi Bhabha, *The Location of Culture* (London, UK & New York, NY: Routledge, 1994), 77.
26 James Clifford, "Of Other Peoples: Beyond the "Salvage Paradigm," in *Discussions in Contemporary Culture No. 1*, ed. Hal Foster, (Seattle, WA: Bay Press, 1987), 121, and Andrew Nurse, "But Now Things have Changed: Marius Barbeau and the Politics of Amerindian Identity," *Ethnohistory* 48, no. 3 (2001): 433–72, accessed from <http://muse.jhu.edu/journals/ethnohistory/v048/48.3.nurse.html>, p. 7 of 26, p. 10 of 26.
27 For a good overview of the basic tenets of primitivism discourse see Marianna Torgovnik, *Gone Primitive: Savage Intellects, Modern Lives* (Chicago, IL: University of Chicago Press, 1990).
28 For a discussion of attitudes expressed by missionaries, anthropologists, and government officials on this topic see C.T. Loram and T.F. McIlwraith (eds.), *The North American Indian Today* (Toronto, ON: University of Toronto Press, 1943).
29 For examples of this view see Diamond Jenness, "Canada's Debt to the Indian," *Canadian Geographical Journal* 18, no. 5 (May 1939), and *The Indians Speak to Canada* (radio show), aired on the Canadian Broadcasting Corporation (CBC) between October and December of 1937. This show was arranged in collaboration with the Indian Affairs Branch and included commentaries from seven educated First Nations leaders from across Canada. Their primary focus was the fact that First Nations people were not dying out, but thriving. They claimed that continued help from the Canadian government was needed for further successful transitions. Interestingly, the closing speaker, who was the minister of the Department of Mines and Resources (in 1936 this department took over the Department of Indian Affairs), glorified the government's existing help and stated that what was currently needed was public support and sympathy for the plight of Indians across

Canada, who were in the process of assimilating. For amateur anthropological tales see Philip H. Godsell, *The Vanishing Frontier: Saga of Traders, Mounties and Men of the Last North West* (London, UK: Robert Hale, 1939), and Philip H. Godsell, *Red Hunters of the Snow: An Account of Thirty Years Experience with the Primitive Indian and Eskimo Tribes of the Canadian North-west and Arctic Coast, with a Brief History of the Early Contact Between White Fur traders and the Aborigines* (London, UK: Robert Hale, 1938).

30 Leach, *RCMP Report*, 31 February 1939.
31 Ibid., 31 February 1939.
32 Ibid., 8 February 1939.
33 Ibid., 14 February 1939.
34 Leach, "Redskins and Redcoat Visit the Antipodes," 54.
35 Leach, personal letter in the possession of Peggy Maxwell, 1939.
36 Leach, *RCMP Report*, 9 March 1939.
37 Ibid., 2 April 1939.
38 Leach, "Redskins and Redcoat Visit the Antipodes," 61.
39 Ibid., 57.
40 Ibid., 60.
41 Lucien M. Hanks and Jane Richardson Hanks, *Tribe Under Trust: A Study of the Blackfoot Reserve of Alberta* (Toronto, ON: University of Toronto Press, 1950) 147–48.
42 Ibid., 147.
43 Ibid., 148.
44 Ibid., 147. In 1939, Hanks and Hanks explained that white, Anglo-Saxon people predominantly populated Alberta. White towns and villages surrounded all of the reserves, and the First Nations people were reliant on them for commodities and services.
45 "Paternalism," *Wikipedia, the free encyclopedia*, <http://en.wikipedia.org/wiki/Paternalism> (accessed 10 January 2004). Also see "Paternalism," *Oxford English Dictionary*, 2nd ed., <http://dictionary.oed.com> (accessed 1 May 2004).
46 Honourable Jane Stewart, Notes for an Address on the Occasion of the Unveiling of Gathering Strength – Canada's Aboriginal Action Plan, Minister of Indian Affairs and Northern Development, 7 January 1998, Ottawa, Ontario, <http://sisis.nativeweb. org/clark/jan0798can.html> (accessed 10 March 2003).
47 Letter, C. Pant Schmidt to A.W. Skidmore, 13 February 1939, Blackfoot Indian Agency (BIA) fonds, #M 1783, Glenbow Archives (GA).
48 The trip lasted eighty days and Leach only reported eight incidents where he felt the men had committed an offence.
49 Leach, *RCMP Report*, 6 March 1939.
50 These phrases were sprinkled throughout both Leach's *RCMP Report* and the article in the *RCMP Quarterly*.
51 Leach, *RCMP Report*, 20 Feb 1939. Leach mentioned that he and Joe Crowfoot had tea with the captain on 6 March 1939.
52 Ibid., 16 March 1939.
53 Ibid., 23 March 1939.

54 Ibid., 24 March 1939.
55 Ibid., 24 March 1939.
56 Ibid., 6 April 1939.
57 Ibid., 28 March 1939.
58 Ibid., 29 March 1939.
59 Ibid., 6 April 1939.
60 Ibid., 7–8 April 1939.
61 Ibid., 12 April 1939.
62 Ibid., 5 May 1939.
63 Leach, "Redskins and Redcoat Visit the Antipodes," 62.
64 Barry Cooper and Royce Koop. "Policing Alberta: An Analysis of the Alternatives to the Federal Provision of Policing Services." In *Public Policy Sources*, No. 72, Vancouver, BC: The Fraser Institute (Nov. 2003): 1–20, pp. 3–5. As seen on <http://www.fraser institute.ca/admin/books/files/AB-Police.pdf> (accessed 10 November 2005).
65 Joy Leland, *Firewater Myths: North American Indian Drinking and Alcohol Addiction* (New Brunswick, NJ: Publications Division, Rutgers Centre of Alcohol Studies, 1976).
66 Robert Campbell, *Sit Down and Drink Your Beer: Regulating Vancouver's Beer Parlours, 1925–1954* (Toronto, ON: University of Toronto Press, 2001), 95, 104.
67 Neuberger, *Royal Canadian Mounted Police*, 59; Haydon, *The Riders of the Plains*, 67; Atkin, *Maintain the Right*, 110; Horrall, *The Pictorial History of the Royal Canadian Mounted Police*, 68; MacDonald, *The Royal Canadian Mounted Police*, 5, and Sealey, *The Mounties and Law Enforcement*, 21.
68 Leach, *RCMP Report*, 26 March 1939.
69 Ibid., 24 March 1939.
70 Ibid., 29 March 1939.
71 Ibid., 2 April 1939.
72 Ibid., 3 April 1939.
73 Ibid., 26 March 1939.
74 Ibid., 7 April 1939.
75 Leach, "Redskins and Redcoat Visit the Antipodes," 55.
76 Ibid., 56; also in the *RCMP Report*, 2 March 1939 and 2 May 1939.
77 Leach, *RCMP Report*, 4 March 1939 and Leach, "Redskins and Redcoat Visit the Antipodes," 56.
78 Leach, *RCMP Report*, 26 April 1939 and Leach, "Redskins and Redcoat Visit the Antipodes," 62.
79 Leach, "Redskins and Redcoat Visit the Antipodes," 62.
80 Julia Harrison explains that although tourists are "generally aware of the limitations of their cross-cultural engagements," they view them as genuine. One of her informants describes how notions of others can be dramatically altered from revulsion to trust during brief visits to foreign countries. See *Being a Tourist: Finding Meaning in Pleasure Travel* (Vancouver, BC: UBC Press, 2003), 88–90.
81 Leach, "Redskins and Redcoat Visit the Antipodes," 62.
82 Ibid.

Chapter 5: The Australian Audience's Reaction to their Canadian Visitors

1. "Show Indians Too Far From Home," *Daily Telegraph* (Sydney), 3 April 1939, 14.
2. Corporal S.J. Leach, *RCMP Report, January 1939 – April 1939* (supplied by Peggy Maxwell, July 2003), entry for 11 March 1939.
3. Gillian Poulter, "Becoming Native in a Foreign Land: Visual Culture, Sport and Spectacle in the Construction of National Identity in Montreal, 1840–1885" (PhD thesis, York University, 1999), 11.
4. Here I argue against Teun A. Van Dijk, who explicitly states that the "hypothesis that the Press writes 'what people think' may safely be rejected." *Racism and the Press* (London, UK & New York, NY: Routledge, 1991), 251–52.
5. Throughout this chapter I use the words "ordinary" and "average" to describe the way that Australian journalists viewed Canada's First Nations cowboys. These terms are problematic and are not intended to suggest actual social categories. They are used to indicate categories of identification (including religious affiliation and marital status) that white, middle class Australians would consider "average" and "ordinary."
6. See Gregory Jay, "'White Man's Book No Good': D.W. Griffith and the American Indian," *Cinema Journal* 39, no. 4 (2000): 3–26.
7. See Robert F. Berkhofer, "White Conceptions of Indians," in *The Handbook of North American Indians IV*, ed. Wilcomb Washburn (Washington, DC: Smithsonian Institute Press, 1988), 522–547; Rayna Green, "The Indian in Popular American Culture," in *The Handbook of North American Indians IV*, 587–606; Karl Markus Kreis, "'Indians' on Old Picture Postcards," *Native American Studies* 6, no. 1 (1992): 39–48 and John Ewers, "Emergence of the Plains Indians as the Symbol of North American Indians" *The Smithsonian Report* (1984): 531–44.
8. Ters Ellingson, *The Myth of the Noble Savage* (Los Angeles, CA: University of California Press, 2001), xv–xvii, 26–34.
9. Berkhofer, "White Conceptions of Indians," 27–28.
10. Hoxie Fairchild, *The Noble Savage: A Study in Romantic Naturalism* (New York, NY: Russell & Russell, 1961), 2.
11. Works discussing "noble savage" ideology in respect to visual representations during this time include Marcia Crosby, "Construction of the Imaginary Indian," in *Vancouver Anthology: The Institutional Politics of Art*, ed. Stan Douglas (Vancouver, BC: Talonbooks, 1991); Robert Linsley, "Painting and the Social History of British Columbia" in *Vancouver Anthology*; Daniel Francis, *The Imaginary Indian: The Image of the Indian in Canadian Culture* (Vancouver, BC: Arsenal Pulp Press, 1992); Marilyn Burgess, "'Dark Devils in the Saddle': A Discursive Analysis of Tourist and Entertainment Formations Constituting Western Canadian Regional Identity" (PhD diss., Concordia University, 1992), and Gerta Moray, "Wilderness, Modernity and Aboriginality in the Paintings of Emily Carr," *Journal of Canadian Studies* 33, no. 2 (Summer 1998): 43–65.
12. Francis, *The Imaginary Indian*, 105–107.

13 Quote from Carr seen in Francis, *The Imaginary Indian*, 46. For a discussion of this emphasis in Carr's work see Crosby, "Construction of the Imaginary Indian," 267–91; Linsley, "Painting and the Social History of British Columbia," 225–45; Moray, "Wilderness, Modernity and Aboriginality in the Paintings of Emily Carr," 43–65. Philip Deloria also discusses "dying race" theory or the "salvage paradigm" in reference to the United States in *Playing Indian* (London, UK & New Haven, CT: Yale University Press, 1998).

14 Emily Carr's work actually did not become popular until the late 1920s and 1930s when she was "discovered" by Lawren Harris. Comments he made about her work can be seen in Lawren Harris, "Emily Carr and her Work," *Canadian Forum* 21 (December 1941): 277–78. For discussions concerning the importance of the work of the Group of Seven in creating a unique Canadian style of painting see Joan Murray, *Northern Lights: Masterpieces of Tom Thomson and the Group of Seven* (Toronto, ON: Key Porter, 1994); Linda Morra, "Re-viewing the Cultural Landscape: Representations of Land in Ralph Connor, Tom Thompson, the Group of Seven, and Emily Carr" (PhD diss., University of Ottawa, 2002) and David P. Silcox, *The Group of Seven and Tom Thomson: Tom Thomson, Lawren Harris, J.E.H. MacDonald ... [et al.]* (Toronto, ON: Firefly, 2003). For discussion which critiques the work of the Group of Seven see Robert Maxwell Gill, "Pedagogies of Nation: Terra Nullius, the Group of Seven and the Experience of Art," (PhD diss., York University, 2001), and Leslie Allen Dawn, "How Canada Stole the Idea of Native Art: The Group of Seven and images of the Indian in the 1920s," (PhD diss., University of British Columbia, 2002).

15 For a detailed account of the implications of Emily Carr's work in the creation of imperial nostalgia, see Bruce Braun, "Colonialism's Afterlife: Vision and Visuality on the Northwest Coast," *Cultural Geographies* 2 (2002): 202–47. For references that connect Canada to wilderness ethos, see Carl Berger, "The True North Strong and Free," in *Nationalism in Canada*, ed. Peter Russell (Toronto, ON: McGraw-Hill Canada, 1966), 3–26; S.D. Grant, "Myths of the North in the Canadian Ethos," *The Northern Review* (1989): 15–41; Roderick Nash, *Wilderness and the American Mind* (New Haven, CT: Yale University Press, 1974).

16 This emphasis on differential treatment is in no way meant to detract from the atrocities of assimilation policies in Canada or to suggest that the "dying race" theory was not alive and well in North America.

17 D.J. Mulvaney, "The Darwinian Perspective," in *Seeing the First Australians*, ed. I. Donaldson and T. Donaldson (North Sydney, NSW: Allen & Unwin, 1985), 69. Elizabeth Edwards focuses on the photographic work of Huxley in Elizabeth Edwards, "Representation and Reality: Science and the Visual Image," in *Australia in Oxford*, ed. Howard Morphy and Elizabeth Edwards (Hartford, UK: Stephen Austin and Sons, 1988), 27–45 and in "The Image as Anthropological Document, Photographic Types: The Pursuit of Method," *Visual Anthropology* 3 (1990): 235–58.

18 Richard Broome, *Aboriginal Australians: Black Responses to White Dominance, 1788–1994*, 2nd ed. (Sydney, NSW: Allen & Unwin, 1994), 160.

19 Anne Maxwell, *Colonial Photography and Exhibitions: Representations of the "Native" and the Making of European Identities* (London, UK & New York, NY: Leicester University Press, 1999), 156.
20 For a discussion of O.V. Neville's policies in the 1930s see Mark Francis, "Social Darwinism and the Construction of Institutionalized Racism in Australia," *Journal of Australian Studies* 50/51 (1996): 90–105.
21 Broome, *Aboriginal Australians*, 160.
22 Edwards, "The Image as Anthropological Document," 28–29.
23 Broome, *Aboriginal Australians*, 91.
24 Margaret Maynard, "Projections of Melancholy," in *Seeing the First Australians*, 93–95.
25 Kreis, Markus Karl. "'Indians' on Old Picture Postcards," *Native American Studies* 6, no. 1, (1992): 39–48, p. 44.
26 Edwards, "The Image as Anthropological Document," 36–37. One of few amateur photographers to elevate the view of Aboriginal people in Australia, Thomas Dick was motivated strictly by the "Salvage Paradigm." The Aboriginal people in his photographs were often posed to look like noble savages, yet his work never became publicly popular or even publicly seen until after his death in 1927. For a comprehensive discussion of Dick's work see Isabel McBride, "Thomas Dick's Photographic Vision," in *Seeing the First Australians*, 137–63.
27 Ian Mclean, "Aboriginalism: White Aborigines and Australian Nationalism," *Australian Humanities Review*, <http://www.lib.latrobe.edu.au/AHR/archive/Issue-May-1998/mclean.html> (accessed 20 January 2004), 4.
28 This theory is gleaned from Myers' discussion of the political and economic influences that turned Australian Aboriginal acrylic painting into a national object. See Fred Myers, *Painting Culture: The Making of an Aboriginal High Art* (London, UK: Duke University Press, 2002), 201–202.
29 Andrew Lattas, "Nationalism, Aesthetic Redemption and Aboriginality," *The Australian Journal of Anthropology* 2, no. 3 (1991): 307–24. Lattas emphasizes the spiritualization of Aboriginal people through their art and the way that mythic truths and spirituality focused on the land are used by white Australians to recapture a new sense of nationalism based on healing the evils of modern industrialization and colonialism.
30 Andrew Lattas has written several articles on this topic. A good starting point is "Aborigines and Contemporary Australian Nationalism," *Social Analysis* 27, no. 3 (1990): 50–69. Also see Jeremy Beckett, "Aboriginality, Citizenship and Nation State," *Social Analysis* 25, no. 24 (1988): 3–18.
31 This was the phrase used in many Australian newspapers. It is still common today.
32 "Descendants of the Nomads of the Western Plains are Becoming Ambassadors of Commerce," *Calgary Herald*, 19 December 1938. For a similar description see "Indians From Alberta's Reserves to Sell Relics at Australia Exhibition," *Calgary Herald*, 19 January 1939.
33 For an example see "Indian Cowboys Sail for Sydney," *The Daily Province* (Vancouver) 8 March 1939.

34 Daily Telegraph Staff Reporter, "Meaty Man are these Braves of the Prairie.... 'Whoo'!" *Daily Telegraph Home Magazine* (Sydney), 3 April 1939, 2.
35 Ibid.
36 Ibid.
37 Ibid.
38 Ibid.
39 Ian Radforth explains how this contradiction plays itself out in colonial rhetoric. He describes the typical nineteenth-century press representation of First Nations people in Canadian newspapers as a combination of "fascination and revulsion" and consequently reflective of "Victorian perceptions of race and racial hierarchies." He claims there was a focus on visual appearance, traditional weaponry and costume as well as a general vacillation between aspects of savagery and "noble savagery." The European press followed suit in its depictions of travelling Buffalo Bill's Wild West shows in the late nineteenth century. The emphasis here was varied, but also hinged on the dualistic nature of "Indians" as noble warriors and conversely as beast-like people. Appearance was also important, as was the fact that they were a dying race, primitive, beautiful, and colourful. See "Performance, Politics and Representation: Aboriginal People and the 1860 Royal Tour of Canada," *Canadian Historical Review* 84, no. 1 (2003): 22–23.
40 Kreis, "'Indians' on Old Picture Postcards," 43.
41 Van Dijk, 250.
42 Van Dijk, 246.
43 For a discussion about the validity of feelings of connectedness that occur while travelling see Alma Gottlieb, "American Vacations," *Annals of Tourism Research* 9 (1982): 325–42.
44 I would like to make it clear that I am not trying to erase the incidents of racist attacks that took place in press reports, but simply explain another emphasis that was also present in reports at this time.
45 "Wild West as Woolloomooloo: Eddie One-Spot Visits Day Nursery," *Sydney Morning Herald Women's Supplement*, 3 April 1939.
46 Ibid.
47 Ibid.
48 Ibid.
49 Ibid.
50 Ibid.
51 "Indians Pack Good Punch," *Daily Telegraph* (Sydney), 13 March 1939.
52 "War Dance on Liner," *Sydney Morning Herald*, 13 March 1939.
53 "They are Wards of Canadian Government: Without a Whoop, 'Injuns are here'," *The Auckland Star*, 6 March 1939.
54 "War Dance on Liner."
55 "Alberta Indians and Cowboys Return from Australia," *The Calgary Herald*, 8 May 1939.
56 This is specifically reiterated in the second article, "Australia Hospitable, Says Alberta Indians," *Albertan* (Edmonton), 8 May 1939. Here the author begins by

stating, "Alberta looked pretty good to eight Indians, three cowboys and a Royal Canadian Mounted Police constable, because most of them were a little tired of shaking hands and signing autograph books in hospitable Australia."
57 "Show Indians Too Far From Home," *Daily Telegraph* (Sydney), 3 April 1939, 14.
58 This phrase was used repeatedly and can be seen in the caption of the photo taken while they were walking up the steps of City Hall, *Sydney Morning Herald*, 13 March 1939.
59 For listed names, see "They are Wards of Canadian Government: Without a Whoop, 'Injuns are here'," *The Auckland Star*, 6 March 1939; "Redskins and 'Mountie' For the Show," *The Sun* (Sydney), 11 March 1939; "Indians Pack Good Punch."
60 "Exhibitions Pour in For Women's Industrial Section," *Country Life and Stock and Station* (Sydney), 17 March 1939; and "War Dance on Liner."
61 "Redskins and 'Mountie' For the Show."
62 Andrew Lattas, "Primitivism, Nationalism and Individualism in Australian Popular Culture," in *Power, Knowledge and Aborigines*, ed. Bain Attwood and John Arnold (Melbourne, VIC: La Trobe University Press, 1992), 47.
63 "Great Scenes at Show: Fine Pageantry," *Sydney Morning Herald*, 6 April 1939, 13.
64 "Redskins and 'Mountie' for the Show."
65 "Exhibitions Pour in For Women's Industrial Section."
66 "Canadian 'Mountie's' Wife Among Niagara Arrivals," *Sunday Sun* (Sydney), 12 March 1939.
67 Ibid.
68 Van Dijk, *Racism and the Press*, 246.
69 Ibid., 251–54.
70 Letter, A.W. Skidmore to C.P. Schmidt, 16 March 1939, BIA files, # M 1783, GFA.
71 Ibid.
72 Ibid.
73 Ibid.
74 Ibid., 30 March 1939.
75 Russell McGregor, "Protest and Progress: Aboriginal Activism in the 1930's," *Australian Historical Studies* 101 (1993): 555–68, 560–61. For a detailed description of the actual events surrounding the "Day of Mourning" see Gavin Souter, "Skeleton at the Feast," in *Australians: 1938*, eds. Bill Gammage and Peter Spearritt (Sydney, 1987), 13–26; and Jack Horner and Marica Langton, "The Day of Mourning," in *Australians: 1938*, 29–35.

Conclusion

1 Andrew Lattas, *Cultures of Secrecy: Reinventing Race in Bush Kaliai Cargo Cults* (Madison, WI: University of Wisconsin Press, 1998), 149.
2 This was the first North American royal tour. The British party was to arrive in Calgary on 26 May 1939. Confirmed in circulated letter, H.W. McGill, Ottawa,

7 February 1939, Blackfoot Indian Agency (BIA) files, # M 1782, Glenbow Foundation Archives (GFA).
3 Ibid., cable from C.P. Schmidt to the Secretary of the Indian Affairs Branch, 1 February 1939.
4 Ibid., letter from S.H. Middleton to C.P. Schmidt, 11 February 1939.
5 Ibid., letter from G.H. Gooderham to C.P. Schmidt, 9 May 1939. He stated that he expected two thousand Indians to come, but that the department was only going to provide a subsidy to those who were invited.
6 Ibid., list of signatures of those who were paid, 23 May 1939.
7 Ibid., committee report, W.G.B. Dailley, 17 May 1939.
8 Ibid., letter from C.P. Schmidt to H.W. McGill, 10 February 1939.
9 For a map of all the stops and dates see R.B. Fleming, *The Royal Tour of Canada: The 1939 Visit of King George VI and Queen Elizabeth* (Toronto, ON: Lynx Images, 2002), 34. There were twelve stops between Saskatchewan and British Columbia.
10 Richard Foot, "Royal Tour of Canada 1939: 'It made us, the King and I'." <http://www.canada.com/national/features/queenmother/story.html> (accessed 30 May 2004).
11 There has yet to be a study that interviews First Nations elders in Alberta to get their impressions of the royal tour of 1939. Several texts document the tour and offer discussions of white Canadian's responses. For examples see Gustave Lanctaot, *The Royal Tour of King George and Queen Elizabeth in Canada and the United States of America, 1939* (Toronto, ON: E.O. Taylor Foundation [c 1964]); Arthur Bousfield, *Royal Spring: The Royal Tour of 1939 and the Queen Mother in Canada* (Toronto, ON: Dundurn Press, 1989); Tom MacDonnell, *Daylight Upon Magic: The Royal Tour of Canada, 1939* (Toronto, ON: Macmillan of Canada, 1989); and Fleming, *The Royal Tour of Canada*. MacDonnell actually altered Schmidt's quote and did not include his reference to the trip to Sydney in order to emphasize that the royal tour of 1939 would be the "highlight in the lives" of "the Indians." MacDonnell, *Daylight Upon Magic*, 130.
12 Anja Nygren, "Struggles over Meanings: Reconstruction of Indigenous Mythology, Cultural Identity, and Social Representation," *Ethnohistory* 45, no. 1 (Winter, 1998): 31–63.
13 Ibid.

Bibliography

Primary Sources

Archival Sources
Glenbow Archives, Calgary, Alberta
Blackfoot Indian Agency series, 1938–39.

National Archives of Canada, Ottawa, Ontario
Indian Affairs, Record Group 10, Volume 7557, File: 1120-1, Correspondence Regarding Indian Participation at the Calgary Exhibition, 1933–1947.
———. Volume 7558, File: 1167-1, Correspondence Regarding Indian Participation at the Pacific National Exhibition in Vancouver, 1928–1938.
———. Volume 4010, File: 253430, General Correspondence Regarding Indians Travelling to Various Exhibitions Around the World (New York, Paris and Sydney, Australia), 1904–1939.

Published Primary Sources
Alexander, Joseph A., ed. *Who's Who in Australia, 1944*. Melbourne, VIC: The Herald and Weekly Times, 1944.
Godsell, Phillip H. "The Vanishing Stoney Indians." *Canadian Geographical Journal* (Oct. 1934): 179–88.
———. *Red Hunters of the Snow: An Account of Thirty Years Experience with the Primitive Indian and Eskimo Tribes of the Canadian North-west and Arctic Coast, with a Brief History of the Early Contact Between White Fur Traders and the Aborigines*. London, UK: Robert Hale, 1938.
———. *The Vanishing Frontier: Saga of Traders, Mounties and Men of the Last North West*. London, UK: Robert Hale, 1939.
Hanks, Lucien M., and Jane Richardson Hanks. *Tribe Under Trust: A Study of the Blackfoot Reserve of Alberta*. Toronto, ON: University of Toronto Press, 1950.
Jenness, Diamond. "Canada's Debt to the Indian." *Canadian Geographical Journal* 18, no. 5 (1939): 269–76.
Leach, Corporal S.J. "Redskins and Redcoat Visit the Antipodes." *RCMP Quarterly* 7, no. 1 (1939): 52–60.
Lighthall, Alice. "Indian Work." *Annual Report of the Handicraft Guild*. Montreal: Canadian Handicraft Guild, 1937: 21–23.

———. "Report of the Indian Committee." *Annual Report of the Handicraft Guild.* Montreal, PQ: Canadian Handicraft Guild, 1938: 25–27.

———. "Report of the Exhibition Committee." *Annual Report of the Handicraft Guild.* Montreal, PQ: Canadian Handicraft Guild, 1939: 17–18.

Loram, C.T. and T.F. McIlwraith, eds. *The North American Indian Today.* Toronto, ON: University of Toronto Press, 1943.

Lyons, The Right Honourable J.A. "An Address." *The Empire Club of Canada Speeches*, 1935–1936. Toronto, ON: The Empire Club of Canada, 1936: 1–18. <http://www.empireclubfoundation.com/details.asp?SpeechID=305&FT=yes> (accessed 10 January 2004).

MacFarlane, T.B. "Rodeo Popular in Australia." *Hoofs and Horns*, July 1940.

Page, The Right Honourable Sir Earle. "Australia and the Empire." *The Empire Club of Canada Speeches.* Toronto, ON: The Empire Club of Canada, 1939: 1–18. <http://www.empireclubfoundation.com/details.asp?SpeechID=922&FT=yes> (accessed 8 January 2004).

Parmelee, James G. "Canada on Parade at Glasgow." *Canadian Geographic Journal* 16, no. 6 (1938): 306–12.

———. "Canada's Participation in the World's Fair." *Canadian Geographic Journal* 19, no. 1 (1939): 85–100.

Pease, The Honourable Percy. "Trade Relations Between Australia and Canada." *The Empire Club of Canada Speeches*, 1936–1937. Toronto, ON: The Empire Club of Canada, 1937: 223–37. <http://www.empireclubfoundation.com/details.asp?SpeechID=158&FT=yes> (accessed 10 January 2004).

Raley, G.H. "Canadian Indian Art and Industries." *Journal of the Royal Society of Arts* 81, no. 4320 (6 Sept. 1935).

Royal Agricultural Society of New South Wales. *Rodeo Programme: Royal Easter Show, 1939.* Sydney, NSW: W.T. Baker and Co., 1939.

Royal Agricultural Society of New South Wales. *Souvenir Programme: Royal Easter Show, 1939.* Sydney, NSW: W.T. Baker and Co., 1939.

Van Allen, W.H. "Canada and the Glasgow Exhibition." *Canadian Geographic Journal* 16, no. 3 (1938): 153–54.

Wallace, Stewart W. *A First Book of Canadian History.* Toronto, ON: Macmillan, 1928.

Westermeier, Clifford. *Man, Beast, Dust.* Denver, CO: World Press, 1947.

Yellowfly, Chief Teddy. "The Red Man's Burden." *The Indians Speak to Canada.* A series of broadcasts sponsored by *The Canadian Broadcasting Corporation*, in co-operation with the Indian Affairs Branch, Department of Mines and Resources, Ottawa, 1939.

Yellow Robe, Chauncey. "The Menace of the Wild West Show." *Quarterly Journal of the Society of American Indians* (July–Sept. 1914): 225.

Newspapers
Albertan (Edmonton, Alberta)
Country Life and Stock and Station (Sydney, Australia)
Daily Telegraph Home Magazine (Sydney, Australia)
Sydney Morning Herald
The Auckland Star
The Calgary Herald
The Chicago Daily Press
The Daily Province (Vancouver, BC)
The Detroit Free Press
The Sun (Sydney, Australia)
The Toronto Daily Star
Victoria Daily Times (Victoria, BC)

Photograph Collections Consulted
Glenbow Archives, Calgary, Alberta.
Heritage Centre, Royal Agricultural Society of New South Wales, Sydney, Australia

Personal Interviews
Crowfoot, Cecil. Interview undertaken by Deanna Crowfoot. Edmonton, Alberta. October 2003.
Crowfoot, Deanna. Conversation with the author. Strathmore, Alberta. 23 October 2003.
Gingold, Erna. Conversation with the author. Sarcee Reserve, Alberta. 20 October 2003.
Leach, Victor. Telephone conversation with the author. August 2003.
Many Fingers, Floyd. Personal interview with the author. Cardston, Alberta. 21 October 2003.
Many Fingers, Geraldine. Conversation with the author. Cardston, Alberta. 21 October 2003.
Maxwell, Peggy. Conversation with the author. Merrickville, Ontario. August 2003.
Nannelli, Elizabeth (archivist for the RAS). Correspondence with the author through email. 13 July 2003.

Private Papers
Leach, Corporal S.J. *RCMP Report. January 1939 - April 1939.* Supplied by Peggy Maxwell, July 2003.
Leach, Sam. *Memoirs of Sam Leach.* Merrickville, Ontario, 1998.
Royal Agricultural Society of New South Wales (RAS). Annual promotional brochure, 1938–1939. Foreword written by Samuel Hordern. Supplied by archives of RAS of New South Wales, Sydney, Australia.
Skidmore, A.W. and T.B. MacFarlane. "Report of Messrs. T.B. MacFarlane and A.W. Skidmore on their tour through Canada and America, August – November, 1938," supplied by archives of RAS of New South Wales, Sydney, Australia.

Secondary Sources

Books and Chapters in Books

Allen, Michael. *Rodeo Cowboys in the North American Imagination*. Reno/Las Vegas, NV: University of Nevada Press, 1998.

Anderson, Benedict. *Imagined Communities: Reflections on the Origin and Spread of Nationalism*. London, UK: Verso, 1991.

Atkin, Ronald. *Maintain the Right: The Early History of the North West Mounted Police, 1873–1900*. Toronto, ON: MacMillan, 1973.

Baillargeon, Morgan, and Leslie Tepper. *Legends of Our Times: Native Cowboy Life*. Vancouver, BC: UBC Press, 1998.

Bairner, Alan. *Sport, Nationalism and Globalization: European and North American Perspectives*. Albany, NY: State University of New York Press, 2001.

Barris, Ted. *The Rodeo Cowboys: The Last Heroes*. Edmonton, AB: Executive Sports Publications, 1981.

Beckett, Jeremy. "The Past in the Present: the present in the past: constructing a national Aboriginality." *Past and Present: the Construction of Aboriginality*, ed. Jeremy Beckett. Canberra, NSW: Aboriginal Studies Press, 1988.

Belanger, Art. *Chuckwagon Racing: Calgary Stampede's Half Mile of Hell!* Surrey, BC: Frontier Press, 1983.

Bell, Philip and Roger Bell. *Implicated: The United States in Australia*. Melbourne, VIC: Oxford University Press, 1993.

Benedict, Burton. *The Anthropology of World's Fairs*. London, UK & Berkeley, CA: Lowie Museum of Anthropology and Scholar Press, 1983.

———. "Rituals of Representation: Ethnic Stereotypes and Colonized Peoples at World's Fairs." In *Fair Representations*, ed. Robert Rydell and Nancy Guinn. Amsterdam, NL: Amsterdam University Press, 1994.

Berger, Carl. "The True North Strong and Free." In *Nationalism in Canada*, ed. Peter Russell, 3–26. Toronto, ON: McGraw-Hill of Canada, 1966.

———. *The Sense of Power: Studies in the Ideas of Canadian Imperialism, 1867–1914*. Toronto, ON: University of Toronto Press, 1970.

Berkhofer, Robert F. *The White Man's Indian: Images of the American Indian for Columbus to the Present*. New York, NY: Knopf, 1978.

———. "White Conceptions of Indians." In *The Handbook of North American Indians IV*, ed. Wilcomb Washburn, 522–47. Washington, DC: Smithsonian, 1988.

Bernardi, Daniel. *The Birth of Whiteness: Race and the Emergence of U.S. Cinema*. New Brunswick, NJ: Rutgers University Press, 1996.

Bhabha, Homi. "The Other Question: Difference, Discrimination and the Discourse of Colonialism." In *Literature, Politics and Theory*, ed. Francis Barker, 148–72. New York, NY: Methuen Press, 1986.

———. *Nation and Narration*. London, UK & New York, NY: Routledge, 1990.

———. *The Location of Culture*. London, UK & New York, NY: Routledge, 1994.

Bieder, Robert E. "Marketing the American Indian in Europe: Context, Commodification and Reception." In *Cultural Transmissions and Receptions: American Culture in Europe*, ed. R. Kroes, D. Bosscher and R. Rydell, 5–23. Amsterdam, NL: VU University Press, 1993.

Bousfield, Arthur. *Royal Spring: the Royal Tour of 1939 and the Queen Mother in Canada.* Toronto, ON: Dundurn Press, 1989.

Bracken, Christopher. *The Potlatch Papers: A Colonial Case History.* Chicago, IL: University of Chicago Press, 1997.

Bridger, Bobby. *Buffalo Bill and Sitting Bull: Inventing the West.* Austin, TX: University of Texas Press, 2002.

Broome, Richard. *Aboriginal Australians: Black Responses to White Dominance, 1788–1994* (2nd ed.). Sydney, NSW: Allen & Unwin, 1994.

Calf Robe, Ben, with Adolf and Beverley Hunger Wolf. *Siksika: A Blackfoot Legacy.* Invermere, BC: Good Medicine Books, 1979.

Campbell, Robert. *Sit Down and Drink Your Beer: Regulating Vancouver's Beer Parlours, 1925–1954.* Toronto, ON: University of Toronto Press, 2001.

Carr, Helen. *Inventing the American Primitive: Politics, Gender and the Representations of Native American Literary Traditions, 1789–1936.* New York, NY: New York University Press, 1996.

Carter, Sarah. *Lost Harvests: Prairie Indian Reserve Farmers and Government Policy.* Montreal, PQ & Kingston, ON: McGill-Queen's University Press, 1990.

———. With Simon Evans and Bill Yeo. *Cowboys, Ranchers and the Cattle Business.* Calgary, AB: University of Calgary Press, 1999.

Churchward, L.G. *Australia and America, 1788–1972: An Alternative History.* Sydney, NSW: Alternative Publishing Cooperative, 1979.

Clifford, James. "Of Other Peoples: Beyond the "Salvage Paradigm." In *Discussions in Contemporary Culture* No. 1., ed. Hal Foster, 121–30. Seattle, WA: Bay Press, 1998.

Cronin, Mike and David Mayall. *Sporting Nationalism: Identity, Ethnicity, Immigration and Assimilation.* London, UK & Portland, OR: Frank Cass, 1998.

Crosby, Marcia. "Construction of the Imaginary Indian." In *Vancouver Anthology: The Institutional Politics of Art*, ed. Stan Douglas, 267–91. Vancouver, BC: Talonbooks, 1991.

Deloria, Philip, J. *Playing Indian.* London, UK & New Haven, CT: Yale Historical Publications, 1998.

Deloria Vine, Jr. "The Indian." In *Buffalo Bill and the Wild West*, ed. The Brooklyn Museum, Museum of Art, Carnegie Institute Buffalo Bill Historic Centre, 53–62. Philadelphia, PA: University of Philadelphia Press, 1994.

Dempsey, Hugh A. *Crowfoot: Chief of the Blackfeet.* Edmonton, AB: Hurtig, 1972.

———. *Tom Three Persons: Legend of an Indian Cowboy.* Saskatoon, SK: Purich, 1997.

Denis, Claude. "Indigenous Citizenship and History in Canada: Between Denial and Imposition." In *Contesting Canadian Citizenship: Historical Readings*, ed. Robert Adamoski, Dorthy E. Chunn, and Robert Menzies, 113–28. Peterborough, ON: Broadview, 2002.

Dirks, Nicholas, B. "Ritual and Resistance: Subversion as a Social Fact." In *Culture/Power/History*, ed. Nicholas B. Dirks, Geoff Ely, and Sherry B. Ortner, 483–503. Princeton, NJ: Princeton University Press, 1994.

Dyck, Noel. "Political Powwow: The Rise and Fall of an Urban Native Festival." In *The Celebration of Society: Perspectives on Contemporary Cultural Performance*, ed. Frank E. Manning, 165–85. Bowling Green, OH: Bowling Green University Press, 1983.

———. "What is the Indian Problem." *Tutelage and Resistance in Canadian Indian Administration.* St. John's, NF: Institute of Social and Economic Research, Memorial University, 1991.

Eamer Claire, and Thirza Jones. *The Canadian Rodeo Book.* Saskatoon, SK: Western Producer Prairie Books, 1982.

Edwards, Elizabeth. "Representation and Reality: Science and the Visual Image." In *Australia in Oxford,* ed. Howard Morphy and Elizabeth Edwards, 27–45. Hartford, UK: Stephen Austin and Sons, 1988.

———. *Raw Histories: Photographs, Anthropology and Museums.* New York, NY & London, UK: Berg, 2001.

Ellingson, Ters. *The Myth of the Noble Savage.* Los Angeles, CA: University of California Press, 2001.

Ewers, John. *Emergence of the Plains Indians as the Symbol of North American Indians.* The Smithsonian Report – 1984: 531–44.

Fabian, Johannes. *Time and the Other: How Anthropology Makes its Object.* New York, NY: Columbia University Press, 1983.

Fairchild, Hoxie. *"The Noble Savage": A Study in Romantic Naturalism.* New York, NY: Russell & Russell, 1961.

Feest, Christian. *Indians and Europe: An Interdisciplinary Collection of Essays.* Aachen, FDR: Rader Verlag, 1987.

Fleming, R.B. *The Royal Tour of Canada: The 1939 Visit of King George VI and Queen Elizabeth.* Toronto, ON: Lynx Images, 2002.

Fletcher, Brian H. *The Grand Parade: The History of the Royal Agricultural Society of New South Wales.* Sydney, NSW: The Society, 1988.

Florentino, Daniele. "'Those Red-brick Faces': European Press Reactions to the Indians of Buffalo Bill's Wild West Show." In *Indians and Europe: An Interdisciplinary Collection of Essays,* ed. Christian Feest. Aachen, FDR: Rader Verlag, 1987.

Foremen, Carolyn. *Indians Abroad: 1493–1938.* Norman, OK: University of Oklahoma Press, 1943.

Foster, Hal. *Recodings: Art, Spectacle, Cultural Politics.* Port Townsend, WA: Bay Press, 1985.

Foucault, Michel. *Discipline and Punishment: The Birth of the Prison.* New York, NY: Random House, 1991.

Francis, Daniel. *The Imaginary Indian: The Image of the Indian in Canadian Culture.* Vancouver, BC: Arsenal Pulp Press, 1992.

———. *National Dreams: Myth, Memory, and Canadian History.* Vancouver, BC: Arsenal Pulp Press, 1997.

Frederiksson, Kristine. *American Rodeo: From Buffalo Bill to Big Business.* College Station, TX: Texas A&M Press, 1985.

Friesen, Gerald. *The Canadian Prairies: A History.* Toronto, ON: University of Toronto Press, 1987.

Furniss, Elizabeth. *The Burden of History: Colonialism and the Frontier Myth in a Rural Canadian Community.* Vancouver, BC: UBC Press, 1999.

Gelernter, David. *1939: The Lost World of the Fair.* New York, NY: The Free Press, 1995.

Glassberg, David. *American Historical Pageantry: The Uses of Tradition in the Early Twentieth Century*. Chapel Hill, NC: University of North Carolina Press, 1990.
Goldberg, David. *The Racial State*. Oxford, UK: Blackwell, 2002.
Graham, William. *Treaty Days: Reflections of an Indian Commissioner*. Calgary, AB: Glenbow Museum, 1991.
Green, Rayna. "The Indian in Popular American Culture." In *The Handbook of North American Indians IV*, ed. Wilcomb Washburn, 587–606. Washington, DC: Smithsonian, 1988.
Greenhalgh, Paul. *Ephemeral Vistas: The Exhibition Universelle: Great Exhibitions and World's Fairs*, Manchester, UK: Manchester University Press, 1988.
Gunderson Harald, *The Linder Legend: The Story of Pro Rodeo and Its Champion*. Calgary, AB: Sagebrush, 1996.
Hall, Stuart. "Cultural Identity and Diaspora." In *Identity: Community, Culture, Difference*, ed. J. Rutherford, 222–37. London, UK: Lawrence and Wishart, 1990.
———. "Encoding, Decoding." In *The Cultural Studies Reader*, ed. Simon During, 90–104. New York, NY: Routledge, 1993.
Harrison, Julia. *Being a Tourist: Finding Meaning in Pleasure Travel*. Vancouver, BC: UBC Press, 2003.
Haydon, A.L. *The Riders of the Plains: a record of the Royal North-west Mounted Police of Canada, 1873–1910*. Edmonton, AB: Hurtig, 1971.
Heaman, E.A. *The Inglorious Arts of Peace: Exhibitions in Canadian Society during the 19th Century*. Toronto, ON: University of Toronto Press, 1999.
Hinsley, Curtis M. "The World as Marketplace: Commodification of the Exotic at the World's Columbian Exposition, Chicago, 1893." In *Exhibiting Cultures, the Poetics and Politics of Museum Display*, ed. Ivan Karp and Stephen D. Lavine, 344–65. Washington, DC: Smithsonian, 1991.
Hobsbawm, Eric. *The Invention of Tradition*. Cambridge, UK: Cambridge University Press, 1983.
———. *Nations and Nationalism since 1780: Programme, Myth, Reality*. Cambridge, UK: Cambridge University Press, 1990.
Hoffenberg, Peter. *An Empire on Display: English, Indian and Australian Exhibitions From the Crystal Palace to the Great War*. Berkeley, CA: University of California Press, 2000.
Horner, Jack, and Marica Langton. "The Day of Mourning." In *Australians: 1938*, ed. Bill Gammage and Peter Spearritt, 29–35. Broadway, NSW: Fairfax, Syme & Weldon Associates, 1987.
Horrall, S.W. (RCMP historian). *The Pictorial History of the Royal Canadian Mounted Police*. Toronto, ON: McGraw-Hill Ryerson, 1973.
Huttenback, Robert A. *Racism and Empire: White Settlers and Colored Immigrants in the British Self-Governing Colonies, 1830–1910*. Ithaca, NY: Cornell University Press, 1976.
Iverson, Peter. *The Plains Indians of the Twentieth Century*. Norman, OK: University of Oklahoma Press, 1985.
———. *When Indians Became Cowboys: Native Peoples and Cattle Ranching in the American West*. Norman, OK: University of Oklahoma Press, 1985.

———. *Rider of the West: Portraits of the Indian Rodeo*. Vancouver, BC: Greystone Books, 1999.

Johnston, Darlene. "First Nations and Canadian Citizenship." In *Belonging: The Meaning and Future of Canadian Citizenship*, ed. W. Kaplan. Montreal, PQ & Kingston, ON: McGill-Queen's University Press, 1993.

Kaplan, Anne E. *Looking for the Other: Feminism, Film, and the Imperial Gaze*. New York, NY & London, UK: Routledge, 1993.

Kasson, Joy. *Buffalo Bill's Wild West: Celebrity, Memory, and Popular History*. New York, NY: Hill and Wang, 2000.

Kinchin, Juliet, and Perilla Kinchin. *Glasgow's Great Exhibitions: 1888, 1901, 1911, 1938, 1988*. Wendlebury, UK: White Cockade Press, 1988.

Kirshenblatt-Gimblett, Barbara. "Objects of Ethnography." In *Exhibiting Cultures: The Poetics and Politics of Museum Display*, ed. I. Karp and S. Lavine, 386–444. Washington, DC: Smithsonian, 1991.

Lanctaot, Gustave. *The Royal Tour of King George and Queen Elizabeth in Canada and the United States of America, 1939*. Toronto, ON: E.O. Taylor Foundation [c 1964].

Lattas, Andrew. "Primitivism, Nationalism and Individualism in Australian Popular Culture." In Power, *Knowledge and Aborigines*, ed. Bain Attwood and John Arnold, 45–58. Melbourne, VIC: Monash University National Centre for Australian Studies, La Trobe University Press, 1992.

———. *Cultures of Secrecy: Reinventing Race in Bush Kaliai Cargo Cults*. Madison, WI: University of Wisconsin Press, 1998.

Lawrence, Elizabeth Atwood *Rodeo: An Anthropologist Looks at the Wild and the Tame*. Knoxville, TN: University of Tennessee Press, 1982.

LeCompte, Mary Lou. *Cowgirls of the Rodeo: Pioneer Professional Athletes*. Chicago, IL: University of Illinois Press, 1993.

Leland, Joy. *Firewater Myths: North American Indian Drinking and Alcohol Addiction*. New Brunswick, NJ: Rutgers Centre of Alcohol Studies, 1977.

Lindfors, Bernth. "Ethnological Show Business: Footlighting the Dark Continent" In *Freakery: Cultural Spectacles of the Extraordinary Body*, ed. Rosemarie Garland Thomas. London, UK & New York, NY: New York University Press, 1996.

Linsley, Robert. "Painting and the Social History of British Columbia" In *Vancouver Anthology: The Institutional Politics of Art*, ed. Stan Douglas, 225–45. Vancouver, BC: Talonbooks, 1991.

Little, Ken. "On Safari: The Visual Politics of a Tourist Representation." In *The Varieties of Sensory Experience*, ed. D. Howes, 148–63. Toronto, ON: University of Toronto Press, 1996.

MacAloon, John J. "Olympic Games and the Theory of Spectacle in Modern Societies." In *Rite, Drama, Festival and Space: Rehearsals Toward a Theory of Cultural Performance*, ed. John J. MacAloon, 241–80. Philadelphia, PA: Institute for the Study of Human Issues, 1984.

MacClancy, Jeremy. *Sport, Identity, and Ethnicity*. Oxford, UK & Herndon, VA: Berg, 1996.

MacDonald, Molly Anne. *The Royal Canadian Mounted Police*. Toronto, ON: Macmillan, 1973.

MacDonald, Sharon. "Identity Complexes in Western Europe: Social Anthropological Perspectives." In *Inside European Identities: Ethnography in Western Europe*, ed. Sharon MacDonald. Providence, RI: Berg, 1993.

MacDonnell, Tom. *Daylight Upon Magic: the Royal Tour of Canada, 1939*. Toronto, ON: Macmillan, 1989.

Macleod, R.C. "Canadianizing the West: The North-West Mounted Police as Agents of the National Policy, 1873–1905" In *Essays on Western History*, ed. Lewis H. Thomas, 101–10. Edmonton, AB: University of Alberta Press, 1976.

Maguire, Joseph. *Global Sport: Identities, Societies, Civilizations*. Cambridge, UK: Polity Press; Malden, MA: Blackwell, 1999.

Makim-Willing, Gene. *Get Up on his Shoulder: A History of Campdrafting in Australia*. Toowoomba, QLD: Mrs. G. Makim, 1997.

Maxwell, Anne. *Colonial Photography and Exhibitions: Representations of the 'Native' and the Making of European Identities*. New York, NY & London, UK: Leicester University Press, 1999.

Maynard, Margaret. "Projections of Melancholy." In *Seeing the First Australians*, ed. I. Donaldson and T. Donaldson, 106–7. North Sydney, NSW: Allen & Unwin, 1985.

McArthur, Colin. "The Dialectic of National Identity: The Glasgow Empire Exhibition of 1938." In *Popular Culture and Social Relations*, ed. Tony Bennett, Colin Mercer, and Janet Wollacott. Milton Keynes, UK: Open University Press, 1986.

McBride, Isabel. "Thomas Dick's Photographic Vision." In *Seeing the First Australians*, ed. I. Donaldson and T. Donaldson, 137–63. North Sydney, NSW: Allen & Unwin, 1985.

Meijer Drees, Laurie. *The Indian Association of Alberta: A History of Political Action*. Vancouver, BC: UBC Press, 2002.

Mellis, Allison Fuss. *Riding Buffaloes and Broncos: Rodeo and Native Tradition in the Northern Great Plains*. Norman, OK: University of Oklahoma Press, 2003.

Miller, Toby. "Cultural Citizenship." In *Handbook of Citizenship Studies*, ed. Engin F. Isin and Bryan S. Turner, London, UK: Sage, 2002.

Mulvaney, D. J. "The Darwinian Perspective." In *Seeing the First Australians*, ed. I. Donaldson and T. Donaldson, 68–74. North Sydney, NSW: Allen & Unwin, 1985.

Myers, Fred. *Painting Culture: The Making of an Aboriginal High Art*. London, UK: Duke University Press, 2002.

Napier, Rita. "Across the Big Water: American Indians' Perceptions of Europe and Europeans, 1887–1906." In *Indians and Europe: An Interdisciplinary Collection of Essays*, ed. Christian Feest, 383–414. Aachen, GDR: Rader Verlag, 1987.

Nash, Roderick. *Wilderness and the American Mind*. New Haven, CT: Yale University Press, 1974.

Neihardt, John G. *Black Elk Speaks, Being the Life Story of a Holy Man of the Oglala Sioux* (1932; Reprint). Lincoln, NB: University of Nebraska Press, 1979.

Nelles, H.V. *The Art of Nation Building: Pageantry and Spectacle at Quebec's Tercentenary*. Toronto, ON: University of Toronto Press, 1999.

Neuberger, Richard L. *Royal Canadian Mounted Police*. New York, NY: Random House, 1953.

Nicks, Trudy. "Indian Villages and Entertainments: Setting the Stage of Tourist Souvenir Sales." In *Unpacking Culture: Art and Commodity in Colonial and Postcolonial Worlds*, ed. Ruth B. Phillips and Christopher B. Steiner, 301–15. Berkeley, CA: University of California Press, 1999.

Pettipas, Katherine. *Severing the Ties That Bind: Government Repression of Indigenous Religious Ceremonies on the Prairies*. Winnipeg, MB: University of Manitoba Press, 1994.

Phillips, Ruth. *Unpacking Culture: Art and Commodity in Colonial and Post-colonial Worlds*. Berkeley, CA: University of California Press, 1997.

Poulsen, David A. *Wild Ride!: Three Journeys Down the Rodeo Road*. Toronto, ON: Balmur Book Publishers, 2000.

Reddin, Paul. *Wild West Shows*. Chicago, IL: University of Illinois Press, 1999.

Rosaldo, Renato. "Social Justice and the Crisis of National Communities." In *Colonial Discourse/Postcolonial Theory*, ed. Francis Barker, Peter Hulme, and Margaret Iverson. Manchester, UK: Manchester University Press & New York, NY: St. Martin's Press, 1995.

———. "Introduction: The Borders of Belonging." In *Cultural Citizenship in Island Southeast Asia*, ed. Renato Rosaldo. Berkeley, CA: University of California Press, 2003.

Rothfels, Nigel. *Savages and Beast: The Birth of the Modern Zoo*. Baltimore, MD: Johns Hopkins University Press, 2002.

Russell, Don. *The Wild West: A History of Wild West Shows*. Fort Worth, TX: Amon Carter Museum of Western Art, 1970.

Rydell, Robert W. *All the World's a Fair: Visions of Empire at America's International Expositions, 1867–1916*. Chicago, IL: University of Chicago Press, 1984.

———. *World of Fairs: The Century of Progress Exposition*. Chicago, IL: University of Chicago Press, 1993.

———, and Nancy Guinn. *Fair Representations*. Amsterdam, NL: Amsterdam University Press, 1994.

Scheckel, Susan. *The Insistence of the Indian: Race and Nationalism in Nineteenth Century American Culture*. Princeton, NJ: Princeton University Press, 1998.

Sealey, Bruce D. *The Mounties and Law Enforcement*. Agincourt, ON: The Book Society of Canada, 1979.

Sears, John. "Beirstad, Buffalo Bill, and the Wild West in Europe." In *Cultural Transmissions and Receptions: American Mass Culture in Europe*, ed. R. Kroes, R.W. Rydell, and B.F.J. Bossher, 15–23. Amsterdam, NL: VU University Press, 1993.

Sheilds, Rob. "Imaginary Sites." In *Between Views*, ed. Daina Augnitis and Sylvie Gilbert, 22–26. Banff, AB: Banff Centre for the Arts, 1991.

Slotkin, Richard. "Buffalo's Bill's 'Wild West' and the Mythologization of the American Empire." In *Culture of United States Imperialism*, ed. Amy Kaplan and Donald E. Pease, 27–44. London, UK: Duke University Press, 1993. 27–44.

Souter, Gavin. "Skeleton at the Feast." *Australians:* 1938, ed. Bill Gammage and Peter Spearritt, 13–26. Sydney, NSW: Fairfax, Syme & Weldon Associates, 1987.

Standing Bear, Luther. *My People the Sioux* (1928; reprint). Lincoln, NB: University of Nebraska Press, 1975.

Stevenson, Nick. *Culture and Citizenship*. London, UK: Sage, 2001.
Stoeltje, Beverly. "Cowboys and Clowns: Rodeo Specialists and the Ideology of Work and Play." In *"And Other Neighbourly Names": Social Process and Cultural Image in Texas Folklore*, ed. Richard Bauman and Roger Abrahams, 123–51. Austin, TX: University of Texas Press, 1981.
Sturken, Marita, and Lisa Cartwright. *Practices of Looking: An Introduction to Visual Culture* Oxford, UK: Oxford University Press, 2001.
Thomas, Nicholas. *Colonialism's Culture: Anthropology, Travel and Government*. Princeton, NJ: Princeton University Press, 1994.
Treaty 7 Elders and Tribal Council, with Walter Hildebrandt, Sarah Carter, and Dorothy First-Rider. *The True Spirit and Original Intent of Treaty 7*. Montreal, PQ: McGill-Queen's University Press, 1996.
Torgovnik, Marianna. *Gone Primitive: Savage Intellects, Modern Lives*. Chicago, IL: University of Chicago Press, 1990.
Turner, G. *Making it National: Nationalism and Australian Popular Culture*. Sydney, NSW: Allen and Unwin, 1994.
Turner, Victor. *Celebration: Studies in Festivity and Ritual*. Washington, DC: Smithsonian, 1982.
Urry, John. *The Tourist Gaze: Theory, Culture and Society*. 2nd ed. Lancaster, UK: Sage, 2002.
Van Dijk, Teun A. *Racism and the Press*. London, UK & New York, NY: Routledge, 1991.
Walden, Keith. *Becoming Modern in Toronto: The Industrial Exhibition and the Shaping of a Late Victorian Culture*. Toronto. ON: University of Toronto Press, 1997.
———. *Visions of Order*. Toronto, ON: Butterworths, 1982.
White, Richard. *Inventing Australia: Images and Identity, 1688–1980*. Sydney, NSW: Allen and Unwin, 1981.
Whyte, Jon. *Indians in the Rockies*. Banff, AB: Altitude, 1985.
Williams, Raymond. "Selections from Marxism and Literature." In *Culture/Power/History: A Reader in Contemporary Social Theory*, ed. Dirks, G. Ely and S. Ortner, 585–608. Princeton, NJ: Princeton University Press, 1994.
Wooden, Wayne S. *Rodeo in America: Wranglers, Roughstock and Paydirt*. Lawrence, KS: University Press of Kansas, 1996.
Yengoyan, Aram A. "Culture, Ideology and World's Fairs: Colonizer and Colonized in Comparative Perspectives." In *Fair Representations*, ed. Robert Rydell and Nancy Guinn. Amsterdam, NL: Amsterdam University Press, 1994.

Articles and Reports

"Alberta's First Nations: A Note on Terminology." *The Applied History Group: University of Calgary*, <http://www.ucalgary.ca/applied_history/tutor/calgary/nativeterm.html> (accessed 30 May 2004).
Anderson, Kay. "White Natures: Sydney Royal Agricultural Show in Post-Humanist Perspective." *Transactions of the Institute of British Geographers* 28, no. 4 (2003): 422–42.

Apter, Andrew. "On Imperial Spectacle: The Dialectics of Seeing in Colonial Nigeria." *Comparative Study of Society and History* 44, no. 3 (2002): 564–96.

Bankmann, Ulf. "The 'Esquimaux-Indians' in Berlin, 1824–1825: drawings and prints." *European Review of Native American Studies* 11, no. 2 (1997): 21–26.

Barron, F. Laurie. "The Indian Pass System in the Canadian West, 1882–1935." *Prairie Forum* 13 (Spring 1988).

———. "Aboriginality, Citizenship and Nation State." *Social Analysis* 25, no. 24 (1988): 3–18.

Blanchard, David. "For Your Entertainment Pleasure – Princess White Deer and Chief Running Deer – Last Hereditary Chief of the Mohawk: Northern Mohawk Rodeos and Showmanship." *Journal of Canadian Culture* 1, no. 2 (1984): 99–116.

Born, David O. "Black Elk and the Duhamel Sioux Indian Pageant." *North Dakota History: Journal of the Northern Plains* 61, no. 1 (1994): 22–29.

Braun, Bruce. "Colonialism's Afterlife: Vision and Visuality on the Northwest Coast." *Cultural Geographies* 2 (2002): 202–47.

Brito, Silvester John. "The Indian Cowboy in the Rodeo Circuit." *Journal of Ethnic Studies* 5, no. 1 (1977): 52–54.

Broome, Richard. "Seeking Mulga Fred." *Aboriginal History* 22 (1998): 1–23.

Burgess, Marilyn. "Canadian 'Range Wars': Struggles over Indian Cowboys." *Canadian Journal of Communications* 18 (1993): 352–64.

Cooper, Barry. "Could Alberta's Provincial Police Return by 2012" as seen on: <http://www.fraserinstitute.ca/admin/books/chapterfiles/Could%20Albertas%20Provincial%20Police%20Return%20by%202012~Nov03cooper.pdf#> (accessed 5 April 2006).

Corbey, Raymond. "Ethnographic Showcases, 1870–1930." *Cultural Anthropology* 8, no. 3 (1993): 338–69.

Cowell, Elspeth. "The Pavilion at the 1939 New York World's Fair." *SSAC Bulletin* 19, no. 1 (1994): 13–20.

Cruikshank, Julie. "Negotiating with Narrative: Establishing Cultural Identity at the Yukon International Storytelling Festival." *American Anthropologist* 99, no. 1 (1997): 56–69.

Dening, Greg. "The Theatricality of History Making and the Paradoxes of Acting." *Cultural Anthropology* 8 (1993): 73–95.

Dickason, Olive, Patricia. "The Concept of l'homme sauvage and early French Colonialism in the America." *Revue Francaise d'Histoire d'Outre-mer* 63 (1980): 25–35.

Dill, Jordan. "Iron Eyes Cody." *Native-L*, January 30, 1994 as seen on: <http://nativenet.uthscsa.edu/archive/nl/9401/0295.html>

Dyck, Noel. "Powwow and the Expression of Community in Western Canada." *Ethnos* 44 no. 1–2 (1979): 78–98.

Edwards, Elizabeth. "Photographic Types: the Pursuit of Method." *Visual Anthropology* 3 (1990): 235–58.

Foot, Richard. "Royal Tour of Canada 1939: 'It made us, the King and I.'" <http://www.canada.com/national/features/queenmother/story.html> (accessed 30 May 2004).

Foucault, Michel. "On Governmentality." *Ideology and Consciousness* 6 (1979): 5–21.
Francis, Mark. "Social Darwinism and the Construction of Institutionalised Racism in Australia." *Journal of Australian Studies* 50/51 (1996): 90–105.
Frey, James H., and D. Stanley Eitzen. "Sport and Society." *Annual Review of Sociology* 17 (1991): 503–21.
Furniss, Elizabeth. "Cultural Performance as Strategic Essentialism: Negotiating Indianness in a Western Canadian Rodeo Festival." *Humanities Research* 3 (1998): 23–40.
Gittings, Christopher. "Imagining Canada: The Singing Mountie and Other Commodifications of the Nation." *Canadian Journal of Communication* 23 (1998): 507–22.
Gooderham, George H. "Joe Crowfoot." *Alberta History* 32, no. 4 (1984): 26–28.
Gottlieb, Alma. "American Vacations." *Annals of Tourism Research* 9 (1982): 325–42.
Grant, S. D. "Indian Affairs Under Duncan Campbell Scott: The Plains Cree of Saskatchewan 1913–1931." *Journal of Canadian Studies* 18, no. 3 (1983): 21–39.
———. "Myths of the North in the Canadian Ethos." *The Northern Review* (1989): 15–41.
Griffiths, Alison. "Playing at Being Indian: Spectatorship and the Early Western." *Journal of Popular Film and Television* 29, no. 3 (2001): 100–111.
Hollingsworth, David. "Guidelines for non-racist language use in Aboriginal Studies." College of Indigenous Education and Research, University of South Australia. <http://www.unisa.edu.au/unaipon/current/guidelines.htm> (accessed 31 May 2004).
Hoy, James F. "The Origins and Originality of Rodeo." *Journal of the West* 17, no. 3 (1978): 16–33.
———. "Rodeo in Australia: Bushmen's Carnivals and Campdrafting." *Antipodes: A North American Journal of Australian Literature* 8, no. 2 (1994): 55–58.
———. "Americanization of the Outback." *Vision Splendid* (1995): 205–8.
Jay, Gregory S. "'White Man's Book No Good': D.W. Griffith and the American Indian." *Cinema Journal* 39, no. 4 (2000): 3–26.
Kniffen, Fred. "The American Agricultural Fair: The Pattern," in *Annals of the Association of the American Geographers* 39, no. 4 (1949): 264–82.
King, Jonathan C.H. "A Century of Indian Shows: Canadian and United States Exhibitions in London 1825–1925." *European Review of Native American Studies* 31 (1991): 35–42.
Kreis, Markus Karl. "'Indians' on Old Picture Postcards," *Native American Studies* 6, no. 1, (1992): 39–48.
Lattas, Andrew. "Savagery and Civilization: Towards a Genealogy of Racism." *Social Analysis* 21 (1987): 39–58.
———. "Aborigines and Contemporary Australian Nationalism." *Social Analysis* 27, no. 3 (1990): 50–69.
———. "Nationalism, Aesthetic Redemption and Aboriginality." *Australian Journal of Anthropology* 2, no. 3 (1991): 307–24.
LeCompte, Mary Lou. "Wild West Frontier Days, Roundups, and Stampedes: Rodeo Before There was Rodeo." *Canadian Journal of History of Sport* 16, no. 2 (1985): 54–67.

Lerch, Patricia. "Pageantry, Parade, and Indian Dancing: The Staging of Identity among the Waccamaw Sioux." *Museum Anthropology* 16, no. 2 (1992): 27–34.

Lupul, M.R. "The Portrayal of Canada's 'Other' Peoples in Senior High School and Social Studies Textbooks in Alberta, 1905 to the Present." *Alberta Journal of Educational Research* 22, no. 1 (1976): 1–33.

Maddox, Lucy. "Politics, Performance and Indian Identity." *American Studies International* 40, no. 2 (2002): 7–36.

Mathur, Saloni. "Living Ethnological Exhibits: The Case of 1886." *Cultural Anthropology* 15, no. 4 (2000): 492–525.

McGrath, Ann. "Playing Colonial: Cowgirls, Cowboys, and Indians in Australia and North America." *Journal of Colonialism and Colonial History* 2, no. 1 (2001) as seen on: <http://web2.trentu.ca:2088/journals/cch/v002/2.1mcgrath.html>

McGregor, Russell. "Protest and progress: Aboriginal activism in the 1930's." *Australian Historical Studies* 101 (1993): 555–68.

McMaster, Gerald. "Tenuous Lines of Descent: Indian Arts and Crafts of the Reservation Period." *Canadian Journal of Native Studies* 9, no. 2 (1989): 205–36.

Mewett, Peter G. "Fragments of a Composite Identity: Aspects of Australian Nationalism in a Sports Setting." *Australian Journal of Anthropology* 10, no. 3 (1999): 357–75.

Mikkelsen, Glen. "Indians and Rodeo." *Alberta History* 35 (1986): 13–19.

Mitchell, Timothy. "The World as Exhibition." *Comparative Studies in Society and History* 31, no. 2 (1998): 217–36.

Moray, Gerta. "Wilderness, Modernity and Aboriginality in the Paintings of Emily Carr." *Journal of Canadian Studies* 33, no. 2 (1998): 43–65.

Myers, Fred. "Culture-Making: Performing Aboriginality at the Asia Society Gallery." *American Ethnologist* 21, no. 4 (1994): 679–99.

National Aboriginal Health Organisation (NAHO). "Terminology Guide." as seen on: <http://www.naho.ca> (accessed 30 May 2004).

Nicks, Trudy. "Indian Handicrafts: The Marketing of an Image." *Rotunda* (Summer 1990): 14–20.

Nurse, Andrew. "'But Now Things Have Changed': Marius Barbeau and the Politics of Amerindian Identity." *Ethnohistory* 48, no. 3 (2001): 433–72, as seen on: <http://muse.jhu.edu/journals/ethnohistory/v048/48.3.nurse.html>

Nygren, Anja. "Struggles over Meanings: Reconstruction of Indigenous Mythology, Cultural Identity, and Social Representation." *Ethnohistory* 45, no. 1 (1998): 31–63.

Ommundsen, Wenche. "Strictly Australian: Tourism and Ethnic Diversity." *Social Semiotics* 9 (1999): 39–48.

Penrose, Jan. "When All the Cowboys Are Indians: The Nature of Race in All-Indian Rodeo." *Annals of the Association of American Geographers* 93, no. 3, (2003): 687–705.

Poignant, Roslyn. "The Photographic Witness?" *Australian Journal of Media & Culture* 6, no. 2 (1991). <http://wwwmcc.murdoch.edu.au/Reading Room/6.2/Poignant.html> (accessed 30 January 2004): 1–21.

Price, John A. "The Stereotyping of North American Indians in Motion Pictures." *Ethnohistory* 20, no. 2 (1973): 153–70.

Radforth, Ian. "Performance, Politics and Representation: Aboriginal People and the 1860 Royal Tour of Canada." *Canadian Historical Review* 84, no. 1 (2003).

Regular, Keith. "On Public Display." *Alberta History* 34, no. 1 (1986): 1–10.

Raibmon, Paige. "Theatres of Contact: The Kwakwaka'wakw Meet Colonialism in British Columbia and the Chicago World's Fair." *Canadian Historical Review* 81, no. 2 (2000): 157–90.

Riegler, Johanna. "Tame Europe and the Mysteries of Wild America: Viennese Press Coverage of American Indian Shows 1886–1898." *European Review of Native American Studies* 1, no. 1 (1988): 17–20.

Royal Agricultural Society of New South Wales. "R.A.S. History. Sydney Royal Easter Show: The Great Muster Show." As seen on: <http://www.greataustralianmuster.com/aboutus/past.htm> (accessed 15 May 2004).

Ruby, Jay. "Seeing Through Pictures: The Anthropology of Photography." *Camera Lucinda* 3, as seen on: <http://www.temple.edu/anthro/ruby/seethru.html>

Rydell, Robert. *"Visions of Empire: International Expositions in Portland and Seattle, 1905–1909." Pacific Historical Review* 52 (1983): 37–65.

Salsbury, Nate. "The Origin of the Wild West." *Colorado Magazine* 32 (1955): 204–14.

Schieffelin, Edward. "Performance and the Cultural Construction of Reality." *American Ethnologist* 12 (1985): 707–24.

Schneider, William. "Race and Empire: The Rise of Popular Ethnography in the Late 19th Century." *Journal of Popular Culture* 11 (1997): 98–109.

Seiler, Robert M., and Tamara P. Seiler. " The Social Construction of the Canadian Cowboy: Calgary Exhibition and Stampede Posters, 1952–1972." *Journal of Canadian Studies* 33, no. 3 (1998): 51–82.

Sluman, Norma. "The Textbook Indian." *Toronto Education Quarterly* 5, no. 3 (1965): 2–5.

Smithsonian Institution Libraries (SIL). *The Book of Fairs*. Research Guide No. 6. <http://microformguides.gale.com/Data/Introductions/10020FM.htm> (accessed 15 May 2005).

Stewart, Honourable Jane. *Notes for an Address on the Occasion of the Unveiling of Gathering Strength – Canada's Aboriginal Action Plan*. Department of Indian Affairs and Northern Development, Ottawa. <http://sisis.nativeweb.org/clark/jan0798can.html> (accessed 7 January 1998).

Treaty 7 Tribal Council Homepage. <http://www.treaty7.org/> (accessed 16 December 2002).

Wade, Henry. "Imagining the Great White Mother and the Great King: Aboriginal Traditional and Royal Representation at the 'Great Pow-wow' of 1901." *Journal of the Canadian Historical Association* 11 (2000): 156–86.

Walden, Keith. "The Great March of the Mounted Police in Popular Literature, 1873–1973." *Canadian Historical Association – Historical Papers: A selection of the papers presented at the annual meeting held at Montreal* (1980): 33–54.

Weadick, Guy. "Origin of the Calgary Stampede." *Alberta Historical Review* 14, no. 4 (1966): 20–24.

Wikipedia, the free encyclopedia. "Paternalism." <http://en.wikipedia.org/wiki/Paternalism> (accessed 10 January 2004).

Theses and Dissertations

Burgess, Marilyn. "'Dark Devils in the Saddle': A Discursive Analysis of Tourist and Entertainment Formations Constituting Western Canadian Regional Identity." PhD diss., Concordia University, 1992.

Green, Vicki Anne. "The Indian in the Western Comic Book." Master's thesis, University of Saskatoon, 1974.

Hoffenberg, Peter. "To Create a Commonwealth: Empire and Nation at English, Australian and Indian Exhibitions, 1851–1914." PhD diss., University of California, 1994.

Kirshenblatt-Gimblett, Barbara. "Performing Diversity." PhD diss., New York University, 1992.

Ofner, Patricia V. "The Indian in Textbooks: A Content Analysis of History Books Authorised for Use in Ontario Schools." Master's thesis, Lakehead University, 1983.

Poulter, Gillian. "Becoming Native in a Foreign Land: Visual Culture, Sport and Spectacle in the Construction of National Identity in Montreal, 1840–1885." PhD diss., York University, 1999.

Index

A

Aborigines, 94, 141
  in the Australian imagination, 116, 119–20
  in Australian government policy, 118, 119
  in Australian social attitudes, 118
  treatment of, 118, 134
Aborigines Progressive Association, 134
agricultural fairs
  and colonialism, 12, 143, 161
  history of, 12
Alberta, 38, 46, 53
  and First Nations, 5, 62–67, 74, 84, 92–93, 102, 146, 150, 156
  high schools and racism, 29, 60
  Pioneers of, 58, 67
  and RCMP, 108, 152
  and rodeo, 78, 84
All Indian Rodeo Cowboys Association, 85
Ambler, Jerry, 80, 107
anthropology, 98
Armstrong, L.O., 42
Ashby, Corporal D., 92–93
assimilation policy, 99
Auckland, New Zealand, 2, 81, 96, 105, 107
  Zoo, 96
  Star, 128, 168, 169, 173
Australia
  Aboriginal cowboys, 142
  at world's fairs, 49
  colonialism, 11, 118–20
  cowboys, 1, 3, 77, 78, 160
  and economic depression, 13, 30–31
  First Nations performances prior to 1939, 26
  media reports, 70, 71, 121–31, 138, 165
  modernity, 19, 31
  nationalism, 12, 16, 24, 29, 33, 120, 144, 160
  political promotion in North America, 30
  public, 7, 9, 25, 32, 48, 70, 72–74, 76, 87, 93, 104, 106, 110, 115–16, 117, 124–28, 131–34
  and racism, 81–82, 112, 118–20, 138, 147, 166–67, 168
  and rodeo, 14–16, 19–20, 145
  trade with Canada and the U.S., 11, 13, 30, 47
  WWII, 11–12, 30–31
Australia's sesquicentenary celebrations, 134

B

Banff, Alberta, 13, 16, 36, 40, 99
  Indian Days, 38
  Springs, 124
Bear Robe, Joe, 1, 3, 6, 43, 53, 56, 58, 67, 72, 74, 76, 78, 81–82, 94, 101, 109, 111, 133
Bhabha, Homi, 97, 143
Blackfoot, First Nations, 54, 56, 69, 71, 153
  Band, 37, 62, 191
  chiefs of, 92–93
  description of in RAS brochures, 26–27
  Indian Agency, 152, 159, 163, 170
  Reserve, 1, 53, 55, 58, 153, 155, 156
Blood, First Nations, 40, 54, 62, 64, 141
  Band, 37,
  chiefs of, 92–93
  Reserve, 1, 58, 155
bootlegging, 108
Braverock, Ted, 57
buckjumping, 2, 14, 77, 144
Buffalo Bill, 25, 145
  historical work concerning, 67, 145, 155, 168
  performers, 120

promoters of, 54
  as romantic figure, 32, 36, 145, 155, 168
bulldogging, 2
bullock-riding, 14, 144
Bushman's Carnivals, 14

C

Calgary Stampede, 16, 36, 38, 44, 55, 58, 60, 62, 64, 79, 145, 157
  Board, 58
  cultural significance of, 44, 55, 65, 74, 79, 152
campdrafting, 14, 144, 145
Canada
  display at world's fairs, 49–51, 118, 143
  international reputation, 41, 48, 52, 67, 70, 89, 51, 93, 117
  in the media, 70, 120
  and modernity, 49, 93
  nationalism, 12–13, 29, 44, 83, 93, 117–18
  political relationship with Australia, 11, 30, 48
  and primitivism, 98
  and RCMP, 88–90, 91–92, 102–3, 111, 132
  and rodeo, 63–64
  use of First Nations culture, 37–40, 48, 117–18, 124
Canadian Handicraft Guild, 153
Canadian Manufacturer's Association, 11
cattle
  and First Nations domestication, 54, 146
  ranching and First Nations in Canada, 84, 142
  ranching in Australia, 6, 14, 16, 20, 144
  and rodeo, 32, 63–65
  stations, 15
Carr, Emily, 18, 165, 166
CBC Radio, 99
Chicago, 1, 43
  Daily Press, 147
  University of, 43
  World's Fair, 41, 43

chuckwagon racing
  and First Nations, 17, 27, 58, 77–78, 146
  history of, 27, 145, 160
  at Royal Easter show in Sydney, 3, 6, 11, 15, 17, 27–28, 32, 143
Citizens of Sydney Organizing Committee, 16
citizenship
  Australian, 124
  in Australian ideology concerning Aborigines, 119
  in Canadian colonial ideology concerning First Nations, 37–39, 44, 60, 99, 137
  cultural, 8, 80, 84, 138, 159, 160
  international representations of, 84
  in the media, 126
  public declarations by First Nations cowboys, 4–6, 79, 82–83
  public performance of, 84
  regional representations of, 43, 54–55
  representations by Constable Leach, 90, 112
  representations by First Nations, 4, 7, 43, 84, 112, 126–28, 138
  rodeo and, 54, 79
Clements International Chuck Wagon Race, 22, 77
Cody, Iron Eyes, 146
Cole, Fay-Cooper, 43
Colonial and Indian Exhibition of 1886, 97
colonialism
  Australian government policies concerning, 118–19
  in Australian ideology, 12, 52, 88, 118, 134, 138
  in Canadian ideology, 4, 6, 38, 52, 98, 137
  Canadian government policies concerning, 5, 6, 36, 38, 54, 124
  as hegemony, 5, 78, 80, 138–39, 142, 143
  and history, 139
  history of, 139
  in the media, 132

and modernity, 78
oppression, 7, 40–42, 60, 62, 103, 108, 137, 124, 129, 137
in public performances, 9, 12, 39, 43–44, 67, 93, 120
and RCMP, 87, 90, 93, 111
resistance, 7, 79, 82–84,
and rodeo, 44, 54, 67
and stereotypes, 116, 137
theories concerning, 97, 111, 143
collective memory, 78, 92
Cook, Captain James, 119
Cowboy Protection Association, 64
cowgirls, 2–3, 15, 80, 83, 105–6, 109, 129, 157, 159, 160
Crowfoot,
Cecil, 68, 70, 72, 74, 79, 84, 90, 108, 141, 155, 158
Chief, 56, 71, 92, 108, 161
Deanna, 74, 155, 159
Joe, 1, 3, 4, 6, 7, 43, 53, 55, 64, 67–69, 71–72, 74, 76, 78, 81–82, 90, 92, 99, 101, 109–11, 124, 126, 128, 133, 136, 138, 155, 163, 183
Cyclone (horse), 64

D

Darwinism, 39, 118, 167
"Day of Mourning," 134, 169
Deerfoot, 25
dime novels, 16, 117
dying race theory, 119, 166

E

Empire Club of Canada, 11, 30, 147

F

First Nations,
and Australian perspectives, 120–31, 132–34
and cattle ranching, 54
and chuckwagon racing, 17
and citizenship, 82–84
cowboys, 54, 63–67, 165
cultural identity, 67
economy, 27, 36, 43–45, 152, 163
fairs and festivals, 62, 156
farming, 146
and horse racing, 45, 54, 62, 64–65, 157
images of, 19, 21, 29, 33, 39, 168
handicraft sales, 46–48
and modernity, 51
nationalism, 4, 54, 83–84, 136
nationalism and land, 38, 84–85, 138
and oppression, 60–62
and political conflicts, 38
politics in Alberta, 53, 62–63, 65–66, 138, 161–62
and RCMP, 91–93, 102, 110–12, 132
and rodeo, 65, 157–58
and savagism, 25, 29
terminology, 141
traditional attire, 6, 17, 21, 33
flags
Many Fingers, 85
and the Olympics, 84, 160
"Pontiac Welcomes the 'Red Indians'," 72
symbolic importance, 28, 83–84, 87, 129
Union Jack, 28, 83, 129

G

Ghost, Bear, 55
Gingold, Erna, 158, 173
Glasgow Exhibition, 42, 49, 154
Gleichen Agricultural College, 156
Gooderham, G.H., 40, 148, 155, 158, 170
Gowrie, Lord, 87, 93, 95
Gramscian theory, 79
Grande Parade, 87, 129
Great Depression, 6, 13, 30, 43, 46, 51, 60, 98, 148, 152
Great Empire Show, 42

H

handicrafts
Canadian government promotion of, 45–46, 52, 153, 159

and First Nations, 45, 68, 153
and First Nations economy, 46
in the media, 46–47, 121, 153
sales in Australia, 3, 51, 121
hegemony
basic theory, 137
and fairs, 12
colonial, 5, 80, 138, 142
counterhegemony, 5, 79–80
"lived hegemony," 5, 137
historical pageantry, 36–37, 45
Honolulu, 2, 69, 94, 97, 107
Hordern, Sir Samuel, 24, 142, 143, 144, 173
hospitality, 106, 124, 126, 132
Hunt, George, 41, 151

I

identity
Canadian, 121
colonial, 6, 51–52, 67
cultural, 7, 8, 43, 54, 82, 84, 137–38
fluidity of, 9, 113, 137
First Nations, 43–45, 51, 67, 82, 139, 42
general theory, 7, 54, 84
individual, 5, 8, 137
interrelational aspects, 82, 113
and movement, 137
national, 4, 5, 7–8, 9, 51–52, 67, 84, 137–38
and performance, 9, 51, 67, 82–84, 115
and race, 51
regional, 67, 76, 84, 139, 142
and resistance, 54, 82, 84, 113, 139
and sport, 9, 54, 84
transnational, 113, 160
imperial
doctrine, 5–6, 12, 33, 52, 118, 137
nostalgia, 118, 166
power, 12
ties, 11
Indian Act, 60, 62, 76, 108
Section 149, 41, 62
Indian Affairs Branch, 1, 5–7, 9, 29, 35, 90
and CBC Radio, 156

and First Nations handicrafts, 2, 45–47, 76
and the Indian Act, 60, 76
paternalism, 91, 103
preferences for the Royal Easter Show, 17, 44, 136
racism, 78, 137
responses to requests for "Indian" performances, 42–43
and the Royal tour, 135
Indian agents, 35, 135
in Alberta, 36
attitude towards First Nations, 36, 40–41, 44–45, 53, 55, 60, 62, 65, 146, 150, 152, 156
and economic depression, 6
and rodeo, 62, 65, 158
Indian Association of Alberta, 54, 58, 62, 154, 156
Indian Days, 16, 36, 38, 45, 157
Indian rodeo, 58, 68, 85, 142, 152, 155, 158, 161
Cowboy Association, 58
as cultural performance, 64
"Indian Village,"
as an attraction in Alberta, 38, 43, 106, 129
as imagined by show promoters, 16–17, 25–27, 43, 132
at the Royal Easter Show, 2–3, 36, 39–40
as a space for First Nations cultural production, 4, 43, 67–68
international
Buckjumping Contest, 77
Bulldogging Contest, 77
competition, 1, 4, 53, 69, 76–77, 84, 79–90, 113, 138
diplomacy, 90
exhibitions, 39, 43
political ties, 6
public performance, 5–7, 40, 42, 67, 79–80, 134, 143
rodeo, 4, 15, 32, 63, 69–70, 84–85, 113, 145, 157

sport in general, 4, 7, 15, 53, 76, 79–80, 84, 160
stereotypes, 32, 51, 137
trade, 11, 30, 48, 52, 70, 121
travel, 5, 39, 67, 76, 120
"Wild Cow Milking Championship," 77

K

Kainai, First Nations, 141
Kiwanis Club, Toronto, 11
Kwakwaka'wakw, First Nations, 41–42, 151
King George VI, 135
Kootenay, Douglas, 1, 3, 6, 43, 53, 58, 74, 76, 78, 99, 109, 111, 115, 128, 133, 157

L

Lazy "B" Ranch, 58
Leach, Constable Samuel J., 1–7, 58, 63, 72–74, 76–83, 87–91, 93–103, 104, 105–13, 115, 117, 121, 124, 129–30, 131–33, 138, 142, 155–56, 158
Leach, Mrs. Dorothy, 1, 6, 7, 80, 98, 101, 107, 111, 129, 131
League of Indians of Canada, 62
Left Hand, Johnny, 1–3, 6, 43, 53, 58, 76, 78, 99, 109–11, 121, 123, 128, 133, 157
Lescarbot, Marc, 117
Lyons, Prime Minister J.A., 30, 147

M

MacFarlane, T.B., 6, 11, 14–17, 19, 22, 27, 30–32, 36, 45, 69–72, 77, 80, 106, 109, 136, 138, 144–48
  ranch in Merriwa, 2, 105
MacInnes, H.W., 35–36, 60, 145, 148–50, 152–54, 156, 158
Many Fingers,
  Buck, 85
  Geraldine, 80, 160
  Frank, 1, 3, 4, 6, 7, 43, 53, 58, 64, 66–67, 69, 74, 76, 78, 82, 85, 90, 109, 110, 111, 115, 126, 128, 133, 138

Floyd, 65, 68, 73, 77, 79–80, 84, 141, 154, 158
  Ranch, 85, 155
Martin, Mungo, 51
Maxwell, Peggy, 18, 20, 21, 22, 23, 24, 25, 72, 73, 74, 130, 142, 158, 161, 162, 163, 165, 173
McGill, H.W., 13, 35, 42, 135, 141, 143–44, 146, 148–49, 151, 169
Merriwa, Australia, 2, 3, 14, 69, 77, 96, 105, 106
missionaries, 42, 44, 162
modernity
  anti-modernism, 98, 118
  and colonialism, 32, 51, 98, 118, 129, 138
  general promotion of, 5, 49,
  at Royal Easter Show, 19, 29, 51
Moore Park, 2, 18, 19, 26, 32, 74
Morley, Alberta, 16, 24, 36, 40, 150
Murray T.F., 40
Murray, W.B., 40, 150, 156

N

Nakodabi, First Nations, 141
nationalism, 143–44
  Australian, 12, 24, 32, 120, 160, 167
  Canadian, 39, 43, 137, 166
  competitive, 148
  First Nations, 4, 38, 54, 83–84, 136, 138
New York World's Fair, 11, 31, 50, 51, 154
New York Sportsman Show, 42
noble savage ideology
  in Australia, 119–21, 167
  in Canadian nationalism, 118, 168
  in North America, 99, 116–18
  stereotypes associated with, 117
  and Wild West shows, 155
nostalgia
  colonial ideology, 118, 166

O

One Spot, Eddie, 58, 61, 67, 75, 78, 126–27, 133, 136, 168

P

Page, Sir Earle, 11, 30, 147
paternalism
    and Constable Leach, 91, 96, 110, 113
    definition of, 102, 163
    and the Indian Affairs Branch, 76, 103, 110
patriotism, 12, 124, 131
    and Constable Leach, 131
    and historical pageantry, 149
pass system, 60, 156,
Pease, Percy, 30, 147
people shows, 38–39, 43, 149
permit system, 60–62
perspective
    of actors, 6–7, 137–39
    of audience, 7
    of Australian government officials, 132
    of Australian media, 116
    of Canadian government officials, 44, 60
    Constable Leach's, 91, 98, 105, 113
    First Nations, 76, 79, 142
    multiple, 8, 113, 137
    as resistance, 79–80, 139
    transcultural, 138
primitivism, 98, 102, 124, 162, 169
progress
    and First Nations, 40, 44, 51, 120, 156
    and modernity, 5, 19, 51, 138
    and nationalism, 12, 31, 37, 144, 148
Pugh, J.E., 40, 58, 146, 150, 155, 158

Q

Queen Elizabeth, 135

R

race
    in Australia, 119, 167
    discrimination in Australia, 108–110, 97, 119
    discrimination in Canada, 113
    evolutionist theories concerning, 39, 118, 167
    in media, 124, 165
    as political tool, 9, 51–53, 64, 98, 150
    transnational implications, 9, 97
    use of the term "Red men," 25, 27, 42, 146, 151,
races at Royal Easter Show,
    Clements Tonic International Chuck Wagon Race, 22, 28, 77, 143, 145–46
    Taronga Zoological Park Red Indian Bareback Race, 21, 77, 159
RCMP, 1, 3, 107
    duties, 102
    First Nations scouts, 58, 67
    history of, 108, 110
    Leach's official report, 90, 94, 96, 97, 105, 142
    myths concerning, 91–93, 102
    as national symbol, 7, 37, 91, 103, 117
    at the Royal Easter Show, 87
RCMP Quarterly, 63, 73, 81, 90, 91, 93, 94, 99, 100, 101, 107, 155, 161, 163, 171
"Red Indians," 3, 13
    Australian view of, 5–7, 9, 11–12, 120, 139
    promotional stereotype, 19, 21–22, 24–27, 32, 72, 100, 104, 141
    use in Australian media, 124–29, 131, 133, 138, 146, 151
resistance
    acts of, 7, 134
    to colonialism, 7, 62, 79
    and Constable Leach, 111, 139
    and First Nations rodeo, 4, 7, 79
    and international competition, 5, 79
    perception as, 7, 79–80, 139
    performance as, 41, 134
Ring Programme, 13, 16–22
RMMS Aorangi, 3, 107
rodeo
    Association of America, 63
    in Australia, 14–15, 19, 143–44
    in Canada, 44, 63, 142, 145
    Canadian All-Round Championship, 58
    and First Nations, 1–2, 4, 5–6, 25, 29, 45, 53–55, 64–67, 84, 142, 146, 152, 157–58

Index   193

"Indian Rodeo," 68, 85, 142
international competitions, 4, 11, 13, 30, 32, 84, 157
and political diplomacy, 31–32, 70, 84
popular cultural activity, 32–33
and the promotion of nationalism, 6, 27, 32, 44, 70, 84, 152
as resistance activity, 4, 7, 35, 44–45, 54, 62–63, 161
at the Royal Easter Show, 16–19, 20, 23–24, 77–78, 109
Rodeo Programme, 17, 19, 145, 146
Rotary Club, Toronto, 11
Rousseau, Jean-Jacques, 117
Royal Agricultural Society of NSW, 1, 11, 131
1939 mandate, 2, 7, 9, 11–12, 109, 132, 138
attitudes concerning First Nations cowboys, 69, 73, 76–78, 91, 106–9
Australian nationalism, 22
Canadian correspondence with, 2, 6, 35, 51, 91, 103, 124, 131, 144, 146
fair-goers
history of, 12–15, 32, 143–44, 146
modernity, 18–19, 51
negotiations with Constable leach, 106–9, 111
racism, 69, 104, 109–10, 139
and World's fairs, 31–32
Royal Easter Show, 2, 6, 11, 15, 30–31, 42, 69, 74, 96, 106, 136
1911 show, 42
audiences at, 129
brochures, 17–29
and First Nations cowboys, 134
and First Nations handicrafts, 47
history of, 13–14, 83, 143–44
nationalism, 12, 120, 138
and rodeo, 15–16, 23, 32, 67, 80
Royal tour, 136, 168, 169

S

salvage paradigm, 98, 118, 162, 166–67
Sarcee, First Nations, 1, 54, 62, 141
Band, 93
chiefs of, 60, 67, 92
Reserve, 53, 58, 158
savagism, 99
Schmidt, C. Pant, 1, 6, 17, 35–40, 43, 44–47, 51–52, 76, 103, 107, 109, 113, 132, 135, 145–49, 152–56, 158–59, 163, 169–70
Siksika, First Nations, 141
Skidmore, A.W., 6, 11, 14–17, 22, 27, 30–32, 36, 45, 70, 72, 76–77, 80, 103–4, 109, 132, 136, 138, 144–48, 152, 159, 163, 169
Souvenir Ring Programme, 17–19
sport in general
in First Nations communities, 54
and international relations, 4, 15, 44, 51, 63, 70, 84
as a political activity, 67, 84, 117
as popular cultural activity, 44, 46, 117
as resistance, 5, 84
SS Niagara, 1, 2, 69, 71, 94, 104, 115
Stacey, Col., 42
Standoff, Alberta, 64
Starlight, Jim, 1, 3, 6, 43, 53, 58, 59, 67, 74, 76, 78, 106, 109, 111, 133
stereotypes, 32
Australian, 25
Canadian, 29
and cultural identity, 7, 54, 116
and ideology, 116
internationally popular, 9, 32, 67
and noble savagery, 155
Plains Indian, 29, 32, 81, 121
and primitivism, 121
production of, 32, 115
and public performance, 43, 142
and racism, 116
RCMP
resistance towards, 43–45, 54, 81, 120, 124, 126, 128, 137–38
and savagism, 101
Stoney, First Nations, 1, 54, 58, 62, 141
Band, 93
chiefs of, 92

Reserve, 16, 53
Sydney, 2, 16, 17, 26, 35, 40, 47, 49, 58, 64, 69, 72, 74, 77, 79, 87, 96, 101, 106, 115, 132, 134, 135, 159
- *Daily Telegraph*, 121
- Koala Park, 100
- *Morning Herald*, 82

Suva, Fiji, 2, 97, 107,

T

teepees, 16, 35, 36, 40, 73, 147
Three Persons, Tom, 64, 142, 157
Toronto, 11, 30, 49, 144
- Board of Trade, 11
- Daily Star, 144
- Industrial Exhibition, 144

Treaty Days, 45, 62, 156–57
Treaty 7, 37–38, 71, 92,
Treaty 7 Tribal Council, 149
transcultural
- experience, 9, 113
- perspective, 138
- representation, 138

transnational, 25, 43, 52
Tsuu T'ina, First Nations, 141
Turtle Cowboy Association, 64

V

Vancouver, B.C., 1, 3, 11, 13, 99, 100, 107, 152
- *Sun*, 71

vanishing race, 25, 64, 138
visual culture, 12, 118–19, 142, 150, 165

W

Wade, Jack, 80, 107
wardship
- indignity associated with, 77
- legalities of, 4, 53, 60, 76, 107–8
- in the media, 168

Westgate, T.B.R., 88, 99
"White Policy," 147
Wild West shows, 6, 16–17, 25, 32, 36, 44, 63–64, 67, 76, 117–19, 128, 134, 155, 168
Williams, Raymond, 5, 137, 142
Without a Doubt Bear, Susie, 55
Woods, S.T., 92–93, 146, 162
World's Bronco Riding Competition, 64
world's fairs
- and hegemony, 12, 31
- and nationalism, 38–39, 118

Y

Yellowfly, Teddy, 60, 92–93, 136, 156
Young Pine, Joe, 1, 3, 6, 53, 57, 67, 74, 76–78, 80–81, 101, 106, 109, 111, 133